HARPERISM

HARPERISM

HOW STEPHEN HARPER AND HIS THINK TANK COLLEAGUES HAVE TRANSFORMED CANADA

DONALD GUTSTEIN

JAMES LORIMER & COMPANY LTD., PUBLISHERS
TORONTO

James Lorimer & Company Ltd., Publishers acknowledges the support of the Ontario Arts Council. We acknowledge the financial support of the Government of Canada through the Canada Book Fund for our publishing activities. We acknowledge the support of the Canada Council for the Arts which last year invested $24.3 million in writing and publishing throughout Canada. We acknowledge the Government of Ontario through the Ontario Media Development Corporation's Ontario Book Initiative.

Notice to educators

This book is available for purchase in print and ebook form. Copies can be purchased from our website at www.lorimer.ca. Copies of individual chapters or portions of the full text in print or digital form are also available for sale at reasonable prices. Contact us for details at rights@lorimer.ca.

The publisher and the author of this work expect that portions of this work will be useful for education, and expect reasonable compensation for this use. This can be readily achieved by arranging to purchase these portions from the publisher. Contrary to the view of university administrators and their legal advisors, it is unlikely that use of a chapter or 10% of this work for educational purposes with no payment to the publisher or author would be found to be fair dealing under the Canadian Copyright Act.

Cover design: Tyler Cleroux

Library and Archives Canada Cataloguing in Publication

Gutstein, Donald, 1938-, author
    Harperism : how Stephen Harper and his think tank colleagues have transformed Canada / Donald Gutstein.

Includes bibliographical references and index.
Issued in print and electronic formats.
ISBN 978-1-4594-0663-6 (pbk.).--ISBN 978-1-4594-0664-3 (epub)

    1. Harper, Stephen, 1959-. 2. Harper, Stephen, 1959- --Influence. 3. Research institutes--Canada. 4. Neoliberalism--Canada. 5. Canada--Politics and government--2006-. 6. Canada--Economic conditions--21st century. I. Title.

FC640.G88 2014   971.07'3   C2014-903847-X
                                             C2014-903848-8

James Lorimer & Company Ltd., Publishers
317 Adelaide Street West, Suite 1002
Toronto, ON, Canada
M5V 1P9
www.lorimer.ca

Printed and bound in Canada.

To Mae and Josh

CONTENTS

INTRODUCTION

"You won't recognize Canada when I get through with it." Stephen Harper hasn't yet uttered that sentence on the public record, yet Canadians instinctively believe he has said exactly that.

Has he lived up to his promise (or threat)? What has he done to make Canada unrecognizable? He was sworn in as Canada's twenty-second prime minister in February 2006, leader of the recently formed Conservative Party of Canada that won the most seats — but not a majority — in the election a month earlier. The CPC replaced the Progressive Conservative Party as the party of the centre-right, retiring the word "progressive" from use after 60 years. Harper's party is conservative, with no progressive complications, would be our conclusion. And he has lived up to this expectation. Harper carried through on his promise to cut the Goods and Services Tax from 7 to 5 per cent, denying government $14 billion a year in foregone revenue. After seven years in power he had cut an additional $60 billion from the corporate tax bill, leading to another massive shortfall. Budget deficits were the inevitable result, especially after his government was forced to engage in some stimulus spending to fend off the worst consequences of the 2007–08 financial meltdown. To try to balance his budget after the revenue hole created by these tax cuts, Harper cut programs and services and laid off 30,000 federal government employees. The deficit was a justification for slashing the federal work force, but these are still moves you would expect from a conservative government, like those made by Ronald Reagan and Margaret Thatcher. And you would still recognize Canada — we've been here before.

Advancing Alberta's bitumen extraction industry is another Harper government mainstay, a policy option you would expect from a conservative government, especially one with strong Alberta representation. His incessant promotion of the Keystone XL pipeline to the United States and his government's green-light for the Northern Gateway pipeline from Alberta to Kitimat on British Columbia's Pacific coast in June 2014 were evidence of this. And his law and order agenda was well-known since Harper's days as policy chief of the Reform Party in the late 1980s. You'd expect these kinds of policies from a conservative Harper government, like Reagan and Thatcher before him. Even the elimination of Statistics Canada's long-form census questionnaire from the 2011 national census could have been anticipated as a move by a government that felt the questions it asked were too intrusive — the state has no right asking them. Yet after all these dramatic changes, Canada remained recognizable.

Other changes Harper was making, though, could help him achieve the aim of rendering the country unrecognizable. His quiet efforts to bring private-property rights to First Nation reserves, after more than a century of failure to eliminate reserves by Liberal and Conservative governments, bypassing national First Nations leadership in the process, aimed to transform collective into individual ownership. What's unique about this campaign was that it is backed by a think tank discourse about liberating "dead capital" on reserves so First Nations residents can prosper like other Canadians. Canada without First Nation reserves: that would be unrecognizable.

Harper was accused of attacking environmentalists because they obstruct resource development. That is certainly true, but there's more to it than that. Eradicating scientific — and indeed all centralized — knowledge by shuttering research stations and abandoning science libraries is a more fundamental change. What's unique here is the idea that environmental decisions should be based on market signals and not on accumulated scientific knowledge. Here too, Harper's efforts are accompanied by a think tank discourse about free-market environmentalism. What kind of a Canada would that be?

If you focus only on Harper, you can learn a lot about his ruthless control over his party and caucus, his disciplined messaging, his obsessive focus on the economy, his ability to move issues forward in the light of vigorous opposition. But you won't have the complete picture, as *Maclean's* political editor Paul Wells cautions.[1] Many depictions centre on Harper as the lone wolf, the rogue conservative who marches to his own drummer. This way of looking at him, though, won't help you to understand the context in which he has operated. Harper is one side of an ideological coin; missing from the discussion is the other side of the coin — the network of conservative think tanks such as the Fraser Institute working over many decades to change the climate of ideas that make sense to many of us. By climate of ideas, I mean our commonly accepted notions about how government and the private sector should operate, and our understandings of ourselves as self-centred individualists or as compassionate members of society.

Imagine that Stephen Harper was a candidate for the leadership of the federal Progressive Conservative Party in 1983, when the Fraser Institute was not even ten years old, in a contest that was won by Brian Mulroney. In all likelihood Harper would have been knocked off after the first ballot because his views were too radical for most delegates. Twenty years after that, espousing the same policies, he was able to win the leadership of the Conservative Party handily on the first ballot and was soon prime minister. Why this dramatic change? I believe it was thanks to the persistent efforts of think tanks like the Fraser Institute that radical Reform ideas became "common sense."

Once in office, Harper was able to put into practice the principles the think tanks could only talk and write about, tempered of course by the necessities of governing, which frequently frustrates his supporters. Harper's unique approach to changing Canadian society works together with the think tanks' persistent and disciplined messaging. Combining Harper's efforts to bring private-property rights to First Nation reserves with a think tank discourse that claims prosperity and economic development are possible only with such rights, constitutes a classic example of Harperism. Like the heads and tails of the coin, the two sides never have to meet, although on occasion they do. Harper, the newly elected Conservative leader, was a guest speaker at the Fraser Institute's thirtieth anniversary celebration in Calgary in 2004. He didn't attend in person, but conveyed his remarks by videotape. He pointed to the Fraser Institute silk Adam Smith tie he was wearing and confirmed he was a disciple of the institute.[2]

The ideology the think tanks promote is properly called neo-liberalism because, in contrast to libertarians who want a small, powerless state that leaves people alone, neo-liberals require a strong state that uses its power to create and enforce markets, and prop them up when they fail, as happened after the 2007–08 financial meltdown. Their utopian dream is a state governed by market transactions and not democratic practices. It's based on the principle that economic freedom must come before political freedom. Political freedom may not even be necessary. It's fair to say they believe in government, but not in democracy.

The post-war period was a time of great social progress throughout the developed western world. Social democracy and the welfare state were the order of the day, driven by values of social justice and collective well-being. A small group of neo-liberals, led by Friedrich Hayek and Milton Friedman, set out to undo these progressive developments by forming the Mont Pelerin Society in 1947. They knew they couldn't change government without changing the climate of ideas within which politics must operate. So they disseminated their free-market ideas to political, economic and social elites through a burgeoning network of neo-liberal think tanks. It worked better than they could have imagined. Sixty years later social democracy is a fading memory.

How they accomplished this fundamental reordering of society and the economy is becoming clear through recent historical studies of neo-liberalism.[3] These studies identify the direct link between the Mont Pelerin Society (MPS) and Margaret Thatcher's decisive 1979 election victory and the rise of Thatcherism in Britain. The link was activated by the creation of the first neo-liberal think tank, the London-based Institute of Economic Affairs (IEA) in the mid-1950s. This institute worked for 20 years to disseminate pro-market, anti-government ideas that eventually took hold in British political and media elites during the turbulent seventies. When Thatcher came to power she wrote to Ralph Harris, the IEA's director: "It was primarily your foundation work which enabled us to rebuild the philosophy upon which our Party succeeded in the past. The debt we owe you is immense and I am very grateful. With best wishes, Margaret."[4]

The studies also identify links between the MPS and Ronald Reagan through the IEA and the Heritage Foundation. This think tank was set up in the early seventies by Ed Feulner, who brought the IEA's formula for changing elite and public opinion to Washington. Heritage produced *Mandate for Leadership*, a detailed prescription for a government guided by neo-liberal principles. Newly-elected president Reagan gave out copies of the best-selling 1,000-page paperback edition at his first cabinet meeting and it became his administration's blueprint.[5]

There's also a direct link from Mont Pelerin to Harper via the IEA, the Fraser Institute, and its allied think tanks that today spend upwards of $26 million a year to promote neo-liberal ideas in Canada alone. Harper was introduced to Hayek as a graduate student at the University of Calgary in the 1980s; Hayek seems to have guided Harper's thinking since then. The debt Harper owes the neo-liberals, their ideology and their network of affiliated think tanks is just as enormous as that owed by Thatcher and Reagan. These influences and how they underpin what Harper is doing form the subject of this book.

Neo-liberalism came later to Canada than to Britain and the United States because of the re-election of Pierre Trudeau in 1980. But after the 1984 federal election, the Progressive Conservative Mulroney government adopted neo-liberalism as its guiding light, throwing open the country to foreign investment, eliminating the National Energy Program, transforming the Foreign Investment Review Agency into Investment Canada, bringing in the Canada–U.S. Free Trade Agreement and signing the North America Free Trade Agreement. Neo-liberalism became entrenched under the Liberal governments of Jean Chrétien and Paul Martin, who accepted the ideology as their own policy orientation, as Chrétien signed NAFTA and Chrétien–Martin brought in an era of privatization and fiscal restraint. By the time Harper took over the reins of government, neo-liberalism was normalized as the accepted way of running the country. That was Harper's starting point. He earns the "ism" label because of his unique way of furthering neo-liberalism, as the book documents.

Thatcher and Reagan's initiatives — and Mulroney's — were mostly high profile, garnering heated support and provoking fierce opposition. Harper's moves, in contrast, are subtle, low-key, incremental, hidden from view. No wonder most commentators have difficulty seeing them. Incrementalism is both practice and theory for Harper. He was forced to move slowly during his years of minority government to stay in office. He continues to deploy this strategy with a majority because it works. "Any other approach will certainly fail," he told the 2003 conference of the Civitas Society, the secretive association — secretive because it allows no public access to its website — of three hundred conservative academics, politicians, journalists, and think tank functionaries who meet annually, free from media oversight, to debate issues important to conservatives.[6] (Harper was ruling out another method of policy change, the "blitzkrieg" or lightning strike. This strategy also involves "a policy goal radically different from the existing configuration," but is "attained in a short period following a surprise announcement and a very rapid implementation."[7])

Reaganism and Thatcherism are not just about economic policy. Underlying the success of each political leader is a unique blend of neo-liberalism and socially conservative family and cultural values. Harper, who was then head of the Canadian Alliance, laid out his version of the program in his 2003 Civitas address. He claimed that the ideas of the economic conservatives had already been adopted by government. As a result of the Reagan and Thatcher revolutions, Harper argued, both "[s]ocialists and liberals began to stand for balanced budgeting, the superiority of markets, welfare reversal, free trade and some privatization."[8] Of course, much more needs to be done, he reassured them. "We do need deeper and broader tax cuts, further reductions in debt, further deregulation and privatization, and especially the elimination of corporate subsidies and industrial-development schemes" that distort the market. But the arguments for this program "have already been won,"[9] he declared. The task was now to bring social conservatives of various stripes into the Conservative tent. There aren't enough economic conservatives to win a majority government, so alliances must be formed with ethnic and immigrant communities, who historically vote Liberal but espouse "strong traditional views of values and family."

Thatcher and Reagan had "ism" appended to their names because their influence extended beyond their administrations. They have been accorded status as doctrines or systems of beliefs. Thatcherism was promoted even more vigorously by the succeeding New Labour government of Tony Blair. And in the United States, Democratic president Bill Clinton furthered Reaganism through policies such as "ending welfare as we know it" after Reagan had targeted "welfare queens" as the enemy. Is Harper deserving of an "ism"? I believe he is and hope to demonstrate in this book that Harper's program will outlast his years as prime minister. The combined firepower of neo-liberal think tanks over forty years has reshaped the Canadian climate of ideas to such an extent that it will take years — perhaps decades — for those views to change again. On top of these ideological underpinnings, Harper has fundamentally modified the relationship between state and society. The theme is simple: we must remove obstacles to the attainment of a state governed not by duly elected officials but by market transactions, because economic freedom is more fundamental than political freedom. This will not be easily undone no matter who follows. Future Canadian prime ministers, like Tony Blair and Bill Clinton before them, cannot ignore the dominant influences of Harperism and neo-liberalism. They must find their space to operate within these frames.

1

CONVINCE CANADIANS OF THE IMPORTANCE OF ECONOMIC FREEDOM

The Fraser Institute released its 2010 *Economic Freedom of the World* annual report in September of that year. This index, which the institute has published since 1996, purports to measure the degree to which government policies and institutions support what the institute calls economic freedom. "The four cornerstones of economic freedom," the document declares, "are personal choice, voluntary exchange coordinated by markets, freedom to enter and compete in markets, and protection of persons and their property from aggression by others."[1] More simply, economic freedom is "the extent to which you can pursue economic activity without interference from government, as long as your actions don't violate the identical rights of others."[2] In this 2010 index, Canada rated seventh, just behind the United States and ahead of Australia. This was an improvement over Canada's ranking in 1996, the first year the index was published, assessing economic freedom up to 1995. Under Liberal prime minister Jean Chrétien,

Canada came in at fourteenth. Canada's problem that year, the index claimed, was excessive government spending levels which were "looking more and more like those of the European welfare states and less like the United States."[3] But during that year Paul Martin's budget slashed spending on social programs, leading to an improved ranking on the economic freedom index in subsequent years. The 2010 ranking was good news for the government of Stephen Harper, which was negotiating a series of bilateral free-trade agreements, using economic freedom as one supporting argument.

The report was introduced at a Fraser Institute policy briefing at Ottawa's Rideau Club, with guest speaker Peter Van Loan, Harper's minister of international trade, who told his audience that "our government places a high value on the work of organizations such as yours."[4] Van Loan applauded his government's "commitment to free trade, open investment rules, and lower taxes." Free trade was the key to economic recovery, he declared. "In Canada, prosperity and quality of life are dependent on trade with the world." Van Loan reminded his audience of the "fierce debates about North American free trade, and the voices from the fringe" — Liberals, New Democrats, Canadian nationalists, presumably — "telling us that it would somehow erode our sovereignty." He declared that "we need to continue building a broad base of support for the importance of a competitive, globally engaged Canadian economy of the future." He ended with an invitation: "So let's work together to continue convincing Canadians . . . of the importance of economic freedom."

It may seem unusual for a government to invite a think tank to work together, but the collaboration is the culmination of a project that began in 1947. That year Austrian economist Friedrich Hayek invited leading European and American intellectuals of various free-market persuasions to meet at the Hôtel du Parc in Mont Pèlerin, a village overlooking Lake Geneva in Switzerland.

He asked them to consider the rise of post-war demands for social and economic rights and the creation of a welfare state. He also charged them to develop theories and strategies to counter the Keynesian orthodoxy that dominated the intellectual landscape. Developing his theory during the Great Depression, British economist John Maynard Keynes (1883–1946) observed that direct government intervention is required to achieve full employment and assure a sufficient level of demand. In the world under Keynes, "the state held a central role in nation building, modifying the excesses of capitalism and generating some measure of equality of opportunity."[5] To ensure stability and growth, capitalism needed to compromise with labour and government.

Such a vision was the exact opposite of economic freedom, Hayek-style. How could there be personal choice, voluntary exchange, freedom to compete, and security of privately owned property if government was prodding the economy in what it considered the "right direction"? Following the Keynes approach would, Hayek argued in his classic manifesto *The Road to Serfdom*, lead to a nightmare world of collectivism and socialism, to slavery, not freedom.[6] When Hayek invited his free-market colleagues to the lakeside spa, they were a beleaguered minority, outgunned by Keynesians, socialists, and Marxists. During their ten days of talk they agreed to form the Mont Pelerin Society, with a mandate to work towards a market state — an individualistic, non-egalitarian society, governed by market transactions.

However, this would become reality, they understood, only if they could capture and reorganize political power. This activist ambition differentiates Mont Pelerin Society liberals from those who came before, and justifies the use of the term "neoliberal," admittedly a slippery concept to pin down. Those who are described as neo-liberals no longer use the term, preferring to call themselves libertarians (in North America), market liberals, or classical liberals. In the early years, though, they did call themselves neo-liberals: Milton Friedman used the word in the title of a 1951 survey of his comrades.[7] They stopped using the term in the late fifties, because they didn't want to dwell on the fact that the liberalism they espoused differed radically from the liberalism that stretched from Adam Smith (1723–1790) to their time.[8] That earlier liberalism, usually called *laissez-faire*, believed government should not interfere in economic affairs. Neo-liberalism, in contrast, was based on the belief that the market society they desired would not come about without concerted political effort and organization. They were radicals who came to demand dramatic government action to create and enforce markets. As Marxist geographer David Harvey explains in *A Brief History of Neoliberalism*, for neo-liberals "the role of the state is to create and preserve" strong property rights, free markets, and free trade, using force if necessary, to guarantee the proper functioning of markets. "If markets do not exist (in areas such as land, water, education, health care, social security, or environmental pollution) then they must be created, by state action if necessary."[9]

In post-war Europe and North America, these neo-liberals couldn't hope to capture and reorganize political power by entering politics directly, given the hostile climate of ideas and the dominance of the Keynesian consensus. "To capture political power, they would first have to alter the intellectual climate," writes Timothy Mitchell, a political theorist at Columbia University.[10] To alter the intellectual climate, Hayek wrote in an influential 1949 essay, "The Intellectuals and Socialism," neo-liberals would have to influence what he termed "professional secondhand dealers in ideas" who control the distribution of expert knowledge to the public. They are "journalists, teachers, ministers, lecturers, publicists, radio commentators, writers of fiction, cartoonists, and artists." They "may be masters of the technique of conveying ideas but are usually amateurs so far as the substance of what they convey is concerned," he wrote.[11] Nonetheless, they are the people who, more than any others, "decide what views and opinions are to reach us, which facts are important enough to be told to us, and in what form and from what angle they are to be presented."[12] Hayek had outlined a grand scheme of propaganda dissemination.

To accomplish the further task of influencing second-hand dealers in ideas, Hayek soon realized neo-liberals would need their own network of "dealerships," or think tanks, as we know them today. "Backed with funds from corporations and their owners, usually channelled through private foundations," Mitchell writes, "think tanks repackaged neoliberal doctrines in forms that 'second-hand dealers' could retail among the general public. Doctrine was supported with evidence presented as 'research,'"[13] which was then packaged into books, reports, studies, teaching materials, and news stories and distributed to news organizations and other second-hand dealers. Later, think tanks developed a variety of simplistic indexes, because these are more likely to receive favourable distribution to target audiences. Annual indexes are effective in persuading people to reconsider their beliefs, because they cater to many people's discomfort with statistics, and they are repeated year after year. The Fraser Institute has made effective use of this device with its tax-freedom day (forty years), hospital waiting list (twenty years), and B.C. secondary-school report card (sixteen years). The economic freedom of the world index (eighteen years) fits comfortably within this pattern.

Sixty years after Hayek, despondent at the prospect of the Keynesian welfare state and its imagined slippery slope towards totalitarianism, invited his fellow neo-liberals to Mont Pèlerin, the organization they created, with the Mont Pelerin Society at its core, constitutes a worldwide network of over one thousand scholars, journalists, think tank professionals, and corporate and political leaders, with a closely related network of over two hundred partisan think tanks, comprising what a recent book on the history of neo-liberalism calls the "neoliberal thought collective."[14] Marxist scholar Perry Anderson ruefully observes that "[W]hatever limitations persist to its practice, neo-liberalism as a set of principles rules undivided across the globe: the most successful ideology in world history."[15] Its success can be measured by the extent to which it has changed our common-sense understanding of how the world works. Followers of nearly every political persuasion must pay attention to this reality in their calculations. Even when nominally progressive or liberal parties have won elections — Tony Blair's New Labour in the United Kingdom, the United States under Bill Clinton and Barack Obama, Canada under Jean Chrétien and Paul Martin — they have been constrained from introducing progressive measures because of the changed climate of ideas.

Stephen Harper is certainly sympathetic to neo-liberalism and the economic-freedom agenda. He was introduced to Hayek as a student at the University of Calgary after he arrived there to study economics. Hayek's work became the foundation of Harper's graduate thesis, and it continued to influence his thinking as he rose from graduate student to the pinnacle of political power.[16] When he took a break from electoral politics in 1997 to run the National Citizens Coalition, he explained in the NCC newsletter that "I am honoured to join you in your fight. The battle for political and economic freedom will have its victories and setbacks, as it has in the past. It will never end . . . and we shall never surrender."[17] Once prime minister, Harper made economic freedom a centrepiece of public policy, as trade minister Van Loan explained. Much of what Harper has done, especially since winning a majority government in 2011, can be understood as removing obstacles to economic freedom: reducing the powers of the Canadian Wheat Board, moving to eliminate Canada's system of supply management, bringing private-property rights onto collectively owned Indian reserves, attacking trade unions and environmentalists, crafting free-trade agreements with undisclosed clauses that further remove obstacles to the free market. As David Harvey explains, with a lengthy list of areas in which markets are to be imposed, Harper has his work cut out for him.

***

The construction of the economic freedom of the world index illustrates how neo-liberal think tanks repackage doctrine by creating supportive research that second-hand dealers in ideas can retail to elites and the general public. Doctrine was supplied in Milton Friedman's 1962 classic manifesto *Capitalism and Freedom*, which Friedman wrote with ongoing financial support from the William Volker Fund, a leading financial supporter of neo-liberalism in the early years.[18] (Volker paid the expenses of Friedman and nine other American free-market liberals, allowing them to attend the first Mont Pelerin Society meeting in 1947.) "Historical evidence speaks with a single voice on the relation between political freedom and a free market," Friedman wrote. "I know of no example in time or place of a society that has been marked by a large measure of political freedom, and that has not also used something comparable to a free market to organize the bulk of economic activity."[19] Friedman provided little evidence to back these assertions. It would be up to the neo-liberals thought collective to produce and organize the research that would establish Friedman's dictum — political freedom depends on economic freedom — as fact.

The international index project was born at the 1984 meetings of the Mont Pelerin Society in Cambridge, England, when Fraser Institute executive director Michael Walker reminded attendees of Friedman's pronouncement — political freedom depends on economic freedom. They knew this was merely a claim and they would have to prove it. Economic freedom wasn't "out there" like Mount Everest, just waiting to be measured. It was an abstract concept, a utopian dream. They would give it life, bring it into the world, so it could be used to transform reality.[20] Working with Milton and Rose Friedman and sixty-one academics, Walker took on the task of creating an index of economic freedom. They were assisted by the Liberty Fund of Indianapolis, which spends $20 million a year sponsoring conferences and publishing books that promote individual liberty.[21] It took them six symposia and twelve years before they had constructed a working index of economic freedom. As mentioned, the first global ranking was published in 1996 and has been recalibrated and republished every year since.

Following Friedman, the group decided early on that economic freedom must not depend on political freedom, and could actually do better without democracy. In fact, democracy could be a hindrance to greater economic freedom. As Michael Walker noted in his summary of the thought collective's first Liberty Fund–sponsored symposium in Napa Valley, California, in 1986, "not only did our discussions conclude that countries have been able to prosper in spite of having no political institutions but the judgement was that they have prospered because there have been no political institutions!"[22] Friedman claimed that economic freedom had to come first, before political freedom could be achieved. He thus equated capitalism and freedom, with democracy running a distant third, a theme fundamental to the neo-liberal war of ideas. It's the free market and not democracy, Friedman argued, that leads to freedom. Hong Kong, then still under British rule, was a case in point. Walker wrote that Hong Kong "is undoubtedly the most economically free [state] in the world. The lack of political institutions has been an important ingredient in Hong Kong's past economic success . . ."[23] Hong Kong, without meaningful democracy, has led the index every year since it was published. Not coincidentally, however, the city state also leads the developed world in its level of income inequality, a theme that will be taken up in Chapter 7. The Mont Pelerin Society's insistence on the primacy of economic over political freedom illustrates a major difference between neo-liberalism and conservatism as commonly understood: in contrast to neo-liberals, most conservatives would defend democracy as a basic freedom.

The ideological nature of the enterprise became apparent when Walker and his collaborators explicitly rejected an approach to economic freedom developed by Freedom House, a seventy-year-old organization that "supports democratic change, monitors freedom, and advocates for democracy and human rights around the world."[24] Eleanor Roosevelt was the organization's first honorary co-chair. Freedom House began producing an economic-freedom index around the same time as the neo-liberals — with one big difference. Freedom House includes an indicator that measures the freedom to earn a living. "Can individuals form voluntary associations to bargain over wages?" the organization asks, indicating this as one measure of economic freedom.[25] For states that do not interfere with a worker's right to join a union and ban indentured servitude, bonded labour, and child labour, it assigns a three-out-of three, thus boosting a country's ranking on the economic-freedom scale. But following the doctrine established at early Mont Pelerin Society meetings, Michael Walker and the neo-liberals rejected any role for unions in the economy, identifying them as instruments of coercion. (See Chapter 3 for a review of this development.) They rejected the Freedom House approach and used their own measure.

The difference in the two approaches is starkly drawn in the way the two groups rank the city-state of Singapore. In the

Fraser Institute's version of economic freedom, Singapore ranks second in the world, just behind Hong Kong. Freedom House, in contrast, ranked Singapore as only partially free, in a group with Albania, Armenia, Bangladesh, Bhutan, Burkina Faso, and fifty-six other countries. To earn high marks in the Fraser Institute's component that measures the regulation of the labour market, "a country must allow market forces to determine wages and establish the conditions of hiring and firing."[26] Passing laws that establish labour-union rights, a minimum wage, or regulations regarding dismissal lower a country's ranking.

⁕

Participants in the Economic Freedom of the World (EFW) deliberations would reject any attempt to call them neo-liberals. Robert Lawson, an economist at Southern Methodist University in Dallas, Texas, and a long-time participant in the project, calls himself a libertarian, not a neo-liberal.[27] Libertarianism, which is based on a philosophy of individual freedom and personal responsibility,[28] is the North American version of classical liberalism. It is used because the word "liberal" has a very different meaning in North America than it does in Europe. After the Second World War, classical liberals in the United States started calling themselves libertarians to differentiate themselves from New Deal liberals, who were their polar opposites. Like others in North America, Lawson has never referred to himself or his colleagues as neo-liberals. He contributed a self-profile to a book edited by Walter Block — another EFW collaborator — titled *I Chose Liberty: Autobiographies of Contemporary Libertarians* that further consolidates his libertarian bona fides.[29] Libertarian, not neo-liberal. Even Milton Friedman, the inspiration for the EFW project, identified himself as a libertarian. In an interview with *Reason* magazine in 1995, Friedman explained, "I am a Republican with a capital 'r' and a libertarian with a small 'l.'" He told his interviewer "my philosophy is clearly libertarian," and "I would like to be a zero-government libertarian," but he wasn't, because he didn't "think it's a feasible social structure."[30]

Is it fair, then, to label people like Lawson and Friedman, who call themselves libertarians, as neo-liberals? Or is it just name-calling, as Lawson maintains. He says the word neo-liberal is used "almost exclusively by ideological foes of economic freedom" when referring to himself and his colleagues.[31] True, there are major differences between libertarians and neo-liberals, especially in their understanding of the role of government. For libertarians, government's role is strictly limited. Governments "should protect all persons equally against external and internal aggression, but should otherwise generally leave people alone."[32] For their part, as we've seen, neo-liberals want a strong state, one that will create and enforce markets, even if it involves uprooting people's lives in the process.

It's this distinction that leads historian Philip Mirowski to conclude that many self-identifying libertarians are actually neo-liberals. They claim to favour the small state and unfettered market, but surreptitiously support a strong state that uses its powers to impose and support markets. Mirowski proposes that "any idea or person with membership or strong ties to the [Mont Pelerin Society] will qualify as 'neoliberal,'"[33] because the MPS consensus was for a state not afraid to use its powers. Lawson may call himself a libertarian, but, because he is an MPS member, he qualifies as a neo-liberal, according to Mirowski. And even though Milton Friedman, an MPS founder, did call himself a libertarian in the 1990s, in the early years of the MPS he wrote about himself and his colleagues as neo-liberals — though he soon stopped using the term, as this chapter points out.

An analysis of a highly regarded Friedman publication by political scientists Michael MacDonald and Darel Paul provides evidence for Mirowski's insistence on the neo-liberal label. Friedman wrote two books in the early 1960s that cemented his reputation as a leading voice for North American libertarianism. The first, *Capitalism and Freedom*, was his polemic. In it he claimed, among other things, that government regulation caused the Depression. "The fact is that the Great Depression, like most other periods of severe unemployment, was produced by government mismanagement rather than by any inherent instability of the private economy," he wrote. "A governmentally established agency — the Federal Reserve System — had been assigned responsibility for monetary policy. In 1930 and 1931, it exercised this responsibility so ineptly as to convert what would otherwise have been a moderate contraction into a major catastrophe."[34] Friedman thus blamed federal regulation of the money supply for the Depression and vindicated self-regulating capital markets, MacDonald and Paul conclude.[35] As libertarians would have it, if the Fed had left financial markets alone, the downturn would have been brief and self-correcting.

A Monetary History of the United States (further referred to as *MH*), which Friedman published the following year with economist Anna Schwartz, was supposed to put technical flesh on *Capitalism and Freedom's* ideological bones. But MacDonald and Paul's careful reading reveals that Friedman and Schwartz don't explicitly make the government-caused-the-Depression claim that Friedman made in *Capitalism and Freedom*.[36] "Friedman and Schwartz never declare the Fed 'caused' or 'produced' the Depression when they actually address the issue directly and thoroughly," they write.[37] What *MH* actually shows is that financial markets are not self-regulating in practice. These markets inevitably create crises of their own making and depend "ultimately and inextricably on state assistance" during these crises.[38] In a word, "financial markets survive existential crises only through state bailouts." Friedman and Schwartz's theory of the state "rejects libertarianism in favor of the technocratic neoliberal state . . ."[39] In *MH*, the Fed's purpose is to "save the financial sector and, when necessary, to substitute its judgment for market signals." The conclusion MacDonald and Paul draw is that, in his polemic, Friedman blames the Depression on the Fed for intervening at all; in his later technical study, he blames the Fed for not intervening enough. Friedman's disciple Ben Bernanke learned this lesson during the financial collapse of 2007 and 2008, shortly after Friedman's death. The Fed stepped in to save the market, bolstered it with hundreds of billions of dollars in support, and got it up and running again with few state-imposed safeguards against future collapses. Friedman the libertarian would have been aghast; Friedman the neo-liberal would have applauded.

Not all libertarians are neo-liberals, of course, since many have little or nothing to do with the MPS or its affiliated think tanks and university and college strongholds. Many non–MPS libertarians clustered under the leadership of Ludwig von Mises, who, like Hayek, was an Austrian economist and MPS founder. Unlike him, however, he was not prepared to compromise his classical liberal principles. According to Friedman, von Mises stood up at the inaugural MPS meeting and shouted, "You're all a bunch of socialists." The group "was discussing the distribution of income and whether you should have progressive income taxes," Friedman recounted to his interviewer. "Some of the people there were expressing the view that there could be a justification for it."[40] Politically, von Mises was to the right of most MPS members. After his death in 1982, his followers set up the Ludwig von Mises Institute in Auburn, Alabama, which became a leading centre for libertarian research and promotion in the United States.

***

Canada under the Harper government must have been doing something right to continue its ascent up the economic freedom rankings, but exactly what? What kind of beast is economic freedom? Walter Block, the Fraser Institute economist who helped construct the index, was clear that economic freedom should be thought of simply as "an amalgamation of the empirical indices that together comprise it. If a statistic is not included in the index," he cautioned, "it cannot determine the level of economic freedom in a given country." Block, who is also a senior fellow at the Mises Institute, specified that "economic freedom is based on statistics. If a concept cannot be quantified, it cannot enter into consideration."[41]

EFW project participants quickly forgot Block's cautionary note. Amnesia — wilful or not — can be seen regarding the weights that should be assigned to components in determining final rankings. Is the size of government more important to economic freedom than the regulation of credit, labour, and business? If so, why? And how can you quantify the difference? Further, the regulation of credit, labour, and business is itself made up of seventeen components. Are these of equal importance? In the end, Walker and his group decided not to weight anything, but to simply take averages. They averaged the seventeen components of the regulation of credit, labour, and business area to produce a ranking out of ten. They then averaged the four other areas to produce a country's final ranking. They justify their decision to take this approach to constructing the index by comparing economic freedom to an automobile. Just as it is "the interconnected parts [of] the wheels, motor, transmission, drive shaft, and frame . . . that provide the mobility of an automobile," they explain, "it may be the working of a number of interrelated factors that brings about economic freedom." It isn't necessary to assign weightings to the components of economic freedom, because they work together. "If any of the key parts are absent, the overall effectiveness is undermined."[42] How is this possible if the components are not components, as Walter Block insists, but merely statistical constructs? Is economic freedom "an amalgamation of the empirical indices that together comprise it" — something we create based on available data — or is it like an automobile where the parts work together to create mobility — something that exists in the world?

The blurring of statistical construct with reality demonstrates "how neoliberalism makes its world," in the apt phrase of Columbia University's Timothy Mitchell,[43] a world in which the statistical construct is as real as the automobile. With this constructed reality, EFW authors systematically extended the use of the index into what must surely be the most successful neo-liberal franchise of all times. The first index was published by the Fraser Institute in 1996, with nine co-publishers. By 2012, the index claimed eighty-five neo-liberal think tank co-publishers, ranging from the Afghanistan Economic and Legal Studies Organization to the Zambia Institute for Public Policy Analysis. Furthering its reach, the collective published an index of economic freedom for the states and provinces of North America starting in 2005 and for the nations of the Arab world in 2006. Such expansion became possible because of increased funding by three conservative foundations that ramped up support for the war of ideas.

The Charles G. Koch Charitable Foundation became a lead sponsor in 2009. This foundation, owned by the world's sixth-richest person, gained notoriety for pumping more than $25 million into climate-change-denial front groups over the past decade[44] and millions more into American Tea Party groups. The Searle Freedom Trust was set up by Daniel Searle, who sold the family pharmaceutical firm to Monsanto in 1985 for $2.7 billion. His trust funds dozens of neo-liberal, conservative, and libertarian think tanks and front groups. The third foundation, Peter Munk's Aurea Foundation, funds most neo-liberal think tanks in Canada and has taken on funding for North American and Arab-world indices.

The big news from the 2012 global index was the continuing climb of Canada up the rankings during the tenure of Stephen Harper and the rapid decline of the United States under Barack Obama. The Fraser Institute released the index in Toronto and followed with a three-day conference in Mexico City, as EFW participants prepared to launch a Latin American version. At fifth in the world, Canada has crept into hallowed territory, achieving its highest-ever ranking in a tie with Australia. The U.S., meanwhile, plummeted to eighteenth place, its worst performance ever. The *Toronto Sun* exclaimed that "Canadians enjoy more economic freedom than Americans."[45] The *National Post* placed the story on its front page and accompanied it with graphs and charts on page two. As the paper framed the story, this was a historic opportunity to widen the gap with the struggling United States. Niels Veldhuis, the Fraser Institute's newly installed president, explains that "what we have in front of us is a marked opportunity. We can significantly exceed the U.S. in economic freedom over the course of, I would say, the next five to 10 years. The question for Canadians is are we going to seize the opportunity or are we going to let the opportunity go by?"[46] Statistical abstraction had indeed become reality.

To ensure the index would have buy-in from political and media elites, EFW participants moved to gain currency in the academic community. If professors support it, then it must be credible, and journalists and politicians can get behind it. Alvin Rabushka, an academic from the Hoover Institution and a Mont Pelerin Society member, had brought the framework for the index to an early symposium in Vancouver in 1988. He hoped that "a side benefit of a formal rating scheme that achieved acceptance and frequent usage is that it would sensitize scholars to the idea of economic freedom and thus elevate it in stature to the much more frequently analysed topic of political freedom. That in itself would constitute an enormous payoff for this effort."[47] And it seemed to work, as the various indexes list nearly five hundred papers written about economic freedom and its relationship to other socio-economic factors. The problem, though, is that it is usually neo-liberal economists and their students who seem interested in writing these papers, so there is little push-back. The Economic Freedom of North America 2012 index, for instance, provides a list of papers that use or refer to this index.[48] Many of these papers are published in conservative or neo-liberal journals such as *Public Choice, Advances in Austrian Economics, Journal of Private Enterprise,* and *Cato Journal.* Economists with the most publications on this list received grants from the Charles Koch Foundation.

The most prominent and prolific author is Russell Sobel, formerly a professor at West Virginia University, which itself received funding from Koch for two academic and two graduate-student positions. Sobel started the neo-liberal Public Policy Foundation of West Virginia with Koch money and was elected to Mont Pelerin Society membership in 2006. He's been in the media spotlight for his Koch-sponsored studies, which claim that government mine-safety laws increase accident rates[49] (and, more importantly, limit the economic freedom of mine owners). The second-most-prolific author on the list is Nathan Ashby, an assistant professor of economics at the University of Texas in El Paso. Ashby studied under Sobel, received grants from the Koch Foundation and the Fraser Institute, and was a winner of the Hayek Fund for Scholars Award.

Looking back over twenty years of effort to transform the concept of economic freedom from its place in Milton Fried-man's dictum into the propaganda powerhouse it became, Michael Walker seemed satisfied. "I don't think that there is any question but that the index has changed the world in a very fundamental way," he told Fred McMahon, the Fraser Institute vice-president who manages the project and coordinates the network of neo-liberal think tanks that participate in it. "Most importantly, it has provided those who seek freedom a way to discuss it with their governments in an objective, unemotional, and comparative way."[50]

Confident in the success of the project, the neo-liberals took on the social democratic state with the publication of a new product that measures human, and not just economic, freedom. Once again Milton Friedman was the inspiration. In 2002, forty years after *Capitalism and Freedom*, the ninety-year-old Friedman wrote a preface to that year's global index.

> *I think the next big task facing the economic freedom project will be to try to weld the two together and make a combined index of economic and political freedom, especially where they mesh with one another. Property rights are not only a source of economic freedom. They are also a source of political freedom. That's what really got us interested in economic freedom in the first place.*[51]

The think tanks had their marching orders: prove that political freedom depends on property rights. A decade later, they produced the first index combining economic and political freedom. This time the Fraser Institute worked with the Liberales Institut, the think tank of the Friedrich Naumann Foundation for Freedom in Potsdam, Germany, a member of the economic freedom network. They dismiss efforts to measure human freedom that don't put economic freedom front and centre. Following neo-liberal ideology, they also base their work on the "negative" definition of freedom — freedom from coercion or interference. They define human freedom as "the absence of barriers or coercion that prevent individuals from acting as they might wish."[52]

As with the economic-freedom index, this approach defends wealth and those already comfortable — the property-owning class. There is a second and positive view of freedom, as opportunity, such as freedom to obtain an education. British lawyer and administrator Geoffrey Vickers explained that "the negative concept of freedom which expresses itself by 'let me alone' is characteristic of the comfortably situated. The others express their demand for freedom by 'give me a chance.' The comfortable take opportunity for granted, but their allusions only reflect their good fortune."[53] The poor may wish to do all kinds of things, but unless they have the opportunity to improve their lot in life, negative freedom is meaningless.

∗∗∗

Alberta Wildrose Party leader Danielle Smith, a self-identifying libertarian, was following neo-liberal doctrine when she declared that "without economic freedom, all our other freedoms are at risk. And property rights are really the foundation of economic freedom."[54] She referred to property rights three times in her acceptance speech when she won the Wildrose leadership in 2009.[55] She promised to entrench basic property rights in the Alberta Bill of Rights before the 2012 Alberta provincial election.[56] Smith's party didn't win the election, so entrenching private-property rights — making sacrosanct "the exclusive authority to determine how a resource is used"[57] — will have to wait for another day, a day perhaps not that far off given the uncertainty facing Alberta's Progressive Conservative party's fortunes. But it's never far from the top of the neo-liberal agenda. The *Economic Freedom of the World* (EFW) index explains that:

> *Security of property rights, protected by the rule of law, provides the foundation for both economic*

freedom and the efficient operation of markets.
Freedom to exchange, for example, is meaningless
if individuals do not have secure rights to
property, including the fruits of their labor . . .
Countries with major deficiencies in this area are
unlikely to prosper regardless of their policies in
the other . . . areas.[58]

Smith has advocated for stronger private-property rights for more than a decade. In 1996, she spent a year as an intern at the Fraser Institute during the period when the think tank released its first economic-freedom index. She was the keynote speaker at the first Canadian property-rights conference, held at Ottawa's Lord Elgin Hotel in September 2012, after her party lost the Alberta election. Federal Conservative MP Scott Reid and provincial Progressive Conservative MPP Randy Hillier hosted the event, along with the Institute for Liberal Studies, a small Ontario-based libertarian (classical liberal, they call it) organization that spreads libertarian ideology through seminars on university campuses as well as annual summer seminars. From their eastern–Ontario stronghold, Hillier and Reid are at the forefront of a burgeoning movement to entrench private-property rights in the *Charter of Rights and Freedoms*, something that has been unattainable since Pierre Trudeau, as justice minister, raised the idea of a charter of rights in 1968. The goal of the conference, Reid explained, was "to build some of the intellectual underpinnings that are essential to the [property rights] movement growing and expanding."[59] They had devised a new strategy for inserting property rights into the *Charter.* Because the amending formula is so onerous — passage by Parliament and agreement of seven provinces with 50 per cent of the population — they decided to work through Section 43 of the *Charter*, under which an amendment can apply only to Ontario and requires passage by Parliament and the Ontario legislature.[60] If successful, other provinces with conservative governments, such as an Alberta led by Danielle Smith, could follow the same route. Reid certainly knows his constitutional ins and outs; he was constitutional adviser to Preston Manning and senior researcher for the Reform caucus during the nineties.

Smith claims that many of the seats her party won in the Alberta election were due to its stance on property rights. She had a simple message: "Property rights have been eroded incrementally and they will be won back incrementally."[61] She applauded the Harper government for its progress based on this incremental approach: abolishing the gun registry, opening up the Canadian Wheat Board (CWB) to competition — "what an incredible blow for economic freedom," she enthused[62] — and working with First Nations advisors to bring property rights to reserves. University of Calgary political scientist Tom Flanagan, a long-time Stephen Harper associate, gave an update on this latter campaign that he was masterminding. (See Chapter 4.) He endorsed incrementalism, "the importance of small incremental changes that are not based on some abstract notion of property rights," as Scott Reid summarized Flanagan's presentation, "but become part of the architecture. You can measure their success and build on them."[63]

***

The Harper government kept the increments coming. Ending the long-standing single-desk selling of wheat and barley by the Canadian Wheat Board was celebrated as a victory — the "incredible blow," described in Danielle Smith's words — for economic freedom. Six months after Harper's 2011 majority victory, Parliament passed the *Marketing Freedom for Grain Farmers Act*, which transformed the CWB from a mandatory into a voluntary organization. The CWB had been established during the Great

Depression to protect grain farmers devastated by the collapse in grain markets. It benefited most grain growers, but remained a thorn in the side of corporate farmers. "Western Canadian farmers have waited far too long for the freedom to market wheat and barley that they pay to plant, spends months to grow and tirelessly harvest," federal agriculture minister Gerry Ritz declared.[64]

In fact, most farmers support the system. The CWB held a plebiscite in 2011, with 62 per cent of farmer-members voting to keep the single-desk system for wheat and 51 per cent for barley.[65] But majority support for the CWB is irrelevant, because, as the economic-freedom project makes clear, economic rights trump political rights. The day the legislation went into effect in August 2012, Harper was on a farm near Kindersley, Saskatchewan, where he and Ritz celebrated market-freedom day. Harper issued "royal pardons" for farmers who had been convicted during the nineties of driving grain across the border into the U.S. in contravention of the *Canadian Wheat Board Act*. "For these courageous farmers, their convictions will no longer tarnish their good names," he declared. "It is to them that much of this victory is owed."[66]

With that victory in his pocket, Harper moved on to the next increment — Canada's long-standing supply-management system. Like the Canadian Wheat Board, this system was intended to support small farmers, but neo-liberals and libertarians alike saw it as another obstacle to economic freedom. Supply management was implemented in the 1970s to benefit milk and, later, chicken, egg, and cheese producers by assuring them a stable income and protecting them from lower-priced, usually subsidized, imports. Supply-management marketing boards gave small farmers economic clout when dealing with large corporations, given the reality that farmers receive a miniscule proportion of the retail price of their products.[67] Here too, neo-liberals saw the system as a distortion of the market, which had to be eliminated. For five years, Neil Reynolds, the avowed libertarian who died in 2013, beat the drum for economic freedom in the pages of the *Globe and Mail.* He mentioned supply management in thirteen columns, including five after Harper's majority victory. Supply management was "a protectionist scam that coddles dairy farmers and severely limits Canada's ability to feed the world," he claimed in one column.[68]

New Zealand ended its supply-management system in the early 1980s, Reynolds reported in one of his last columns for the *Globe,* and "an industrial revolution followed." His sole source for this assertion is an essay published by the Cato Institute, an EFW Index co-publisher.[69] Reynolds should have used other sources, because New Zealand never had supply management, but a system of tariffs and subsidies to support the entire agricultural sector.[70] Reynolds also failed to mention that the dairy sector is based on farmer cooperatives — anathema to market fundamentalists — permitting "a strong marketing and distribution presence in world markets."[71] After they ended supply management, Reynolds erroneously reported, New Zealand farmers began to operate more efficiently and increased their productivity by leaps and bounds. It wasn't the non-existent supply management that was ended (in 1984), but a system of tariffs and supports. New Zealand's success was based on its long-standing orientation to export markets, not freedom from supply management. Reynolds then informed readers that, according to an economic-freedom index developed by the Heritage Foundation, the largest American neo-liberal think tank, New Zealand was the fourth-freest country in the world and Canada was sixth (having moved up again under Harper's steady hand). "This difference in ranking comes down to supply management," Reynolds concluded. If Canadians — especially those whose dream was a Canadian market state — seek to further improve Canada's ranking on the economic-freedom index, supply management has to go.

Intellectual support for this position came from the massed power of neo-liberal think tanks. Just a decade after supply-management boards were established in British Columbia in 1972, the Fraser Institute asserted in a study that Vancouver consumers paid thirty cents a dozen more for eggs than Seattle residents. The reason for this disparity was the provincial "egg marketing cartel."[72] The institute continued its attacks on marketing "cartels" over the ensuing decades. On the prairies, the Frontier Centre for Public Policy went after the cartels in the pages of the *Winnipeg Free Press, Regina Leader Post*, and *Saskatoon Star Phoenix*. The Montreal Economic Institute took a different — and creative — tack. It claims marketing boards contribute to the country's obesity epidemic by raising milk, egg, and chicken prices beyond the reach of the poor, driving them to eat junk food instead.[73] In Ottawa, the Macdonald–Laurier Institute (MLI), the most recent addition to Canada's neo-liberal think tank network, coordinated its attacks on supply management with reported developments within the Harper government, a relationship that will be explored in Chapter 2. The MLI released its study, with the predictable title "Milking the System," just as the American government's invitation to Canada to join the Trans–Pacific Partnership talks, the free-trade deal being negotiated by nine nations on either side of the Pacific Ocean, was made public. News stories speculated about Canada's supply-management system being put on the table as a requirement for Canada to get into the talks.

The MLI report was greeted with a media feeding frenzy, led by the *National Post*. The MLI's Brian Lee Crowley and Jason Clemens, in a *Post* opinion piece, tied the fate of supply management to Harper's trade ambitions. "Supply management is becoming a painful obstacle to opening international markets for Canadian goods and services," the two wrote, "at a time when trade liberalization is a vital part of the government's economic strategy."[74] The same day, the *Post* published an op-ed by MLI senior fellow Laura Dawson and an editorial lauding the report. The Crowley–Clemens commentary was republished in papers across the country, and Crowley was on CTV and CBC. The *National Post*'s Chris Selley referred to the MLI piece and exclaimed, "It's a no-brainer. Do it."

A paper by former Liberal MP Martha Hall Findlay had even greater impact on the campaign. Following her 2011 election loss, Findlay was appointed an executive fellow at the University of Calgary's School of Public Policy, by school director Jack Mintz. The institutional setting for Findlay's paper is important, because of the school's close ties to Harper, as Chapter 2 will discuss. Findlay sat across the aisle from Harper and his caucus in Parliament, but, as a business Liberal in the mould of former Liberal finance minister John Manley, who resurfaced as the head of the Canadian Council of Chief Executives, she is not far from Harper on economic issues. Tom Flanagan, who had joined her at the School of Public Policy, says that Harper was opposed to supply management, but decided not to dismantle the system because he worried it would hurt him in Ontario.[75] Findlay's paper demonstrates this is not the case. Getting rid of supply management will not cost him many seats.

Focusing on milk production, the largest protected industry, Findlay notes that the number of dairy farms has declined by 90 per cent since 1970, when supply management was introduced. So the number of votes involved are much reduced. Her analysis shows further that farms are concentrated in electoral districts where one or another party won by a commanding margin in 2011. Even if some electors change their votes, she argues, few, if any, districts will see their results change. Only thirteen ridings contain more than three hundred dairy farms. Five of these are in Ontario, and are strongly held by Conservatives who won by a margin of at least 10,000 votes. Even if Harper loses all five, plus three more in Quebec that the Conservatives won by overwhelming margins, he will still have his majority. Harper has nothing to fear on the electoral front, Findlay, the former

Liberal Party leadership candidate advises Harper.

Findlay's paper received royal treatment from the so-called second-hand dealers in ideas. Media coverage commenced with a Findlay column in the *Globe and Mail*. The same day she received a positive column in the *Ottawa Citizen* and an editorial and front-page story in the *National Post*. Next day, Andrew Coyne's glowing tribute was reprinted in nearly every Postmedia paper across the country.[76] The Liberal-leaning *Toronto Star* published a positive editorial and a column by Richard Gwyn. Of course, the *National Post's* crusty libertarian ideologue Terence Corcoran weighed in, along with positive offerings from Chris Selley, economist William Watson, and trade lawyer Lawrence Herman. It wasn't until three weeks later that one column critical of the Findlay study appeared in the *Winnipeg Free Press*,[77] but it was ignored. The results were in. The media spoke with one voice, and their message was clear: supply management must go.

***

Like many enemies of supply management, Findlay tied its elimination to the negotiations underway for a new trade agreement.

> *With lucrative free trade agreements being considered, and in particular the prospect of joining (or being refused access to) the Trans-Pacific Partnership, now is the time for the Harper government to reach out to the provinces and farmers, and move away from supply management for the good of all Canadians.*[78]

When Findlay wrote her paper, the Trans-Pacific Partnership was a nine-member, American-led effort to further entrench corporate rights in the global economy, in what U.S. trade representative Ron Kirk called "an ambitious, 21st century" agreement. The original members were the United States, Chile, and Peru on one side of the Pacific, and Australia, New Zealand, Singapore, Malaysia, Brunei, and Vietnam on the other. In 2011, the U.S. "arm-twisted" Japan into agreeing to join the talks. International-affairs columnist Jonathan Manthorpe reported on the skepticism about the feasibility of such an agreement ever coming to pass, as well as the "suspicion bordering on paranoia" in China that the TPP is a "Washington plot to contain and constrain China's economic rise."[79]

In June 2012, President Obama invited NAFTA partners Canada and Mexico to join the TPP talks. The apparent price for Canada's admission: putting supply management on the negotiating table. Findlay's paper came out the same month. It was neatly executed. Canada already has trade agreements with four TPP partners: the U.S., Peru, Chile, and Mexico.[80] As Unifor economist Jim Stanford notes, the other six members combined account for less than 1 per cent of Canada's exports.[81] There's barely any trade advantage for Canada. The partnership could be significant for Canada if Japan joins, since Japan is Canada's second-largest destination for agricultural exports.

Ottawa greeted the invitation to join the TPP with enthusiasm. Peter Van Loan was no longer international trade minister. After the 2011 election, Harper had installed Abbotsford, B.C., MP Ed Fast in the portfolio. Just after the TPP announcement, Fast was in Winnipeg speaking at a Canadian Manufacturers and Exporters luncheon. He bragged about his government's accomplishments on the trade front: "Our government believes that trade is the new stimulus and that freer and more open trade around the world is critical for the global economic recovery." This approach was already paying off, he told the business audience. "Friends, our pro-trade plan has already made Canada one of the most open pro-trade economies in the world.

Indeed, the Economic Freedom Index ranks Canada sixth in the world in terms of the openness of its economy."[82]

Openness seemed to be relative, though. Removing other obstacles to the market state were under intense discussion by TPP partners, but this only came out later, because talks take place under extreme secrecy. Even Democratic Senator Ron Wyden of Oregon, who chairs the Senate committee with official jurisdiction over TPP and who is a staunch supporter of free-trade agreements, was denied access to the U.S. proposals for the talks. Over six hundred corporate advisers, in contrast, have direct access to TPP documents and texts. Leaked documents, published by citizen-advocacy organization Public Citizen, outline new and enforceable corporate rights and privileges and constraints on government regulation.[83] It's a virtual checklist for economic freedom — but for corporations, not individuals: extending the length of patent protection for drugs, entrenching the right of companies to offshore jobs, giving foreign corporations the right to challenge a country's environmental, land-use, health, and other laws before international tribunals, and entrenching greater copyright protection. With these new rules, Canada's ranking on the EFW index will surely improve, especially if eliminating Canada's supply management regime is part of the deal, and Harperism will move another step forward.

***

The EFW Index may be the Mont Pelerin Society's most brilliant creation. It sounds so much more positive than the policies on which it is based: deregulation, low taxes, weak unions, the primacy of property over human rights and trade over jobs. And it can be used to justify these policies. Who can be against economic freedom? And who doesn't want to be rising in the rankings, not sinking, as is the case with the Obama administration in the

United States? Left unsaid, though, is why the American ranking is declining: intervening in the market to save financial institutions and car makers from collapse, raising the minimum wage, reinstating higher taxes on the wealthy, to name a few. The EFW Index casts what many believe to be positive moves as negative drags on economic freedom. And it's working. The release of the index each year further entrenches neo-liberal thinking in the public mind. That makes the job to sell more all-encompassing trade deals or to entrench property rights in the *Charter of Rights* — at least for a single province — that much easier. If economic freedom and property rights are locked in a struggle with democracy and political rights, it's an unequal contest, and one side is winning. Friedrich Hayek died before the first EFW index was published, but Milton Friedman lived to experience ten years of publication. Through the Mont Pelerin Society, the EFW index's phalanxes of think tanks and academics and Stephen Harper's diligent application, his legacy burns brighter than ever.

2

SEND IN THE THINK TANKS TO WIN THE BATTLE OF IDEAS

Brian Lee Crowley was having a very good year. In 2012 his Macdonald–Laurier Institute (MLI) had been operating less than three years, but was already influencing federal policy-making. Crowley was everywhere in the media that year, writing a biweekly column in the *Ottawa Citizen* and a column a month for the influential *Hill Times*. He wrote three opinion pieces in the *Globe and Mail* and five in the *National Post*. His pieces were published twenty-three times in the *Calgary Herald*, sixteen in the *Vancouver Sun,* and dozens more times in other Canadian papers. He was seen and heard multiple times on television and radio. His staff and senior fellows magnified the think tank's impact, with commentaries in all major news media on a wide range of subjects.

During the same year, MLI produced many papers on issues crucial to the neo-liberal project: why we must expand energy exports; why some Canadian provinces are in danger of hitting the debt wall; why agricultural supply management has to go;

why provinces should be encouraged to experiment with two-tier health care; why we must welcome more foreign investment; why all provinces benefit from Alberta bitumen exports; why inequality is not such a big deal; why we should allow oil tankers off the West Coast; and much more. The institute started a bimonthly magazine, *Inside Policy*, releasing the first issue on the twenty-fifth anniversary of the Canada–United States Free Trade Agreement. Crowley was named one of the hundred most influential people in Ottawa by the *Hill Times*. MLI was rated the fifth best new think tank (established in the past 18 months) in the world by the University of Pennsylvania's International Relations Program.[1] And the institute was one of only two new think tanks to win the 2012 Templeton Freedom Award for special achievement by a young institute, awarded by the Atlas Economic Research Foundation.[2]

With his think tank's credibility firmly established, Crowley expanded his messaging in subsequent years, with biweekly columns in the *Globe and Mail* (where he had earlier spent two years on the editorial board) and the *Ottawa Citizen*, the papers with the greatest impact in Ottawa. MLI studies were cited in major Canadian media and MLI fellows and authors wrote dozens of opinion pieces.

It was quite the beginning for the Macdonald–Laurier Institute, a new type of think tank for Canada, one established after a party with a neo-liberal agenda had taken over the reins of government. Crowley frames MLI as "a rigorously non-partisan organization open to new ideas based on solid factual evidence."[3] To ensure the organization follows this mandate, Crowley set up a research advisory board, whose members may be non-partisan, but certainly not non-ideological, as all eight members cluster at the conservative end of the political spectrum.[4]

Crowley is well positioned for the task at hand. He is an ardent devotee of Friedrich Hayek, neo-liberalism's high priest.

His friend, pundit Andrew Coyne, tells the story of how Crowley went to the London School of Economics — Coyne was there too — with the goal of writing a thesis debunking Hayek. Crowley soon found himself unable to answer Hayek's arguments, and finally was persuaded by them. He "had become a convert," Coyne wrote in the foreword to Crowley's book *Fearful Symmetry*.[5]

Crowley the convert wrote a lengthy and adoring polemic about Hayek for *Next City* magazine — a short-lived publication funded by the Donner Canadian Foundation and published by Lawrence Solomon, then head of Toronto-based Energy Probe — on the hundredth anniversary of Hayek's birth.[6] (Coyne was a contributing editor to this magazine.) Titled "The Man Who Changed Everyone's Life," the article compared Hayek's assault on "central planning and government regimentation of individual life" with the Allied invasion of Normandy "in the military battle against the totalitarian Axis powers in Europe." In this, he was following Hayek's lead in associating government planning with totalitarian dictatorship. Crowley trashed Hayek's rival John Maynard Keynes, whom he claimed Hayek regarded as a glib, amoral homosexual and intellectual dilettante, whose theories, unlike Hayek's, would not stand the test of time. Delusional intellectuals were determined to press interventionism to achieve "mastery of our social and economic life." In contrast, the Hayek-inspired Thatcher revolution reinvigorated British life and "removed the dead hand of government control and political interference from vast swaths of the economy." He lauded Thatcher's moves to privatize everything she could. Crowley concluded with the observation that Hayek "can truly be said to have shaped the course of the century" and he offered us a way "back onto the road of freedom and progress." On the twentieth anniversary of Hayek's death (2012), Crowley republished parts of his essay in the *National Post* under the headline "We're all Hayekians now," repeating his critique of Keynes — except for the part about Keynes's alleged homosexuality — and his adulation of Hayek.[7]

***

As was mentioned in Chapter 1, Friedrich Hayek astutely pointed out in his influential 1949 article, "The Intellectuals and Socialism," that a key target in the war of ideas is what he called second-hand dealers. Hayek had a solution to the problem of how to reach and influence them and recruited British businessman Antony Fisher to put his plan into operation. Fisher had made a fortune by introducing factory-farmed chicken in Britain after the Second World War. He had also read a condensed version of Hayek's *The Road to Serfdom* in the *Reader's Digest*, and it had a profound impact on him. He sought out Hayek, then teaching at the London School of Economics, where Crowley and Coyne would study forty years later. Hayek advised Fisher not to waste his time going into politics to fight the socialists. Instead, Hayek counselled Fisher to become involved in the "great battle of ideas" by creating "a scholarly research organisation to supply intellectuals in universities, schools, journalism, and broadcasting with authoritative studies of the economic theory of markets and its application to practical affairs."[8] Fisher became lifelong friends with Hayek and, in 1954, was invited to join the Mont Pelerin Society. The following year Fisher established the Institute of Economic Affairs (IEA) in London. This would be the prototype for MLI, the Fraser Institute, and the hundreds of neo-liberal think tanks that followed.

"It was ten years before the IEA could truthfully claim to be exerting an appreciable influence on debate, and at least another five before its success looked beyond doubt," Fisher's biographer reports.[9] The organization's preferred product was a lively ten-thousand-word monograph aimed at journalists writing for quality newspapers, urging them to review or write about the publication. Each monograph was accompanied with an executive summary and news release for busy readers. Make no concessions to existing political or economic realities, but stick to neo-liberal doctrine, was the guiding principle of all IEA publications.[10]

Fisher provided a model that conservative and libertarian business executives could use to turn public and elite opinion away from support for interventionist governments and back to a favourable view of capitalism and the market. Their collective impact was instrumental in shifting the British climate of ideas to such an extent that Margaret Thatcher could sweep into office with an agenda to bring "the British economy under the discipline of market forces."[11] One supporter declared that "had it not been for the Institute of Economic Affairs, there would have been no Thatcher Revolution. They prepared the ground."[12] Not only did the Fisher model colonize Britain, it was exported to the United States, Australia, and further afield. In Canada, the Fraser Institute was established in 1974, with hands-on support from Fisher.

With the continued activism of the early Trudeau government in Ottawa and the election of the New Democratic government of Dave Barrett in British Columbia, with its ambitious social-democratic agenda, business executives became alarmed. Noranda Mines chairman, Alf Powis, felt "what was needed was a think tank that would re-establish the dominance of free enterprise ideas, the values of the market, and property rights."[13] Fisher was invited to Vancouver by economist Michael Walker (who knew of Fisher's work through Walker's lifelong friend, Milton Friedman) and forestry executive Patrick Boyle. They asked Fisher to replicate the success of the IEA, and followed Fisher's formula for funding, projects, experts, and dissemination:[14] employ a core group of researchers and contract with sympathetic academics to conduct specific studies that support neo-liberal doctrine; disseminate the results through conferences, books, reports, and news and opinion pieces to reach relevant second-hand dealers in ideas in academia and the media; finance the enterprise by appealing to wealthy conservative business executives and their foundations and to corporations that can benefit from institute activities.[15] At first the new institute was greeted with a lukewarm response from the business press. But within a few years, it achieved success on all fronts, lining up corporate and foundation supporters, academic collaborators, and media cheerleaders.

Fisher established two more think tanks, the Manhattan Institute for Policy Research with William Casey, a Wall Street speculator and later Ronald Reagan's CIA director, and the Pacific Research Institute, with local business leader James North in San Francisco. As with the Fraser Institute, they chose geographical names rather than trumpeting their ideological purpose. Fisher received requests from business executives around the world to help them set up similar organizations in their own countries to promote the free-market and individual liberty. In 1981, he established the Atlas Economic Research Foundation to automate the process of setting up and running such think tanks. Atlas is based in Arlington, Virginia, and is named after Ayn Rand's libertarian screed *Atlas Shrugged*. In 2013 it worked with 478 neo-liberal — Atlas calls them "market-oriented" — think tanks around the world.[16] Atlas's executive director, Alex Chafuen, is a long-standing Fraser Institute trustee.

During the 1990s, a new wave of neo-liberal think tanks swept across the nation. With organizational support from Atlas and start-up funding from the Donner Canadian Foundation, local business executives and neo-liberal policy entrepreneurs founded regional think tanks in Halifax (Atlantic Institute for Market Studies, 1994), Montreal (Montreal Economic Institute,

1999), and Winnipeg (Frontier Centre for Public Policy, 1999). The Fraser Institute set up a branch office in Calgary to tap into neo-liberal and neo-conservative academics at the University of Calgary, started a Toronto satellite office to support the work of the Mike Harris government, and opened a branch office in Montreal to urge the province to back away from its social democratic leanings. The regionalization of corporate-sponsored think tanks followed the American model, where such organizations were created in most states to provide a neo-liberal perspective on policy issues at state and municipal levels.[17] Montreal Economic Institute executive director Michel Kelly-Gagnon explained to the *National Post* that "we are trying to change the climate of opinion in Quebec." The Fraser and Howe institutes "do good work but they fail to penetrate Quebec. The message needs to come from within the tribe"[18] (or at least from the tribe's chiefs — the institute's corporate backers). Donner also backed the creation of single-issue advocacy groups like the Dominion Institute (to attack the social-history approach to history education), the Canadian Constitution Foundation (to defend individual liberty against the state's supposed onslaught), and the Society for the Advancement of Excellence in Education (to promote choice and charter schools in public education). Finally, in 2008, the Macdonald–Laurier Institute was established in Ottawa to backstop the Harper government's incremental move to the market state.

When Atlas celebrated its twenty-fifth anniversary, it could boast of affiliated think tanks in six Canadian provinces, forty-four American states, nearly every country in Central and South America, eleven African and Middle Eastern countries, nearly every country in Greater Europe, and most countries of South and Southeast Asia.[19] Eighty-five Atlas-related think tanks participate in the Fraser Institute's Economic Freedom of the World project, as we have seen. It was an instructive display of ideological power. But, as was the intention of the project from the beginning, corporate power is supporting seemingly independent research.

***

Crowley started his career as a neo-liberal policy entrepreneur at the Atlantic Institute for Market Studies in Halifax, which he launched with over a million dollars of Donner funding and Atlas support. As with all neo-liberal think tanks, the confluence of neo-liberal doctrine and corporate interests seemed to guide AIMS's work. AIMS proposed privatizing New Brunswick Power and allowing electricity rates to rise; the president of Emera Inc., the largest private utility in the region, which would be a prime beneficiary of the policy, chaired the AIMS board. AIMS proposed "modernizing" the Newfoundland fishery by allowing industry to shut down "inefficient" plants; the president of Fishery Products International, which owns dozens of these inefficient plants, was on the board. AIMS proposed doing away with zoning and planning regulations on land development; the CEO of Empire Co., an owner of shopping malls and office buildings and a residential land developer, was on the advisory council.[20] AIMS became a neo-liberal and Stephen Harper favourite. During its tenth-anniversary year (2004–05), then-Opposition leader Harper called AIMS "dollar for dollar the best think tank in the country."[21]

The following year, Crowley was appointed Clifford Clark Visiting Economist in the Department of Finance by deputy minister Rob Wright. Occupants of this prestigious post — there have been eleven — advise the department "on emerging economic issues and take part in policy development at the highest level,"[22] the department website explains. In his preface to *Fearful Symmetry*, Crowley reports he had been invited by his friend Kevin Lynch, who had just been made clerk of the Privy Council by newly installed prime minister Stephen Harper, to be on a panel "about the chief economic challenges facing the country"[23] at an Ottawa retreat for the new flock of deputy ministers. Wright attended the panel session and must have foreseen the winds of change set to sweep through Ottawa — Jim Flaherty, late of Ontario premier Mike Harris's "common-sense revolution," had just been appointed finance minister. So Wright invited Crowley to join the department and help him and Flaherty fashion a budget for the Harper era. Four months later, Crowley incorporated the Macdonald–Laurier Institute.[24]

Flaherty later hosted a private dinner at Toronto's Albany Club to raise support for the think tank. He wrote a letter inviting corporate executives to the event. He was "giving [the think tank] my personal backing," he wrote, "and I hope that you will consider doing the same . . . This important national initiative deserves to succeed," the letter continued. "Please join me in ensuring that it does. My office will follow up with you."[25] The finance minister seemed to be using his office to raise funds for the new think tank to promote certain ideals, which Flaherty enumerated: smaller government, lower taxes, and greater personal responsibility. It was a "level of coziness between [Flaherty's] department and right-wing think tanks that might make many Canadians uncomfortable," *Toronto Star* columnist Linda McQuaig suggested.[26]

The Harper government and MLI maintained their cozy relationship. Harper's 2008 election platform was titled "The True North Strong and Free"; Crowley's motto for his think tank is "True North in Canadian Public Policy." Coincidence perhaps, but there have been many coincidences.

- In 2010, MLI published a paper arguing that Canada Mortgage and Housing Corporation, the Crown corporation that provides most mortgage insurance, enjoyed an unfair competitive advantage over private firms that should be eliminated. In 2012, the MLI recommended a thorough review of how CMHC finances mortgages. One recommendation was to bring CMHC under the oversight of the Office of the Superintendent of Financial Institutions. Eight weeks later Flaherty did this and even mused about privatizing CMHC, something MLI was also urging, laying out a detailed plan to accomplish this.[27]

- When the Harper government renamed the Museum of Civilization the Canadian Museum of History, Crowley was quick off the mark to attack critics of the change, "civilization" being an unwelcome term in the neo-liberal market-driven universe,[28] while a Canadian-history focus on the prime ministers and wars was a key ingredient in Harper's quest to promote patriotism. (See Chapter 8.)

- When the Harper government had eighteen tough-on-crime bills before Parliament in the months before the 2011 election, even though crime rates were in decline, the MLI produced a study saying there was no decline. Crime rates are up if you include unreported crime. MLI repeated the study in 2013 with the same conclusion.[29] The think tank even produced a scorecard assessing which of its recommendations the Harper government was pursuing.[30]

- An October 2011 paper by MLI senior fellow Benjamin Perrin recommended strategies Canada should pursue to deter immigrant smuggling. Some of these were adopted by Citizenship and Immigration Minister Jason Kenney in proposed legislation (Bill C-31: *Protecting Canada's*

Immigration System Act, 2012). Perrin subsequently spent a year in the Prime Minister's Office as a legal adviser on justice, public safety and citizenship and immigration.[31]

- In 2013 the Institute laid out a plan for how the Northern Gateway pipeline project could be put on a sounder footing. Key was a strategy for aboriginal engagement, a quest the Harper government had already embarked on.[32]

- Also in 2013 the Institute provided legal backup for the Harper government's decision to turn health-care delivery back to the provinces. This would allow private health care, private insurance, user fees and extra billing, the study suggested.[33]

Harper certainly approved of the relationship. On MLI publications since April 2012, the prime minister is quoted as saying, "I commend Brian Crowley and the team at MLI for your laudable work as one of the leading policy think tanks in our nation's capital. The Institute has distinguished itself as a thoughtful, empirically-based and non-partisan contributor to our national public discourse."

MLI didn't open its doors for nearly a year after Flaherty's pitch, while Crowley raised additional funds. Donner gave him $48,000 in seed money, plus an additional $390,000 over the following four years.[34] Crowley solicited contributions from four of the five big banks. (Remember his close connections to the finance minister.) He picked up funding from Genworth Financial, the private-sector competitor to CMHC. Crowley also received donations from Pharmaceutical Research and Manufacturers of America, the drug industry's lobby group, along with Merck, Pfizer Canada, Johnson & Johnson, and AstraZeneca Canada. From the oil-and-gas industry, he received sponsorships from Encana and the Canadian Petroleum Products Institute, an industry lobby group. And on the media front, CTV is a sponsor. Perhaps that explains the subject of MLI's first debate in its Great Canadian Debates series: "Resolved that Canada no longer needs the CBC." (Andrew Coyne spoke for the motion.)

***

While Crowley was working with Flaherty in Ottawa, another initiative was being constructed in Calgary. Corporate lawyer and former University of Calgary chancellor James Palmer donated $4 million to the university to set up yet another unusual type of organization for Canada — a neo-liberal think tank embedded within a university. To announce its creation, the School for Public Policy (SPP) invited Condoleezza Rice, George W. Bush's secretary of state, to be the keynote speaker at a $500-a-plate dinner for 1,100 guests (raising another half-million dollars for the school). Despite anti-war demonstrators outside, Rice was an appropriate choice for the launch because she is a member of Stanford University's political science department and a senior fellow at the neo-liberal Hoover Institution, which is affiliated with the university.[35] Stanford-Hoover seems to be the model Palmer and his advisers followed in Calgary, though a school is a different creature than an institute (which implies more autonomy). The SPP benefits from the university's reputation for scholarship and independent research and, at the same time, promotes neo-liberal ideology in which research serves a different purpose, as Chapter 1 explains. Crowley at the MLI didn't have to worry about the competition from the West, though. Palmer and Crowley were old allies. Palmer, a native of Prince Edward Island, was an original financial supporter of Crowley's Atlantic Institute for Market Studies and remained on the AIMS board for over a decade. It was just more massing on the neo-liberal end of the political spectrum.

The university brought in tax specialist Jack Mintz, CEO of the C.D. Howe Institute, to head the SPP and occupy the Palmer Chair in Public Policy. Like C.D. Howe, corporate influence in this new organization is heavy — but unusual, given that this is a university operation dealing with public policy. Palmer was one of Canada's top oil-and-gas lawyers (he died in 2013), specializing in corporate mergers and acquisitions.[36] He was on the boards of numerous oil and gas companies, and for a few years lobbied the federal government for Imperial Oil and its parent company ExxonMobil, promoting their oil pipeline proposals. Imperial Oil's CEO, Tim Hearn, had just retired and joined the SPP's advisory council; his company subsequently donated $1 million to the school. (Head of the SPP, Jack Mintz is a director of Imperial Oil and of the Imperial Oil Foundation that distributes six-to-seven million dollars a year to organizations in communities where Imperial Oil operates.) Hearn's successor at Imperial Oil, Bruce Marsh, was a featured speaker at SPP's kick-off conference the day after Rice's speech. That the school would be top-heavy with fossil-fuel-industry support shouldn't be surprising, given its location in Calgary and given the makeup of the university's board of governors. Board chair Bonnie DuPont was a senior executive at Enbridge, while other governors were from Suncor and the Canadian Energy Pipeline Association. The university's president Elizabeth Cannon is a geomatics engineer, a director of Enbridge Income Fund Holdings, and a trustee of Enbridge Income Fund, which operates the company's oil and gas pipelines.

The school seems to be a marriage of business and ideology. A decade before SPP was established, a group of political scientists, historians, and economists at the university emerged as the intellectual backup for neo-liberal and social-conservative causes.

Dubbed the Calgary School, these academics coalesced around arguments forged to attack special-interest groups (except business and neo-liberals): slash social programs, downsize government, deregulate the economy, and cut taxes.[37] Led by political scientist Tom Flanagan, the Calgary School had enormous influence on federal policy and politics. It helped shape the direction of the Reform Party and Canadian Alliance and dominated the thinking of Stephen Harper, who studied under Calgary School professors, selected one — Flanagan — as a close adviser, and picked the student of another — Ian Brodie, who studied under Calgary School political scientist Ted Morton — as his first chief of staff.

After SPP was up and running, the entire Calgary School — with the exception of political scientist Barry Cooper — moved over into its ranks: historian David Bercuson as area director of international policy; Rainer Knopff (faculty); Flanagan (distinguished fellow); and Morton (executive in residence).[38] Finally, in 2013, Brodie joined the organization as its research director, reinforcing the ties between SPP and Harper. Darrel Reid, who occupied various senior positions in Harper's PMO, and ended up as deputy chief of staff, was already at SPP as an executive fellow. Economist Robert Mansell, a Calgary School affiliate, became the SPP's academic director. He had been one of Harper's professors, and arranged the meeting between Harper and Preston Manning that brought Harper into the Reform Party fold. (In his thesis, Harper acknowledges Mansell's support for "both my academic and non-academic pursuits."[39]) Calgary School academics met with Harper and Manning to formulate Reform Party policy, which Harper assembled in the party's Blue Book.

The school's neo-liberal credentials are indicated by its phalanx of Fraser Institute fellows (past and present) who are program directors: Eugene Beaulieu is the school's director for international economics; Herb Emery, director of health policy;

Ron Kneebone, director of economic and social policy; and Ken McKenzie, director of tax and economic growth. Given the lineup of neo-liberal and libertarian personnel, even allowing for a scattering of centrists and progressives, it's not surprising that SPP's research follows a well-trodden path: Alberta needs to cut its spending; governments need to privatize services; business taxes need to be cut; private pension plans are the route to enhanced retirement income; the mandatory long-form census is an overuse of state power; income inequality is not a bad thing; and supply management has to go (as SPP executive fellow Martha Hall Findlay concluded in her paper discussed in Chapter 1).

Nor is it surprising that the school emphasizes research supporting the oil industry, given the industry's influence, at least at the administrative level. In one paper written in collaboration with American oil pipeline consultants, SPP authors sound the alarm that Alberta must get its bitumen to markets in the Pacific Rim as quickly as possible, or risk losing out to competitors. Canada needs to get on with the Northern Gateway and Trans Mountain expansion projects as quickly as possible, the paper urges.[40] Another paper trashes the idea of green jobs, calling them "illusory" because only the market can create economically efficient jobs based on "the intensity of energy use and greenhouse gas emissions per unit of output." The study ignores the nature or quality of the output.[41] SPP research seems to downplay negative impacts of energy development. One paper asserts that "Canada's plentiful resources are an indisputable blessing, and those critics of federal industrial policy who compare this country to illiberal and corrupt 'petro-states' are being either ignorant or deceitful."[42] Another paper claims the Canadian economy suffers, not from Dutch disease, but from Canadian disease. This newly diagnosed affliction is due to "Canada's extraordinarily heavy reliance on the United States as a trading partner." But since a third of Canadian exports to the U.S. are oil and gas products, isn't it still Dutch disease? No, the SPP author counters. It's perhaps "a Dutch Affair," which could become Dutch disease if left untreated.[43] Most recently an SPP paper about "the facts" on Canada's energy trade presents as one fact the claim that promoting energy trade "requires lowering investment barriers and creating a predictable and stable investment climate for foreign direct investment."[44]

***

Stephen Harper hasn't yet appeared at the SPP — close connections notwithstanding — but he has courted the neo-liberal infrastructure throughout his political journey. As leader of the Canadian Alliance, he spoke at a luncheon sponsored by the Montreal Economic Institute in 2003, where he declared "the Quebecois sovereigntist movement as we've known it is dead. And Pierre Trudeau's vision of Canadian sovereignty is already dead."[45] (Harper appointed Montreal Economic Institute executive vice-president Maxime Bernier as his first minister of industry.) The following year, as leader of the Conservative Party, Harper spoke by videotape at the Fraser Institute's thirtieth-anniversary celebration as the Introduction explains.[46] He attended the tenth anniversary of Brian Crowley's AIMS in person the same year, and, as we have seen, called the organization "dollar for dollar the best think tank in the country." He also spoke that year at the Frontier Centre for Public Policy on tax policy, and in 2009 gave his special greetings at that centre's tenth anniversary. "Frontier's ongoing contribution to serious, informed, public-policy debate in Canada has been outstanding," Harper insisted.[47]

***

The project to influence second-hand dealers in ideas requires serious cash to set up think tanks, support conservative scholars, publish their works, and disseminate the results widely in the media. During the 1990s, the Donner Canadian Foundation was the lifeblood of this activity. Buoyed by its success in funding the Reagan Revolution through its American foundation, the Donner family decided to move the Canadian foundation to the right as well.[48] After consulting with leading conservative academics and journalists (including Andrew Coyne), the foundation launched a new grant-making program, pouring two- to three-million dollars a year into conservative efforts, and helping establish the regional think tanks and single-issue advocacy groups.[49] This foundation, "with real money to spend, has accelerated the growth of a conservative intellectual network," Stephen Harper and Tom Flanagan acknowledged in a lengthy analysis in the *Next City*, the magazine Donner set up to accelerate the growth of the conservative intellectual network.[50]

Flying under the radar as a financial angel for the neo-liberal project is the foundation of Canada's second-wealthiest family, the W. Garfield Weston Foundation, whose fortune comes from food wholesaling (Weston Foods) and retailing (Loblaw Companies). Most Weston Foundation funding goes to "good works," such as Canadian Merit Scholarships that enable high-school students to attend university. Weston also leads in donations to the Royal Ontario Museum and to the Nature Conservancy of Canada to purchase ecologically significant properties. The foundation is also a dedicated supporter of the Fraser Institute. Between 2000 and 2012, Weston donated nearly $22 million to this think tank and virtually nothing to any others.[51] Most of the money went into Fraser Institute initiatives to undermine public education. Once again, Milton Friedman was the inspiration. His 1995 *Washington Post* editorial said it all: "Public Schools: Make Them Private."[52] Three years later, largely with Weston funding, the institute began manufacturing report cards that ranked all secondary and elementary schools, first in British Columbia, then in Alberta, Ontario, and Quebec. Each year, the rankings find private schools that control entry and schools in wealthier neighbourhoods top the list. Weston provides awards for these schools and for those that show the greatest improvement from the previous year, bringing competition and choice into the system, as Friedman advised. In a second program that lasted nine years (2003–2012) and accounted for nearly half the funding, Weston financed the Fraser Institute's school-vouchers program, which sent poor children to private and religious schools. The program was called Children First, implying that, as Friedman claimed, in the public system, teachers and bureaucrats come first, and not children.[53] Weston provided private scholarships of up to $3,500 a year to 2,100 disadvantaged students in Ontario and Alberta, so they could attend non-public schools. Children were supported to the end of Grade 8. What happened to them after that was someone else's problem.

The institute's ability to obtain such vast sums from Weston may be influenced by the fact that several Weston family members are active in the think tank. Schoolteacher Claudia Rebanks Hepburn is a niece of Weston chairman, Galen Weston, and a trustee of the foundation. She was the Fraser Institute's director of education policy (1999–2008) and founder of the Children First program. Mark Mitchell, a Galen Weston nephew and also a foundation trustee, is a Fraser Institute vice-chairman. Mitchell's family provided two million dollars to the Fraser Institute for its work on economic freedom.[54]

In 2006, a new foundation began funding neo-liberal infrastructure after Donner cut back its direct support. Peter Munk, who made a fortune as head of Barrick Gold, created the Aurea ("golden," in Latin) Foundation. The foundation grabbed public attention as sponsor of the Munk Debates, which pits high-profile liberals against conservatives to debate controversial topics such as: "I would rather get sick in the United States than Canada," "Climate change is mankind's defining crisis and demands a commensurate response," and "Foreign aid does more harm than good."[55] The debates serve two purposes. They elevate conservative positions to parity with long-standing liberal viewpoints, crowding out progressive ones. They also mask the foundation's more financially significant activities: doling out nearly two million dollars a year to Canadian neo-liberal organizations.[56] Major recipients (2007–2012) include the Frontier Centre for Public Policy ($1.3 million), the Canadian Constitution Foundation ($767,000), the C.D. Howe Institute ($644,000), and the Macdonald–Laurier Institute ($450,000). The Fraser Institute, which received over one million dollars from Aurea and a second Munk family foundation, in 2010 awarded Munk the T.P. Boyle Founder's Award at a gala dinner in Toronto "in recognition of his unwavering commitment to free and open markets around the globe and his support for enhancing and encouraging democratic values and the importance of responsible citizenship,"[57] thus equating "free and open markets" with "democratic values," as Milton Friedman instructed. During this year Harper appointed Nigel Wright as his chief of staff. Not only was Wright a well-connected Bay Street functionary, he was an Aurea trustee and another link between Harper and the think tanks that support Harperism. Wright lasted more than two years in the Prime Minister's Office before resigning due to the $90,000 cheque he wrote for controversial senator and Conservative fundraiser Mike Duffy.

Money is also supplied to think tanks by corporate Canada, but little is known about this funding. Few Canadian think tanks reveal their sources of corporate backing, which is not required by the *Income Tax Act*.[58] If they do provide any information about their corporate supporters, as the Macdonald–Laurier

Institute does, they don't reveal the amount of the contributions. Think tanks must pay for studies by academics whose work is compatible with the think tank's goals. Think tanks must also build staffs of reliable researchers and analysts who do much of the day-to-day research, writing, and promotion of the institute's products. With a budget of just over ten million dollars in 2012, the Fraser supports a staff of forty-three, plus forty-one senior fellows, making it by far the largest neo-liberal think tank in Canada.[59]

The Fraser hasn't released a list of corporate members or the amount of member contributions since the 1980s. A partial understanding of corporate backing can be gained by examining think tank boards, since board members are likely recruited because of their potential financial contributions. In 2012, the board contained two executives from the private health-care industry; a major institute activity is attacking Medicare and promoting private health care. On top of this, the Lilly Endowment of Indianapolis, Indiana, whose assets come from multinational drug company Eli Lilly, is a long-standing funder ($600,000 in 2011). The board also includes ten financial-industry executives from Vancouver and Toronto; cutting corporate and income taxes and deregulating the economy are Fraser mainstays. Oil and gas money from Calgary is represented on the board by seven directors; the Fraser has supported global-warming deniers for a decade, and promoted oil pipelines more recently. As well, the institute's long-standing attacks on environmentalists are supported by ongoing funding from the Charles G. Koch Foundation ($415,000 between 2010 and 2012), a well-known funder of global-warming denial.

The extent to which corporate funding drives institute research is unknown. What is known, though, is that the Fraser Institute has courted funding from corporate interests it believes will support specific ventures. Such was the case when the institute requested financial support from the tobacco, food, biotechnology and chemical industries to back a centre that would provide research downplaying the risks emanating from the use of their products. In one case in 2000, the institute asked British American Tobacco Co. (BAT) for $100,000 a year to support its work attacking research that demonstrated a link between lung cancer and second-hand smoke.[60] The CEO of BAT's Canadian subsidiary was on the Fraser Institute board at the time.

***

As Hayek foresaw, second-hand dealers in ideas — especially the news media — are crucial to the success of the neo-liberal project. By providing research reports accompanied with news releases, op-eds, and tailored news stories, think tanks subsidize news. They make the work of news media easier, reducing the time and resources journalists must commit to a story for research and comment. As the nation's largest neo-liberal think tank, the Fraser Institute has the greatest media presence. "Reaching decision makers, policy makers, and the public through the mainstream media remains one of our primary tactics," the institute reports.[61] The institute's leaked 1997 draft five-year plan, "Towards the New Millennium," reveals an ambitious media-relations program. This document, though dated, provides a rare glimpse of think tank thinking. Each new project area the institute undertakes "will have a component focusing on the approach to the media and to other second-hand dealers in ideas," a characterization that harkens back to Hayek's 1949 paper. Devising these strategies for media dissemination was a key element in determining which projects to adopt. Projects that "provided a tangible empirical focus for the policy concern" are crucial in the media-penetration efforts, as the five-year plan predicted. These are endeavours like Tax Freedom Day, the hospital-waiting-list survey, the Economic

Freedom of the World Index, and the school report card.[62] They attract media attention because they can grab headlines and are easy to report. They are also effective, because most people tend to accept statistics as being authoritative. Canadians would hear little about the economic-freedom index or other items on the neo-liberal agenda if they weren't mentioned in the press. Almost everyone reads newspapers, listens to radio talk shows, or watches news on television, at least some of the time.

The political tenor of Canadian media shifted dramatically when Conrad Black took over the Southam newspaper chain in the mid-1990s. He remade the *Ottawa Citizen* and *Montreal Gazette* into more conservative papers, started a dedicated conservative daily, the *National Post*, and moved the entire Southam chain rightwards by hiring half-a-dozen conservative commentators from outside the organization (including Andrew Coyne).[63] Black fostered a close relationship with the Fraser Institute. His company, Hollinger Inc., donated $99,000 to the institute's building fund, and his two long-time business partners, David Radler and Peter Whyte, and his journalist wife, Barbara Amiel, joined the institute's board of trustees. The think tank kept a picture of Black on its wall near the Hollinger south wing on the fourth floor of its Vancouver building.[64] Black brought Fraser Institute staffers into the editorial rooms of the *Vancouver Sun* (Fazil Mihlar), *Calgary Herald* (Danielle Smith), and *Ottawa Citizen* (John Robson). The Asper family maintained the conservative complexion of the chain when it bought out Black in 2001. Son David Asper joined the boards of the Fraser Institute and Frontier Centre before he became *National Post* publisher. And the company that took over the papers in 2010 — Postmedia Network — continued the chain's rightward slant. CEO Paul Godfrey was *National Post* publisher and had started the *Toronto Sun* as a conservative daily in the 1970s.

Other media owners followed the same path. In 2005, billionaire tycoon Ted Rogers made his flagship magazine, *Maclean's*, into a more conservative organ by hiring as his new editor Ken Whyte, former editor at the *National Post* and a trustee of the Donner and Aurea foundations. Whyte soon populated his newsroom with former *National Post* staffers. The Corus Radio Network, owned by the billionaire Shaw family, presents a lineup of mostly conservative talk-show hosts, such as Charles Adler and Roy Green; the family now owns the Global Television Network as well. *The Globe and Mail* gave a twice-monthly column to retired oil-industry executive and Fraser Institute vice-chairman Gwyn Morgan, who donated a million dollars to the Fraser Institute Foundation the same year,[65] and a twice-weekly column to long-time newspaper editor and former Libertarian Party of Canada president Neil Reynolds, an unabashed cheerleader for neo-liberalism. His musings on supply management are described in Chapter 1. In 2011, media tycoon Pierre Karl Péladeau, who bought the *Sun* newspaper chain from Paul Godfrey and his backers, launched the conservative television news channel Sun TV — dubbed Fox News North. Sun TV lived up to expectations as a relentlessly conservative media attack-dog, similar in function to Fox News. With the launch of Sun TV, neo-liberals can command sympathetic attention in all major media.

Andrew Coyne is mentioned frequently in this chapter, because he occupies the interface between think tanks and media, crucial territory in the neo-liberal war of ideas. He's been a journalist for nearly thirty years, writing for all major print publications except the liberal *Toronto Star*. He's a regular participant on CBC-TV's "At Issue" panel. Since 2012, Coyne has been a syndicated columnist for the *National Post* and Postmedia Network. With a daily circulation of 1.1 million, these papers provide a far-reaching pulpit from which Coyne can disseminate neo-liberal and conservative ideas. In just one month in 2013, he:

- Argued that we need to take power away from government bureaucrats, school boards, and union leaders and give it to schools, parents, and individual teachers (Jan. 5);
- Attacked aboriginal activist and academic Pam Palmater, because she sees the advancement of aboriginal peoples as a collective, not an individual, issue (Jan. 8);
- Argued that, to lift themselves out of poverty, aboriginals need what we need: human capital (education) and physical capital (the right to own property) (Jan. 12);
- Attacked the Harper government for engaging in stimulus spending in the auto and high-tech industries (Jan. 17);
- Lambasted Sun TV for wanting to get on basic cable and the CBC for existing; instead, he argued, the market should decide people's viewing preferences (Jan. 24).

But Coyne is more than a conservative commentator on political affairs; he's an active participant in them. When the Donner family decided to shift its Canadian foundation to the right in the early 1990s, it organized a meeting of a dozen conservative journalists and academics at the Intercontinental Hotel in downtown Toronto. Coyne was on the guest list, and, when asked how their ideas could have greater influence on public discourse, Coyne suggested a magazine. It was two years later, with a Donner grant of $1.4 million, that the *Next City* commenced publication, with Coyne as a contributing editor. Margaret Thatcher was the magazine's patron saint.[66] *Next City* published articles calling for parent-run charter schools, the privatization of Medicare, and an end to government subsidies to the arts. It published Brian

Crowley's article on Friedrich Hayek and the Harper–Flanagan analysis of the conservative movement in Canada.

Coyne moved from the *National Post* to Ken Whyte's *Maclean's* as national editor in the mid-2000s and assumed a more central role in the neo-liberal/social-conservative infrastructure. He joined the council of advisors of the Manning Centre for Building Democracy, Preston Manning's project for expanding the conservative movement and the Conservative Party.[67] Coyne spoke at various Manning Centre conferences in Ottawa on the nature of conservatism and where the Harper government was going wrong. Perhaps most importantly, Coyne became a trustee of Peter Munk's Aurea Foundation, putting him, along with Ken Whyte and Nigel Wright, at the forefront of funding for neo-liberal think tanks and single-issue advocacy organizations like the Canadian Constitution Foundation (CCF).

Coyne subsequently joined the board of directors (and later the advisory board) of the CCF, Canada's first conservative public-interest law firm, which was started with $200,000 from Donner. It was headed by lawyer John Carpay, a former Alberta director of the Canadian Taxpayers Federation and an unsuccessful Reform Party candidate. The CCF is modelled on American libertarian law firms, such as the Institute for Justice, with a mission to launch legal actions that promote individual freedom, economic liberty, and equality before the law. In its quest to achieve these goals, CCF has supported challenges to health-care laws that make private health care and health insurance illegal and to labour laws that require workers to pay union dues.

Does Coyne's activist role influence the quality of his commentary? In February 2013, the Supreme Court of Canada ruled unanimously that flyers distributed by born-again Christian Bill Whatcott, of Weyburn, Saskatchewan, promoted hatred against gays and lesbians. The flyers called homosexuals sodomites and equated them with child abusers. The court ruled that the flyers used "vilifying and derogatory representations to create a tone of hatred."[68] Coyne wrote two columns attacking the decision, the first calling it "calamitous" and lacking in "supportive evidence." The court didn't even seek to discover if attacks on gays and lesbians increased because of Whatcott's flyers, he protested.[69] In his second column, Coyne accused the court of being twenty years out of date.[70] The CCF intervened on Whatcott's side, but Coyne didn't disclose his connections to the CCF or to Aurea, which donated $767,000 to CCF's work.

Coyne's reporting on think tanks that Aurea may have funded also raises questions — at least of the need for disclosure and transparency, values he frequently espouses. A critical stance is lacking, especially for work emanating from the Macdonald–Laurier Institute, run by his friend Brian Lee Crowley, to which Aurea has donated $450,000. Coyne writes:

- "A new study for the MLI calculates most provinces face a better than 50-per-cent probability of default over the next 30 years";
- "The MLI has just put out a study debunking the 'Dutch Disease' thesis";
- "According to figures compiled by Brian Lee Crowley, president of the MLI, Canada's labour force grew the fastest of any advanced economy."

Coyne was challenged on this practice of non-disclosure by Kevin Grandia of DeSmogBlog for two columns Coyne wrote for *Maclean's* in which he cites studies by the Fraser Institute, AIMS, and Frontier Centre, with no mention of the Aurea funding. Coyne chose not to address Grandia's concerns in his brief reply.[71]

Coyne developed a formula for promoting conservative ideas without being seen to be standing behind them. A column he wrote in June 2013 exemplifies this approach. He has "some good news to report," because the "first shoots of independent thought have begun to reappear." We're beginning to move away from the years of "suffocating consensus." It was published in the *Vancouver Sun, Calgary Herald, Edmonton Journal, Regina Leader Post, Saskatoon Star Phoenix, Windsor Star, National Post, Ottawa Citizen,* and *Montreal Gazette* under headlines such as "Fresh Ideas Are Starting to Sprout Up in Canadian Politics" and "Time for Fresh Debate." But the news he has to report is good for just some Canadians. The rest have to ask just how independent and fresh these shoots of thought are.[72] The ideas he lauds are:

- Eliminating supply management: Coyne claims this policy "makes food more costly for millions of families, for the benefit of a few thousand farmers." He gives no thought to the fact that the purpose of the policy is to ensure the continued existence and viability of a domestic agricultural industry. That would be getting in the way of the market.
- Promoting toll roads: Coyne applauds Ontario's Mike Harris government for financing a new highway with tolls, and claims it is the wave of the future. (He was wrong here. It was Bob Rae's New Democratic government that initiated the financing of the toll road.) The market should determine usage. He does not deal with the fact that not everybody can afford to travel on toll roads and bridges.
- Bringing in right-to-work: Coyne bemoans the fact that workers in unionized workplaces have to pay dues because they benefit from the union's efforts to raise wages and improve benefits and working

conditions. The union shop must go, because it gets
in the way of the market. He gives no thought to the
fact that right-to-work pits individual employees
against their bosses, and that usually doesn't end up
well for employees.

- Introducing private ownership on First Nation
reserves: Coyne credits Stephen Harper for moving
forward on this file, which would give Natives living
on reserves the same rights as other Canadians.
Collective ownership is anathema to the market and
must go. He does not address the fact that such a
policy would undermine the ability of First Nations
to make collective decisions about the future of their
communities.

Coyne asks "why so many log-jams have come unstuck at the
same time," and suggests possible answers. It could be the influence of the Internet and social media, he offers, resurrecting the
myth of technological determinism. Or it could be the "knock-
on effect" of previous "reforms" such as free trade, although he
doesn't explain how this would work. His strongest suggestion is
that the "log-jams" became unstuck because of "individual acts
of political courage" by politicians such as Martha Hall Findlay,
Kathleen Wynne, Tim Hudak, Stephen Harper, Joyce Murray,
Nathan Cullen, Stéphane Dion, and Mark Warawa, covering
most political bases. Coyne's speculation on the role of a handful
of disparate individuals diverts attention away from the impact
of the organizations he's had a hand in funding.

***

As of this writing in mid-2014, a tightly knit, smoothly operating
neo-liberal propaganda system has been installed in Canada. The

foundations of wealthy businessmen, corporations, and individuals are investing more than $26 million a year in neo-liberal think tanks and single-issue advocacy organizations.[73] (This figure doesn't include Calgary's School of Public Policy, whose financial statements are buried within the university's accounts.) The long-term goal is to discredit government as a vital institution and to champion market alternatives. The system hinges on the writings of Friedrich Hayek, Milton Friedman, George Stiglitz, James Buchanan, and other members of the Mont Pelerin Society (MPS) that provide neo-liberal doctrine. Think tanks transform the doctrine into research; sympathetic academics provide research studies compatible with the think tank's goals; corporate executives and the foundations of wealthy businessmen finance the research; and sympathetic media owners and commentators disseminate the research to target audiences. It's a package deal. Canada's neo-liberal think tanks rarely discuss the connection, but they operate comfortably within the MPS orbit. Most Canadian policy entrepreneurs — Crowley at AIMS–MLI, Michel Kelly-Gagnon at the Montreal Economic Institute, Peter Holle at the Frontier Centre, and Michael Walker at the Fraser Institute — are MPS members. Two generations of Canadians — the Fraser Institute celebrated its fortieth anniversary in 2014 — have been exposed to neo-liberal ideas. The repetition of these ideas, especially through the vehicle of annual indexes, has been effective in incorporating them into the common-sense understanding of the world held by Canadians of all political stripes.

Of course people are not automatons who blindly internalize neo-liberal messages. But gradually, and especially as a result of constant repetition, some ideas rise to prominence, while others fade away. People are presented with a changing set of ideas from which they must make selections to make sense of their world.

The Fraser Institute represents the first generation of think tanks, established when social-democratic ideology ruled public opinion. Then, during the 1990s, as neo-liberalism gained traction in Western democracies, a second generation of think tanks extended neo-liberal perspectives into provincial and municipal policy arenas. Finally, a third generation of think tanks is being put into place since the turn of the century. These think tanks demonstrate the flexibility and creativity of the neo-liberal project as it finds unoccupied niches to extend its influence. The Macdonald–Laurier Institute was designed to backstop the Harper government, but it will promote neo-liberalism no matter which party forms the government. The School of Public Policy at the University of Calgary is a more audacious experiment and requires the participation, or at least blessing, of senior university administrators. This shouldn't be a problem though, because the university is heavily engaged in research collaborations with industry — the Alberta Ingenuity Centre for In-Situ Energy, the Consortium for Heavy Oil Research by University Scientists, and the Enbridge Centre for Corporate Sustainability, to name three that were investigated by the Canadian Association of University Teachers to determine any limitations on academic freedom the collaborations imposed on their university participants.[74] The university has always courted neo-liberal and conservative scholars to counter the supposed liberal, socialist, and Marxist leanings of other universities.

As a result of the massing on the right, the political space is crowded with a seemingly endless flow of studies, reports, and commentaries supporting neo-liberal perspectives. In 2013, neo-liberal think tanks outgunned their progressive rivals — the Canadian Centre for Policy Alternatives, Parkland Institute, and Broadbent Institute — by a factor of four to one in mentions in major Canadian dailies. If neo-liberalism's allies are added to the equation — the Canadian Taxpayers Federation, the Manning Centre for Building Democracy, the National Citizens Coalition (NCC), and the C.D. Howe Institute — the ratio rises to seven to one.[75] Constant repetition over many decades has achieved the

desired result, as some ideas have become familiar and even common-sense: economic freedom and school choice are unqualified
good things; the tax burden is burdensome and requires relief;
government is inefficient because it harbours bloated bureaucra-
cies and overpaid public employees; the private sector is hobbled
by red tape; and so on.

The success of the Fraser Institute's school report card exemplifies the strategy. To advance Milton Friedman's doctrine that
competition in education is the only way to improve it, with
Weston Foundation funding, the institute has ranked schools in
British Columbia, Alberta, and Ontario annually for over a decade. It created a research technique that purports to demonstrate
that a school itself — its administration, teaching and counselling
— is the key factor in student achievement. The methodology is
flawed because the indicators the institute selects and the weightings it gives them "exaggerate the differences between schools
and school systems," writes retired teacher Dietmar Waber,
and make the school the factor being measured and ranked.[76]
To appear to do this the institute ignores information about
socio-economic status, race, ethnicity, disability, ESL, and school
location in determining its rankings. To create seemingly large
differences among schools it magnifies small differences in test
results by double-counting them.[77] Nonetheless, the rankings
are an unqualified success, as real-estate agents tout properties
near high-ranking schools, mothers-to-be discuss where to buy
houses, and divorcing parents fight over child custody based on
which parent lives closer to a higher-ranking school. The Fraser
Institute brought choice and competition into the public education system; there's no going back.

Neo-liberalism largely supports the Harper government, but
that's not its main purpose. Its role is to change the climate of
ideas to such an extent that it doesn't matter who forms the government. Of course, its ultimate goal is to see the election of a

Margaret Thatcher, a Ronald Reagan, or a Stephen Harper, who can then use state power to accelerate the transition to a market state. Harper has used that power assiduously, as if he was born for the job, creating a philosophy of government that will outlast his administration. He's hobbled government's long-standing social-democratic obligations by slashing revenues to their lowest levels — in relation to the size of the economy — they've been at in fifty years, when the state first implemented its major social programs. One estimate pegs Harper's tax cuts at $45 billion a year in foregone revenues.[78] With total revenues at about $250 billion, that's nearly a 20 per cent cut. Call it privatization by default. If there's not enough money in the public coffers to finance health care, post-secondary education and old age security needs, they will have to be provided by the private or voluntary sectors or by individuals.

Brian Crowley comments that there's "basically a strong political consensus now" for a smaller government and lower government revenues and expenditures. It was the Jean Chrétien government, with Paul Martin as finance minister, that started Canada on the track to reduced resources through its massive spending cuts in the mid-nineties, Crowley notes approvingly.[79] Both Liberals and New Democrats have indicated they will not stray far from the economic consensus. The New Democrats' Tom Mulcair pledged to not raise personal income tax nor the sales tax, and to increase corporate taxes only for large corporations.[80] Justin Trudeau of the Liberals says "we are not going to be raising taxes."[81] They've accepted Harperism, the new reality. But Harperism is more than fiscal conservatism. While he's cut government's ability to look after its citizens, Harper has involved his government assertively in issues that traditionally haven't been part of government's mandate, as he inches forward toward the market state. The opposition parties may not even be aware of the extent to which the changed climate of ideas will constrain their actions.

3

REJECT UNIONS AND PROSPER

Stephen Harper's response to labour disputes involving postal workers, Air Canada employees, and Canadian Pacific Railway workers wasn't as dramatic as Ronald Reagan's take-no-prisoners approach to air-traffic controllers, but it served a similar purpose. When the Professional Air Traffic Controllers Organization (PATCO) went on strike in August 1981, Reagan gave the workers forty-eight hours to return to work. When eleven thousand of the thirteen thousand PATCO members ignored his order, he fired them and imposed a lifetime ban on rehiring them. Several months later, PATCO was decertified. The PATCO strike was a pivotal event in the establishment of neo-liberalism in America. Reagan served notice on organized labour there was a new game in town, and labour unions were not going to be players, as the Mont Pelerin Society had concluded. Writing in *Dissent* magazine, labour historian Jefferson Cowie argued that the result of Reagan's action was to "break unions, strip them of the right to strike, redistribute wealth upward, and create massive economic insecurity."[1]

The PATCO strike marked an acceleration in the decline of union membership and the rise of the top 1 per cent of the population. By 2012, American private-sector union membership had plummeted from 18.7 per cent to 6.6 per cent, a level not seen since 1916.[2] And the income share of the top 1 per cent soared from 10 per cent to 20 per cent, reaching a level not seen since 1928.[3] As organized labour goes, so goes the middle class. The evidence for this relationship is "just about bulletproof," the *Toronto Star*'s Antonia Zerbisias notes. Studies by the Center for American Progress and the Economic Policy Institute demonstrate direct correlations between the decline in union membership, the decline in the middle-class share of income, and the rise in the share of income captured by the top 10 per cent of income earners.[4]

Harper won a majority government just shy of thirty years after Reagan went after air-traffic controllers. Much had changed in Canadian labour relations since PATCO. Following American trends, the proportion of workers belonging to a union declined markedly, from 37.6 per cent in 1981 to 29.7 per cent in 2011, a drop of 7.9 percentage points, but a decrease of 21 per cent of the organized work force. The decline in union fortunes is even more dramatic, since only 16 per cent of private-sector workers were unionized in 2011, compared to 29.8 per cent in 1981, a decline of 46 per cent.[5] When Harper launched all-out war on unions in 2011 — without declaring he was so doing — he faced an organized labour sector much weakened from its heyday in the 1970s, particularly in the private sector.

Following his preferred method of accomplishing an objective, Harper rolled out a succession of forays into enemy territory, few of which could be tied directly to him or the Prime Minister's Office. His goal was to chip away at union power until it no longer threatened the realization of the market state. During his first year in power, he achieved this in a variety of ways: intervening in the collective bargaining procedures of workers who work in industries under federal jurisdiction; reducing long-established roles of unions in the employment-insurance system; and introducing legislation that would undermine unions by requiring them to vastly increase the amount of financial information they must report to the Canada Revenue Agency — and to employers. In his second year of majority government, he threatened to bring in right-to-work legislation for workers under federal jurisdiction.

Using the mantra that strikes threaten Canada's "fragile" economic recovery, Harper and Minister of Labour Lisa Raitt moved decisively to destabilize the collective bargaining system for federally regulated industries. Six weeks after Harper's 2011 election victory, Raitt introduced back-to-work bills for postal workers and Air Canada service-counter and call-centre agents. Both unions soon settled for contract terms their members had already rejected. Coming in rapid-fire succession, the actions served notice that trade unions were in the Conservatives' crosshairs. Two months later, the Canadian Union of Public Employees, representing Air Canada flight attendants, decided it had no choice but to accept the employer's offer, because the Harper government would not let it go on strike. The members, however, rejected the tentative agreement by 88 per cent, and later voted 98 per cent in favour of a strike mandate.

Just before the members walked off the job, Raitt summoned the parties to Ottawa and told the House of Commons she would introduce another back-to-work bill if the union and Air Canada didn't reach a settlement. Once again the threat of government action forced the union to accept an offer it might not otherwise have deemed adequate. When members again rejected the proposed deal and prepared to go on strike, Raitt responded with a different tactic. She took advantage of a section of the *Canada Labour Code* intended "to prevent an immediate and serious danger to the safety and health of the public" and referred the case to the Canada Industrial Relations Board (CIRB).[6] She asked this independent, quasi-judicial tribunal to determine which services affected by the proposed strike were essential. It was a dubious proposition, because other airlines could fill the gap, but served the goal of pre-empting strike action, removing the union's most important power: the right of its members to withdraw their labour. The two sides eventually agreed to binding arbitration, and the flight attendants ended up with a contract they had voted down.

In March 2012, Raitt blocked two further possible disruptions of Air Canada services by referring the disputes — a lockout of the airline's three thousand pilots and a strike by 8,600 baggage handlers and mechanics — to the CIRB. "This is not what the economy needs and it is certainly not what the travelling public needs at this time of year," Harper told reporters at Billy Bishop Toronto City Airport, referring to labour action over the busy March spring-break travel period.[7]

To wrap up its year of intervention in long-established collective-bargaining practices, the Harper government moved once more, this time into the dispute between Canadian Pacific Railway and the Teamsters Canada Rail Conference, which represents engineers, conductors, and traffic controllers. Raitt called the two sides to meetings in Ottawa after the union issued a seventy-two-hour strike notice. Workers went on strike after talks broke down. Several days later, Raitt introduced back-to-work legislation in Parliament; within a week, rail workers were back on the job.[8]

What motivated the Harper government's actions in labour relations? Several sources suggested ideology, but didn't define what they meant. Paul Cavalluzzo, lawyer for the postal-workers union, charged that Conservative moves to block work stoppages were based on ideology, rather than hard evidence of potential economic damage if a strike occurred.[9] Charlotte Yates, a labour-relations professor at McMaster University, agreed, noting that governments like Harper's weren't just trying to keep deficits in check. They were also cutting for philosophical reasons. "The kind of attacks on labour we're seeing are much more fundamental. They're going into ideological attack mode," said Yates.[10] *Toronto Star* columnist Tim Harper saw mixed motives. "These will be tumultuous times because it is not only austerity that is driving this government in its war with labour. It is being driven by ideology and plain old politics," he wrote. "The Conservatives are trying to draw the next NDP leader into the fray so he or she can be caricatured as beholden to big union bosses."[11]

On several occasions labour minister Raitt went out of her way to deny her actions had anything to do with ideology. After she referred the flight attendants' dispute to the CIRB, she said she was merely being practical. "This isn't about having a fight with anybody," she argued. "This is about making sure that in the bigger picture, the economy continues to work."[12] After referring Air Canada's disputes with baggage handlers and pilots to the CIRB, she reaffirmed that her decisions weren't driven by political ideology, but by how a strike or lockout might send ripples across the economy.[13]

EKOS Research pollster Frank Graves suggested the Tory moves were less about ideology and more about politics, and the fact that being tough with labour plays well with their Conservative constituency. "I do think that, right now, the attitudes to organized labour and unions are probably not that favourable," said Graves. Making war with the unions might not be bad politics, he added.[14] Gerry Nicholls, a political commentator and former Harper colleague at the National Citizens Coalition, said the only real "ideology" driving the Harper government is the prime minister's determination to "eliminate the Liberal Party."[15] *Globe* reporter Jane Taber, however, saw that the Conservatives had switched targets. "In these recent labour fights," Taber wrote, "Ms. Raitt and her government are distinguishing themselves from their biggest threat, the NDP, by pushing back against the unions. This is a government, after all, that has gone hard against the NDP, painting it and its principals as being in the pockets of unions."[16]

Practical politics or ideology? George Smith, an adjunct professor and fellow in the School of Policy Studies at Queen's University, remained puzzled: "Intervening like this, it just doesn't add up."[17] Smith should know. He was senior director of employee relations at Air Canada before and after its privatization in 1988. Smith complained that the Conservative government was "going to be in the business of collective bargaining rather than the business of governing." Smith warned that the swift legislation from Lisa Raitt stripped relevance from parts of the *Canada Labour Code* that allow companies and unions to reach a collective agreement. Perhaps that's the point. If the purpose of the neo-liberal state is to create and enforce markets, as many careful observers claim, then the Harper government may have been reshaping the labour market incrementally to remove collectivity — an unforgiveable abomination to Mont Pelerinians — and replace it with a system of individual employees negotiating contracts with employers. Such an outcome would surely vault Canada to the top of the Economic Freedom of the World tables and enshrine Harper in the hallowed halls of neo-liberal freedom fighters. As the headline in a *National Post* column by the Fraser Institute's Niels Veldhuis and Amela Karabegovic lauding right-to-work laws and the consequent decimation of unions put it, "Reject Unions and Prosper."[18]

Harper's multiple interventions in labour relations to save a "fragile" economic recovery reveals a subtle change in how we view the economy. In the nineteenth century, the economy was something that happened outside government. Consequently, laissez-faire made sense: government should just keep its hands off the economic levers and all would be well. When that approach led to the Great Depression, socialist and Keynesian analyses both saw a vital role for government, although the extent of required intervention differed dramatically. Then, in the 1980s, with its mandate for government to create and enforce markets wherever possible, neo-liberalism became the dominant ideology with Thatcher and Reagan. Harper follows that tradition by espousing the view that the economy needs his government, which has a duty to remove anything standing in the way of economic recovery. His job is to nurse the economy back to health, but he's not afraid to administer tough medicine, if necessary. Margaret Thatcher and Ronald Reagan made no secret they were sworn enemies of organized labour. Harper follows in their footsteps, but incrementally — moving the goalposts whenever an opportunity arises — and without declaring he is against unions. Instead, his mission is to create and maintain a healthy, unfettered economy. Unions are an obstacle to the accomplishment of that mission and must be removed. His unique brand of neo-liberalism is another example of Harperism.

***

Labour unions preoccupied the Mont Pelerin Society from its earliest days. In *The Road to Serfdom*, Friedrich Hayek accused organized labour of colluding with capital to obtain a better share of "monopoly profits at the expense of the community and particularly at the expense of the poorest, those employed in the less-well-organized industries and the unemployed."[19] In a peculiar twist of logic, Hayek accused those who were union members of supporting monopolies of power, because not every worker was a member of a union. By the 1930s, unions had been legalized in most countries. This development, Hayek believed, would almost certainly "lead to the destruction of democracy," because it doomed individual freedom. Legally recognizing unions would lead to union members being paid more than non-union workers.[20] Rather than conclude that non-union workers should have the benefit of being represented by a union in negotiations over wages and working conditions, Hayek's view was that every worker should be free to negotiate with the employer on his or her own.

At the inaugural meeting of the MPS three years after the publication of *The Road to Serfdom*, Hayek identified the trade-union issue as the "thorniest question" neo-liberals would have to tackle in the post-war world.[21] Hayek insisted that "if there is to be any hope of a return to a free economy, the question of how the powers of trade-unions can be appropriately delimited by law as well as in fact is one of the most important of all the questions which we must give our attention."[22]

Swiss researcher and journalist Yves Steiner undertook a careful analysis of MPS meetings and discussions over the decade following the establishment of the society. His analysis reveals sharp divisions over the union question. Those "who considered some form of arrangement between employers and trade unions [to be] beneficial" to the economy were in the majority, Steiner reports.[23] Some went so far as to advocate a role for labour in the operation of the corporation, but felt that it should be limited to social and personnel matters. Such discussions within the MPS "formed the ideological basis of the German employer associations' discourses on co-determination in postwar Germany and during the 1950s," Steiner notes.[24] (Codetermination, or the practice by which employees participate in management decisions, was introduced by the federal government of Germany in 1952 and spread in various forms to other countries of Western Europe.[25])

Those who, like Hayek, considered any arrangement with

labour to be a dangerous departure from classical liberal principles were in the minority. But by the end of the decade, the
minority prevailed. The view that business has a duty to restrict
its cooperation with organized labour became dominant in
neo-liberal circles.[26] This conviction, Steiner reports, gained
ascendancy largely because of the deep pockets of anti-union
business executives who financed MPS meetings and supported
individuals who espoused the anti-union cause, such as Milton
Friedman and Hayek himself. Howard Pew of Sun Oil Co., Jasper
Crane of DuPont, and Harold Luhnow, who ran the Volker Fund,
were staunch anti-communist, anti–New Deal businessmen who
supported the MPS financially and became MPS members. At
Crane's insistence, Hayek organized a full session of the MPS on
the problems of unions that was stacked in favour of the view that
"coercive" practices, such as the union shop, had been integrated
into the American legal framework. Laws protecting a worker's
right to join a union should be undone, because they merely lead
to a monopoly of union power, the session concluded, much
to the delight of its anti-union backers.[27] Hayek's position on
unions was the most radical of those expressed in MPS meetings during the fifties. Unions represented the foremost threat to
economic order and the free society, he argued, and they should
be legally disenfranchised. By the 1960s, with financial support
from "the ultraconservative fraction of employers," the view that
unions had too much power and must be removed from economic calculations became the dominant neo-liberal perspective
on unions.[28]

Neo-liberals didn't seem to have similar concerns about the
market-distorting tendencies of corporate monopolies. Within
the MPS the view gradually formed that monopoly was almost
always undone by the forces of competition, so there was no need
to worry about either monopoly or large corporations. That view
was reinforced by Milton Friedman's 1962 polemic, *Capitalism*

and Freedom, which was supported by the Volker Fund over the half-dozen years it took Friedman to write it. Monopoly capitalism was not a problem for Friedman. "The most important fact about enterprise monopoly is its relative unimportance from the point of view of the economy as a whole," Friedman asserted.[29] And regarding a particular industry, economic theory couldn't help determine if a monopoly existed in it. "[T]here can be no clear-cut determination of whether a particular enterprise or industry is to be regarded as monopolistic or as competitive." He then diverted his readers' attention away from problems of corporate monopolies by urging them to worry more about the "governmentally operated or supervised sector," which "had grown greatly over the past half-century," than about monopolistic sectors of the economy, which had not increased and may well have decreased.[30] Based on scant evidence, Friedman concluded that Americans overestimate the importance of monopoly in their economy. In his later manifesto, *Free to Choose*, written with Rose Friedman, monopoly capitalism had disappeared. Private monopoly did not distort the price system nearly as much as government, "the major source of interference with a free market system."[31] In fact, the Friedmans assured their readers, the United States contained no heartless monopoly capitalists.[32]

The monopoly in labour, on the other hand, should not be ignored. Unions have the ability to "raise wage rates in a particular occupation or industry," thus reducing employment in that industry and forcing down wages in other occupations. Because of unions, Friedman claimed, high-paid workers receive even higher pay at the expense of lower-paid workers. "Unions have therefore not only harmed the public at large and workers as a whole by distorting the use of labor," he concluded. "[T]hey have also made the incomes of the working class more unequal by reducing the opportunities available to the most disadvantaged workers."[33] In *Free to Choose*, unions receive a full chapter's worth of the Friedmans' scorn. Unions lead to greater unemployment and lower wages for workers who are not members of unions, they declare. Unions are not the reason for "the enormous improvement in the conditions of the working person." That occurred because of the free market.[34]

Friedman and Hayek's portrayals of unions became the final word on the "union problem." Think tanks then had the task of packaging this doctrine in "research" and distributing the product to the appropriate second-hand dealers of ideas in academia and the media. During the early period, the MPS could count on only one think tank, the Institute of Economic Affairs, which didn't become influential until the 1970s when it provided the ideas that fuelled the Thatcher revolution (see Chapter 2). By this time, however, other anti-union business executives saw the wisdom of investing in neo-liberal think tanks.

First to step up to the plate was Joseph Coors, president of Coors Brewing Company, and, according to the *Chicago Tribune*, a member of "one of the nation's premier union-busting families."[35] The *Tribune* was referring to Coors's brutal — but successful — no-holds-barred campaign to rid the company of its last union in 1978. During the company's decertification drive, the Teamsters, the union representing the workers, disclosed "that Coors required all employees to take lie detector tests, which included questions about whether they were loyal Americans, homosexuals, dishonest, loyal to the company, or drug users."

Five years before lashing out at his workers, Coors had put up $250,000 to cover the first-year's budget of the Heritage Foundation, one of the first American neo-liberal think tanks, and he contributed a further $300,000 each year for several years thereafter.[36] Coors was a staunch supporter and financial backer of the National Right to Work Committee, which was lobbying vigorously for state right-to-work laws. Heritage was co-founded by Ed Feulner, who was then an assistant to a Republican congressman and staff director for the Republican Study Committee. This group briefed Republican congressmen and senators about legislative developments, so they might generate a common conservative view.[37] Feulner saw the Heritage Foundation filling a similar function as the study committee, but seemingly at arm's-length from partisan interests, just like the Institute of Economic Affairs. Feulner was already well-acquainted with Hayek, the Mont Pelerin Society, and the IEA. He studied at the London School of Economics in the sixties and became an intern at the IEA, based on a letter of introduction he carried from Milton Friedman. Feulner spent two terms at IEA while he finished his Ph.D., joined the MPS, and became the society's long-serving treasurer.[38]

When Ronald Reagan defeated Jimmy Carter for the American presidency in 1980, Heritage presented Reagan with a thick report, entitled *Mandate for Leadership*. It contained two thousand recommendations that offered a blueprint for a conservative revolution, program by program, department by department. Along with other institutions that provided intellectual credibility for the shift to the right, Heritage's report was an "across-the-board drive to reduce the scope and content of the federal regulation of industry, the environment, the workplace, health care, and the relationship between buyer and seller," journalist Thomas Edsall noted at the time.[39] Budget cuts, deregulation, and "the appointment of anti-regulatory, industry-oriented agency personnel" to key positions would accomplish this goal.[40]

Heritage funder Coors was a long-time Reagan supporter and a member of Reagan's "kitchen cabinet" of wealthy backers and advisers. Heritage claimed that, by the end of the Reagan presidency, two-thirds of its recommendations had been put into effect, including one on how to handle labour disputes with air-traffic controllers. *Mandate for Leadership* anticipated an air-traffic-controllers' strike, because the contract would expire several months after Reagan took office, and the two sides were "very far away from agreement on a new contract." It noted that "all signs point toward an illegal strike or 'withholding of services' by the controllers."[41] *Mandate* recommended that the new administration "should get on top of this problem well before Inauguration Day." Reagan should take "a tough stance against an illegal strike" by identifying "which individuals were participating" and "prosecut[ing] them with criminal charges."[42] Reagan didn't go quite as far as Heritage recommended, but he still achieved the desired outcome.

***

Stephen Harper didn't have a Heritage–style manual to help him rid Canada's fragile economy of the alleged deleterious impact of unions, but he could benefit from Fraser Institute research on the subject. The institute's most important anti-union product is its ongoing research to prove that better economic performance is a result of weaker union structures, as Friedman predicted in 1962's *Capitalism and Freedom*. The study *Measuring Labour Markets in Canada and the United States* was first published in 2003 and reissued yearly. As we saw, Friedman had the backing of the rabidly anti-union Volker Fund for his work, but the sponsors of *Measuring Labour Markets* are not clear. The report says only that it is financed by "those members of the Fraser Institute who generously made available resources to undertake this study," but these members remain unnamed.[43]

The study ranks all ten Canadian provinces and fifty American states on five measures that it claims identifies healthy, high-performing labour markets. The researchers take averages over five years for total employment growth, private-sector employment growth, unemployment rate, duration of unemployment, and labour productivity. These five indicators yield an overall score for labour-market performance. Not surprisingly in the 2012 study, given their booming resource economies, the four Western provinces score well on these measures, with Alberta leading all Canadian provinces and, in fact, all of North America. It is followed by Saskatchewan, North Dakota, and Alaska. All top ten jurisdictions are in the oil, gas, and mining regions of North America.[44] Perhaps labour-market performance has more to do with the economy and less with labour issues. Nor are the indicators without their own problems. Total employment growth and total private-sector employment growth, for instance, are not independent. The former contains the latter, so this is little more than double-counting, which magnifies small differences, a common Fraser Institute technique.[45] Similarly, unemployment rates and duration of unemployment are intertwined, so these two indicators add to the double-counting. Missing from calculations are indicators measuring part-time versus full-time jobs, and any qualitative or quantitative measures of wages and benefits, items that would be of interest to workers.

The report is timed to be released annually for Labour Day to garner additional media coverage. The first-year's study (2003) received widespread media attention. A story in the *Globe and Mail's* business section claimed that "Alberta was not only the leader in Canada, it was the only province whose labour market was able to compete with any of the United States, the . . . study found. It said Alberta has the fewest provincial public-sector workers, the lowest unionization rate in Canada, and the lowest effective minimum wage,"[46] as if these were undeniably good things. The *National Post* outdid the *Globe*, with a business-section front-page story, followed by an opinion piece by two study authors who claimed that, because unions "knee-cap" the economy, we need right-to-work laws.[47] Danielle Smith, then an editorial writer at the *Calgary Herald*, lauded such laws, citing an unnamed relative who "had the grave misfortune of spending most of her adult life working in closed-shop public-sector jobs."[48] The study was also reported in the *Ottawa Citizen*, *Times Colonist* (Victoria), *Toronto Star*, and *The Province* (Vancouver).

The media report on the study each year it is released, reinforcing the message that unions are a blight on the economy, and even putting a number to it. The study concludes annually that Canadian provinces lag behind American states because Canadian labour-relations laws are too inflexible. It cites examples of inflexibility, such as the fact that mandatory union membership is not prohibited in Canadian jurisdictions as it is in American right-to-work states. And mandatory union dues are allowed in Canada, while they are not in right-to-work states.

Implicit in this work is a connection between labour-market performance — the rankings measured by the indicators, as imperfect as they may be — and labour-market "flexibility." These are items such as the degree of unionization and the existence and magnitude of a minimum wage. Certainly the media make that connection, as the *Globe* did the first year the index came out, highlighting Alberta's stellar ranking on the index, along with its lower unionization rate and low minimum wage.[49] Eleven years later, the connection was still being made in the pages of the *National Post*. Comment editor Jesse Kline, who wrote previously for the libertarian *Reason* magazine and Ezra Levant's economically and socially conservative *Western Standard*, reported that "Alberta has the best-performing labour market on the continent. Alberta also has the lowest rates of unionization in Canada."[50] But *Measuring Labour Markets* doesn't utilize rates of unionization to determine labour-market performance. There is no such connection, according to the report's own figures. Nineteen states have unionization rates under 10 per cent.[51] These are the right-to-work (RTW) states of the Deep South and Midwest. Of these nineteen, only six are in the top fifteen highest-performing jurisdictions (Texas, Virginia, South Dakota, Wyoming, North Dakota, and Louisiana). Five of these — the exception is Virginia, whose economy is based on neighbouring Washington, D.C. — have economies based on resource extraction and processing. Five more of the RTW states (North Carolina, Georgia, South Carolina, Florida, Arizona) are in the fifteen lowest-performing jurisdictions. There is no relationship between labour market performance and rate of unionization. Despite its flaws of omission and commission, *Measuring Labour Markets* executed its mission faithfully, feeding anti-union facts and figures to the news media that reported them widely over a ten-year period. The 2012 study seems to be the last in the series though, as the institute moved on to other anti-union products, such as one highlighting the benefits of right-to-work laws, tracking events in Stephen Harper's PMO.

***

Harper's views on unions became clear when he joined the National Citizens Coalition in 1997, first as vice-president and then as president. The NCC was well-known for its anti-unionism because of its financial backing of the legal battles of one Merv Lavigne, an instructor at the Haileybury School of Mines in Northern Ontario.[52] Lavigne refused to join the Ontario Public Service Employees Union (OPSEU), which was the exclusive bargaining agent for all employees at the college. However, because he benefited from the collective agreement the union negotiated with the college, he was required to pay monthly dues. In 1985, Lavigne launched an NCC–supported constitutional challenge in the Ontario Supreme Court, asking that his union dues be used for collective-bargaining purposes only. When they were used for political purposes with which he disagreed, such as the peace movement or abortion rights, he argued, his right to freedom of expression was violated.

Lavigne was victorious in the Ontario Supreme Court, but the Ontario Court of Appeal overturned the lower-court ruling, saying the contract between OPSEU and community colleges didn't breach Lavigne's constitutional rights. The *Charter of Rights and Freedoms* doesn't apply to unions, because they are not government or government-supported bodies. Lavigne and the NCC fought the case all the way to the Supreme Court of Canada, which upheld the Court of Appeal's decision and awarded as much as one million dollars in legal costs to the unions that fought Lavigne. The NCC, which had already raised about $1.5 million to support the case, had to pay up.

Although this case occurred before Harper's tenure at the NCC, the organization kept up its anti-union activity under his leadership. It attacked the Ontario Labour Relations Board for a decision to certify the United Steelworkers of America as the bargaining agent for employees at a Walmart Canada store in Windsor, Ontario. The board overturned the employees' vote against the union, saying Walmart executives subtly threatened employees who supported the Steelworkers' drive. Harper was NCC vice-president when president David Somerville ignored the illegal behaviour of Walmart executives and called the board decision "blatantly anti-democratic."[53] With Harper as president, the NCC supported the Association for the Right to Work, a group of anti-union contractors in Quebec that launched a challenge under the "freedom of association" section of the *Charter*. Quebec law requires construction workers to belong to a union or obtain a government exemption. The NCC, along with Merit Contractors, the Alberta-based anti-union construction organization, provided advice and assistance on the case. It was eventually turned down by the Supreme Court of Canada, which ruled the Quebec law was constitutional.[54]

The NCC also supported a plan by the Mike Harris government for a tax credit to aid private schools. A fundraising letter over Harper's signature claimed the government would save about seven thousand dollars for every student who didn't attend a "union-run public school."[55] It also urged Alberta premier Ralph Klein to bring in right-to-work legislation, so that situations like the strike by newly unionized employees at the *Calgary Herald* wouldn't be allowed to occur. Alberta's labour laws tilt towards employers, because they allow replacement workers to be brought in during a strike. But Harper saw the situation differently. "We think the labour laws are far too pro-union," he told two *Herald* replacement workers. "Workers should have the right to seek employment outside of a union. There should not be forced unionism. If they want a job they should be able to do it."[56]

***

A decade later, as prime minister, Harper was finally able to get to work to weaken union political and economic power, as this chapter describes. He mustered an array of strategies, from niggling to profound, to make life more difficult for unions. A potentially damaging initiative was a private member's bill, C-317, that would require all trade unions to provide extensive financial information to the Minister of Finance. The bill was introduced in October 2011 by Conservative MP Russ Hiebert and reintroduced two months later as C-377, after flaws were corrected. It specified that the information must be posted on a searchable government website for everyone to see. And what a long list of information it was! Not only did the bill require unions to submit financial statements, it also asked for a list of all transactions and disbursements over five thousand dollars with the name and address of the payer and payee, the purpose and description, and the specific amount of the transaction. Unions would also have to provide separate statements of all disbursements on political and lobbying activities, contributions, gifts and grants, administration, general overhead, organizing activities, collective-bargaining activities, conference and convention activities, education and training activities, and legal activities. The bill also asked for statements of disbursements to officers, directors, trustees, all employees, and contractors, including gross salary, stipends, periodic payments, pension and benefits, vehicles, bonuses, gifts, service credits, and lump-sum payments. It also asked for a record of the percentage of time each employee and officer dedicated to political and lobbying activities.[57]

At the very least, making public such detailed filings on union affairs would give anti-union employers a huge and unfair advantage when dealing with their workers, and would provide valuable insights into union plans. Employers weren't required to provide similar information. The bill was roundly attacked by the Canadian Labour Congress. The Canadian Bar Association presented its concerns to MPs: the law would violate workers' privacy and constitutional rights, impose large expenses on taxpayers and unions, and have a negative impact on workers' pensions and benefits.[58] But the bill's defenders were numerous and well-organized, and included the NCC, the Fraser Institute, the Montreal Economic Institute (which wrote a quickie paper on why this was such a good idea[59]), anti-union construction contractors who were members of Merit Canada, and the social conservatives at the Canadian Centre for Policy Studies.

Hiebert claimed the bill would require unions to disclose no more than what other charities already do, an explanation that was readily accepted by most reporters. As Kathryn May wrote in the *Ottawa Citizen*, the bill called "for unions to make massive mandatory financial disclosures to the Canada Revenue Agency similar to the disclosures made by charities."[60] If that's all that was being asked for, who could be against it — unless they had something to hide?

However, this is a far-from-accurate depiction of the very limited information from charities that is displayed on the Canada Revenue Agency (CRA) website. Form T3010, the *Registered Charity Information Return*, requires information on the ten highest-compensated employees, and then only the number of employees whose compensation falls within set categories. The Fraser Institute's 2012 return, for instance, tells us that two employees earned between $250,000 and $300,000, and three employees earned between $160,000 and $200,000.[61] The return does not tell us how much the institute brought in from each of its fundraising activities. Donations from foreign sources are kept confidential by the CRA, although the total of this revenue is reported.

The bill leapfrogged to the head of the long list of private members' bills, most of which never get beyond first reading. By the middle of March, it had received second reading, with Harper's support, and was referred to the Standing Committee on Finance. Rabble.ca's Lori Theresa Waller observed that "far from being a run-of-the-mill backbencher's bill, C-377 was a government darling, with the full weight of the Prime Minister's Office behind it."[62] An NDP filibuster during committee hearings in September and October blocked Conservative MPs from introducing amendments to fix some of the serious flaws in the bill, and it was reported back to the House in its original form. That forced the government to step in with a package of amendments to smooth over some of the worst problems, further indicating Harper's support.

The bill passed third reading and was sent over to the Senate for what was expected to be rubber-stamp approval. However, something unexpected happened on its way to Royal Assent and passage into law. A handful of Conservative senators rebelled. Led by Senator Hugh Segal — a Red Tory who had been appointed

by Liberal Prime Minister Paul Martin — they voted with the
Liberals to approve a series of amendments and send the bill
back to the House of Commons for reconsideration.[63] The Senate banking committee had heard concerns about whether the
bill was a constitutional invasion into provincial responsibility
for labour law, "the protection of personal information, the cost
and need for greater transparency, and the vagueness as to whom
this legislation would apply," the committee reported.[64] Segal
denounced the bill as "bad legislation, bad public policy, and a
diminution of both the order and the freedom that should exist
in any democratic, pluralist, and mixed-market society."[65] The
bill didn't go back to the Commons though. Harper prorogued
Parliament and, when the Senate resumed sitting in October, it
was in a new session. The bill stayed in the Senate.

The corporate media seemed content to report the progress of
the bill without much comment. No one asked how a junior MP
from suburban Vancouver could put together a bill with such
deep knowledge of union affairs. True, Hiebert was a lawyer, but
not a labour lawyer. Before being elected in 2004, Hiebert was
an evangelical lawyer and elder in Vancouver's Tenth Avenue
Alliance Church (which is aligned with Harper's East Gate
Alliance Church in Ottawa). He had also been legal counsel to
Brian Rushfeldt's Canadian Family Action Coalition (CFAC),
an organization whose goal is to see Christian moral principles
established as the foundation of Canadian society.[66] Rushfeldt
and Harper were old friends, going back to the days when Harper
headed the National Citizens Coalition (1997-2000). Journalist
Marci McDonald reports that a photo of Rushfeldt and Harper
"huddled together in the prime minister's office now hangs in
pride of place on Rushfeldt's wall." But it wasn't just their history
that gave Rushfeldt access to the PMO, she writes. CFAC played
a prominent role in Harper's 2006 election victory by mobilizing
evangelicals to vote Conservative. By 2006, Russ Hiebert had

already been elected federally, having been parachuted in to the safe South Surrey riding by party leadership.

Windsor–area NDP MP Joe Comartin suggested one possibility that might account for how a junior MP, who up until then had never said a word about union finances, was able to put forth such an extensive proposal.[67] He pointed to the similarity of Hiebert's bill to legislation in the United States and the role of anti-union politicians like Newt Gingrich.[68] In 1992, Gingrich wrote a memo to Secretary of Labor Lynn Martin, urging her to boost the reporting requirements demanded by the Office of Labor-Management Standards for unions, in order "to weaken our opponents and encourage our allies." This approach became entrenched in Republican thinking. Republican adviser and anti-tax activist Grover Norquist later opined that "every dollar that is spent on disclosure and reporting is a dollar that can't be spent on other labour union activities."[69]

It wasn't until 2005 that the George W. Bush administration put the strategy into effect. Bush's deputy chief of staff, Karl Rove — "Bush's brain," as he was known — had a long-term plan to destroy the finances and political strength of unions, which had spent $200 million on behalf of Democrat John Kerry in the 2004 election. That spending had to be stopped, or else Rove might not be able to execute his plan to make Republicans the permanent governing party.[70] He recruited Don Todd, a former Republican National Committee strategist to head the Office of Labor-Management Standards. Todd was well-known for his relentless hostility to anything to do with the Democratic Party. He made Gingrich's wish come true. Within two years, the amount of information required from unions increased by an estimated 60 per cent, with a parallel increase in the time and money required to fulfill the reporting requirements. The information in the forms filed by unions (called LM-2s) was valuable, and not just to union members, who could see what their leaders were up to. Companies often hire management consultants to advise them on how to remain non-union, and more detail on union spending was certain to reveal strategies being used for organizing. It was also important to the Republican Party, the historic enemy of unions.[71] Unions couldn't prove Karl Rove's involvement behind the scenes, but there were connections: Don Todd came from the Republican National Committee; he worked for Ken Mehlman, who ran the RNC; Mehlman took his orders from Rove. Surely this attack on unions couldn't have happened without Rove's approval and encouragement.

Stephen Harper has been accused of "Rovian tactics" — "highly aggressive, message-controlled and truth-challenged politics" — by his critics.[72] Following Rove and the Republicans, anything Harper and the Conservatives can do to weaken unions will ultimately weaken their new enemy, the NDP, because of the long-standing connections between the party and organized labour. After the 2011 election, NDP front- and back-benches included many MPs with trade-union affiliations.[73]

Harper's incremental attacks on unions kept coming. Buried in the 2012 budget was a clause that repealed the *Fair Wages and Hours of Labour Act*, a law that requires contractors bidding on federal contracts to pay "fair" wages and overtime. Its repeal gives non-union construction companies the upper hand on government contracts.[74] And Bill C-4, the 2013 budget implementation bill, contained a measure changing the balance of power between the federal government and federal public-sector unions. It gave federal employers "the exclusive right" to determine whether any "service, facility, or activity of the government of Canada is essential because it is, or will be necessary for the safety or security of the public or a segment of the public."[75] Historically, employers and unions together made the determination. Currently, 40,000 of the Public Service Alliance of Canada's (PSAC) 187,000 members are essential. "The change would undermine bargaining rights, potentially double the number of essential workers and sap their ability to use job action to press demands," a *Toronto Star* editorial opined.[76]

But the biggest increment loomed in the background. Just a year after Don Todd ramped up reporting requirements for American unions, the Fraser Institute bemoaned the "acute . . . divide" between Canadian and American disclosure laws.[77] "In general, the disclosure requirements for unions are extraordinarily weak in Canada," the Fraser authors warned. "The United States, on the other hand, has rigorous and stringent public reporting requirements for unions."[78] Never mind these had just been imposed by Todd. The Fraser's recommendation was a foregone conclusion: "A Canadian policy should build on the successes of the U.S. system." Soon, Russ Hiebert's bill was doing just that.

The think tank didn't stop there. It highlighted the lower rate of unionization in the U.S. and explained this was a good thing, because American workers have "more choice" about joining a union. Some Canadian workers, "as a condition of employment . . . can be compelled to join a union," the study complained. Worse, "Canadian workers covered by a collective agreement, regardless of union membership status, must pay full union dues."[79] It was the Merv Lavigne–NCC attack all over again. The NCC continued to call this long-established practice "forced union dues." A September 2012 letter on the NCC website claimed that "union bosses are free to spend their members' union dues on political causes without reporting their activities or consulting their membership."[80] Eliminating "forced union dues" was never far from top of mind for neo-liberals, libertarians, and social conservatives alike. Such an act, Brad Walchuk, a McMaster University labour-studies professor, wrote, "would significantly impede Canadian unions."[81]

Harper was waiting for the right time to move.

That time may have arrived just after Labour Day, 2012. Russ Hiebert's bill had passed second reading and was headed to the finance committee. Then the news broke that PSAC regional wings had supported candidates running for the separatist Québec Solidaire and Parti Québécois in the Quebec provincial election. Taking up the cudgels this time was another social conservative in the Conservative caucus, one with close ties to the party's inner circle. Pierre Poilievre, an Ottawa-area MP, said he couldn't "accept a union representing public servants working for the government of Canada which forcefully takes money out of the pockets of Canada's public servants to support parties that want to break up the country."[82] Poilievre had been parliamentary secretary to the prime minister, and earlier an executive assistant to Stockwell Day. He was taking up this issue, he claimed, because some public servants in his riding complained their mandatory dues were going to radical causes and political campaigns they opposed, such as student protests in Quebec. "[T]he law should not force them against their will to pay dues for causes they don't support," Poilievre explained, as he announced plans to press his Conservative colleagues for legislative changes to allow public servants to opt out of paying union dues. He soon extended his proposal to include all employees under federal jurisdiction. These were the workers at Air Canada, CP Rail, and Canada Post that so pre-occupied Harper and Raitt during the first year of majority government. Unlike Hiebert, however, Poilievre couldn't introduce a private member's bill, since he was a parliamentary secretary and thus a member of the government. Poilievre's threat was greeted with enthusiasm by the *National Post* editorial board and by the paper's national-affairs columnist John Ivison, who complained about the fact that such legislation would apply only to unions under federal jurisdiction, whereas Hiebert's bill, because it amends the *Income Tax Act*, applies to all unions. That's its "genius," he enthused.[83]

Poilievre didn't make good on his threat. Harper prorogued Parliament and, in the new session, gave Poilievre a new assignment as minister of state for democratic reform. But right-to-work didn't go away. At the Conservative Party convention in Calgary at the end of October 2013, in a page taken from Milton Friedman, delegates passed a motion — with 66-per-cent support — declaring that "mandatory union membership and forced financial contributions as a condition of employment limit the economic freedom of Canadians and stifle economic growth." The delegates then passed a motion with a clear majority, supporting "right-to-work legislation to allow optional union membership."[84]

Union-dues check-off — "forced financial contributions," in Conservative lingo — came into use in Canada in 1946, the result of an arbitration decision by Supreme Court Justice Ivan Rand after a bitter strike by the United Auto Workers against the Ford Motor Company of Canada in Windsor, Ontario. Under this ruling, called the Rand Formula, workers in a unionized workplace are not required to join the union, but because they benefit from the union's ability to win higher wages and benefits and improved working conditions, they must pay union dues. Coming into effect the year before Friedrich Hayek created the Mont Pelerin Society and focused the society's attention on the "union problem," the Rand Formula epitomizes the union problem in Canada. Its elimination through right-to-work laws, even at the federal level, would be a significant step in the removal of a major obstacle to the market state.

The Fraser Institute works steadily to promote right-to-work and attempt to demonstrate the existence of a link between weaker unions and greater prosperity. "Reject Unions and Prosper," declared the *National Post* headline on a Fraser Institute opinion piece. But prosperity for whom? The studies by the

Center for American Progress and the Economic Policy Institute cited earlier in this chapter suggest a robust correlation between a healthy union movement and a prosperous middle class. As union membership and density declined, the middle class saw its prospects dim. So prosperity must be for the already prosperous.

Labour relations fall largely under provincial jurisdiction, so solving the union problem will require the participation of provincial governments. Possible candidates are British Columbia, Alberta, and Saskatchewan. Ontario is a primary target, especially considering the pro–right-to-work Tim Hudak and his Progressive Conservatives. To bolster Hudak's RTW advocacy, the Fraser Institute produced a study purporting to demonstrate that states with RTW laws experience greater economic growth than states without them.[85] This report followed on the heels of the February 2012 closure of the Electro-Motive Diesel locomotive assembly plant in London, Ontario, and the transfer of operations to a new plant in Indiana. The move, and the loss of 450 jobs, occurred the same month that Indiana — with a Republican governor, Senate, and House of Representatives — became the twenty-third RTW state. Wages at the Indiana plant are about half of what they were in London.[86] Weaker unions, lower wages, and higher profits — both neoliberals and their corporate backers get what they want. Hudak backed off his advocacy for RTW when it became clear such a policy could lose more votes than it could win, and the Harper government went silent. The RTW threat was relegated to the back burner, to return at the next opportune moment.

Despite forty years of Fraser Institute anti-union messaging, Canadian unions still enjoy substantial public support, according to a Harris/Decima poll of December 2013. The poll, commissioned by the Canadian Association of University Teachers, found that 63 per cent of Canadians oppose right-to-work laws, agreeing that, if everyone benefits from a union, everyone should pay.[87] Just over 30 per cent disagreed, saying the individual should have the right to opt out. The survey contains other good news for unions: 70 per cent said unions are still needed; 55 per cent of respondents agreed that unions are a positive force; and 54 per cent felt that our society would be less fair without unions. But not all results are positive: 45 per cent agreed that unions have too much power over governments and businesses (36 per cent disagreed). Respondents were divided on the statement that governments should have the right to impose contracts on public-sector unions (40 per cent agree, 42 per cent disagree), and also on the statement that public-sector unions should not have the right to strike (40 agree, 43 disagree). According to these results, Harper's attacks on public-sector unions will be well received by 40 per cent of Canadians — his margin of victory.

Most Canadians know nothing of these results, though, because the survey was reported only in the *Huffington Post* and did not appear at all in major corporate media. If Canadians don't know what their fellow citizens think about unions, Harper's task is that much easier. Against the backdrop of a gradual decline in union density, Harper has little to risk. No federal government has gone after unions as comprehensively as Harper's, upsetting long-standing labour practices, intervening in contract negotiations, slashing the federal workforce, reducing union membership, and threatening right-to-work legislation. Hayek and the Mont Pelerin Society worked on the union problem for half a century, and the Fraser Institute has published its anti-union studies for forty years. Despite significant public support for unions, Stephen Harper is advancing the cause — removing organized labour as a factor in the operation of the economy — through his unique brand of ideology and incrementalism, another example of Harperism in action.

4

LIBERATE DEAD CAPITAL ON FIRST NATION RESERVES

Rarely does a book about a public-policy issue become government policy overnight. Such an occurrence is extraordinary, because ideas take years to percolate through political elites and public-opinion filters before they end up on a government's agenda. But it has happened twice under Harper, illustrating yet again the success of a Canadian right-wing echo chamber, comprising corporate media, think tanks, the Prime Minister's Office, and policy entrepreneurs. They work together to amplify messages and establish issues as legitimate candidates for public and political consideration. There's nothing conspiratorial about this process, because the actors are doing what they were set up to do. This is how Harperism works.

First was the publication in 2010 of *Beyond the Indian Act: Restoring Aboriginal Property Rights*, by Tom Flanagan, Christopher Alcantara, and André Le Dressay. This book argues that bringing private-property rights onto First Nation reserves is the best hope for lifting indigenous peoples out of poverty. Within a few months of its publication, the Harper government was considering the legislation laid out in the book. It was followed six months later by *Ethical Oil: The Case for Canada's Oil Sands* by Ezra Levant, a former student of Flanagan's at the University of Calgary. This book, which is discussed in Chapter 5, argues that Alberta bitumen is preferable to oil from the Middle East and Venezuela, because it is produced under an ethical system. Four months after that book's publication, ethical oil was a Harper government talking point, if not official government policy.

Beyond the Indian Act's meteoric rise to prominence began at the Rideau Club in Ottawa where the book was launched at an event sponsored by the Macdonald–Laurier Institute (MLI), the think tank closest to the Harper government, as Chapter 2 explains. Co-sponsors for the event were Michael Coates of public-relations powerhouse Hill and Knowlton, whom Tom Flanagan jokingly called the "president of the invisible government," and Rick Anderson, a former Reform Party apparatchik, who was executive vice-president of Interborder Holdings, parent of the giant land-development company Walton International, which subsidized the cost of the book. (Land developers are naturally interested in the results of privatization.) Senators and MPs were "coming and going all evening," Flanagan noted. They could purchase the book for half-price, thanks to Walton.[1]

Beyond the Indian Act forges an alliance between neo-liberal networks and a group of Canadian First Nation leaders. These chiefs, led by Manny Jules, former chief of the Kamloops First Nation, and supported by economist André Le Dressay, want to open reserves to at least a modified form of capitalism. Neoliberals are represented by Flanagan, who makes the case that giving First Nation residents ownership of their homes is the best way to lift them out of poverty, because they can take out mortgages on their houses and start businesses. The Fraser Institute plays a prominent support role in this campaign. Both groups are guided by the work of Peruvian economist — and Mont Pelerin Society member — Hernando de Soto and his doctrine of liberating dead capital. De Soto's endorsement on the back cover of *Beyond the Indian Act* says that "you don't have to travel to Zambia or Peru to see dead capital. All you need to do is visit a reserve in Canada. First Nation people own assets, but not with the same instruments as other Canadians. They're frozen into an *Indian Act* of the 1870s, so they can't easily trade their valuable resources."[2] The book argues that, although most aboriginal people live in poverty, they are potentially wealthy landlords, with land reserves totalling 6.5-million acres. All that needs to happen is for First Nations to obtain the underlying or reversionary title to their reserves. Once they have this, they can create fee-simple titles.[3] By establishing a modern, efficient system of property rights for First Nations, more Indian millionaires will be created and reserve housing will be improved.[4]

Flanagan referred to the book's proposal for a First Nations property-ownership act in his MLI presentation, and stated that the book's publication was "just one phase of a larger campaign to get this legislation developed."[5] The corporate press gave it enthusiastic attention. Flanagan had an op-ed in the *Globe and Mail*, followed by articles in the *Toronto Star* and *National Post*. The *Post* placed its story by John Ivison on the front page, treating Flanagan as a rock star and his proposal for private property on reserves as self-evident. The *Post* followed up with a supportive column from McGill University economist and MLI adviser William Watson, plus an excerpt, and a supportive editorial. Then Flanagan and Jules were off to Winnipeg for a luncheon address at the Frontier Centre for Public Policy and an excerpt in the *Winnipeg Free Press*. Their talk was reported in the *Free Press* and in Postmedia News's two Saskatchewan dailies. After that, it was on to Calgary for a Fraser Institute–sponsored "policy briefing" at the Calgary Chamber of Commerce, and then to Vancouver for a keynote address at the Fraser Institute's annual Harold Walter Siebens lecture and luncheon.

Just weeks after the book's release, the campaign had progressed so rapidly the Canadian Press could report that "a proposed law that would allow First Nations to own the land they live on, reversing hundreds of years of aboriginal policy, is gaining support among native leaders and the country's political class. The government is quietly getting behind the idea, providing the funding for a feasibility study and policy conference."[6] In fact, the Harper government had been quietly backing private ownership of reserve land since it came into office in 2006, as we shall see. For neo-liberals, collective ownership of reserve lands is an obstacle to the market state and needs to be eliminated, or at least neutralized. *Beyond the Indian Act* is the way forward.

"This has to be a First Nations led initiative," Flanagan informed the senators and MPs at the launch. "It won't work if it is imposed from the outside. If it's Flanagan telling Indians what to do, it won't go anywhere. It's really Manny's idea, and it has to be presented that way." Jules was already "consulting with First Nations and attempting to demonstrate that there is some support for this that will culminate in the drafting of legislation," Flanagan said. Jules would be the public face of the government-funded feasibility study and policy conference. Jules's idea, perhaps, but wrapped in de Soto's neo-liberal doctrine.

As chief of the Kamloops First Nation, Jules oversaw the largest real-estate development ever to be built on native land, a $600-million project with 2,000 homes, a 6,700-yard golf course, an entertainment and sports complex, a shopping centre, and a 200-room hotel, all on 240 hectares of reserve land. Under the ninety-nine-year lease with developers, the band acts as the local government, providing services and collecting taxes.[7] Jules wanted to go further. "We want to be able to own our own lands," he told the MLI book launch. "It's about the freedom to choose,"[8] he said, referring, perhaps inadvertently, to Milton and Rose Friedman's classic 1980 polemic, *Free to Choose*, a neo-liberal bible.

For his part, Flanagan pointed to de Soto's research that seemed to demonstrate that giving desperately poor squatters ownership of the land on which they had built their homes could lift them out of poverty. The same could hold true for aboriginals on reserves in Canada, where reserve land was held in trust by the federal government for the Indian band as an entity, he suggested. Transforming collective ownership into individual ownership was the recipe for improving the lot of Canada's aboriginal people. Flanagan had been working on this idea for years. "Collective property is the path of poverty, and private property is the path of prosperity,"[9] Flanagan and Alcantara had written in a Fraser Institute policy study nearly a decade earlier. Why? Because "markets work best when property is privately owned," they claimed, citing Hayek as their source.[10] Through property ownership, First Nation individuals can become equal with other Canadians. In *Beyond the Indian Act*, Flanagan and his co-authors write that

> *Our approach follows in the footsteps of Peruvian economist Hernando de Soto, who has argued in two bestselling books that defective property rights make life miserable for the poor in the Third World . . . Unable to get title to the land on which they live, they cannot use it as security for loans to improve their homes or start a business . . . The problems of First Nations in Canada, though not identical in detail to what de Soto describes, are similar in principle.*[11]

Jules was also a believer. He designed the front cover for *Beyond the Indian Act* as two side-by-side pictographs: one an eagle, representing the aspirations of First Nations of North America, and the other a condor, doing the same for indigenous peoples of the south. "I want to unite the eagle and the condor," Jules told the MLI audience. He was already collaborating with de Soto. "We're working together to achieve what no other peoples have achieved in the Americas, which is recognizing the underlying fundamental title that First Nations have to the lands they occupy."[12]

In his famous book *The Mystery of Capital*, de Soto argues that the Third World is bursting with assets saved and accumulated by the poor. The problem is that they "hold these resources in defective forms: houses built on land whose ownership rights are not adequately recorded, unincorporated businesses with undefined liability . . . Because the rights to these possessions are not adequately documented, these assets cannot be readily turned into capital,"[13] he writes. "The poor have accumulated trillions of dollars of real estate during the past 40 years. What the poor lack is easy access to the property mechanisms that could legally fix the economic potential of their assets so that they could be used to produce, secure, or guarantee greater value in the expanded market."[14] Third World nations do not have a system for documenting assets. Without such a system, "their assets are dead capital."[15] You need a property right before you can make money.

De Soto's work is cited, not just by Flanagan and Jules in Canada, but around the world, to justify projects intended to improve the plight of the poor. His message was a comfort to economic and political elites: "Revolution is not necessary, because capitalism clearly works in the West and — with a little bit of tinkering — can work in the Third World," as one critic explained the implications of de Soto's work.[16] And even "transfers of wealth are not the solution," economist Christopher Woodruff adds. "Formalizing ownership" is all that is needed to bring the poor into the economy.[17]

But how true is this good news? Did de Soto's work in Peru and countries like Egypt and the Philippines, where he applied similar techniques, lead to improved living conditions? Did squatters who obtained title to their homes establish businesses, take out loans, and enter the market economy?

Columbia University political theorist Timothy Mitchell subjected de Soto's Peruvian project to careful scrutiny and came to a startling conclusion: de Soto is wrong. Any positive results were due, not to land ownership, but to how the titling program was rolled out. Property titling had no significant effect on access among the poor to business credit,[18] Mitchell concludes.

De Soto started the program in Lima in the mid-eighties. In 1996, Peruvian president, Alberto Fujimori, expanded the program to cities across the country as a strategy to counter the success of Peru's revolutionary organizations. The World Bank came in with a loan to finish the project. On completion in 2004, over a million households had been registered and over a million titles issued. But studies of the experiment, Mitchell reports, found that mortgage lending increased only after the Peruvian government abandoned the scheme and subsidized low-income mortgages, creating a non-market incentive for the poor to take out mortgages. Government subsidies and not individual ownership drove de Soto's program.[19] By then, however, de Soto had written his bestselling books and moved on to other countries wanting to utilize his services.

A second study of the newly created property owners, however, did find an unexpected result: they began to work harder, with an average increase of 17 per cent in the number of hours worked by a household. Neo-liberals were relieved, Mitchell argues, because this finding confirmed a major tenet of their doctrine, "that the right of private property is the fundamental requirement for economic development and that securing this right and reaping the benefits can be accomplished by establishing the proper rules and institutions."[20] De Soto and the World Bank could ignore the failure of the titling project to produce its intended result, an increase in lending to the poor,[21] and point instead to the unexpected but welcome result of an increase in hours worked. However, in an analytical tour de force, Mitchell demolishes this study, demonstrating why its findings are not true either.[22]

The study compared households that received title to their land with households not yet reached by the program. It was this comparison that found the 17-per-cent differential in hours worked. But the study compared apples and oranges. Mitchell discovered that the majority of titled households are located in Lima, where employment opportunities are greater, and all residents, whether in titled or non-titled housing, are more likely to have jobs and work more hours. The study didn't look at non-titled households in Lima. The majority of non-titled households in the survey are located in cities in the interior with fewer employment opportunities. Here, too, de Soto's work was inaccurate. The results had little to do with property ownership, Mitchell concludes. Success is related to location, not ownership, a phenomenon relevant to the situation facing Canadian First Nations, where reserves near urban centres and resort destinations are generally more prosperous than those in isolated locations with few resources.

Mitchell is not the only critic to expose the flaws in this scheme. In 2000, Brian Ballantyne, then a professor in the Department of Geomatics Engineering at the University of Calgary, led a synthesis of studies of cadastral reforms (changes to the system by which property is registered) in six countries, including Peru. The review found that the reforms "were neither successful in increasing security of tenure; promoting improvements to land; facilitating access to credit; nor creating a viable land market."[23]

However, these findings didn't change the opinions of the

neo-liberal thought collective, which had expended significant effort and funds to demonstrate the doctrine that private property is a fundamental requirement for prosperity. De Soto had published two best-selling books — with endorsements from Margaret Thatcher and Milton Friedman — that claimed this.

Given the influence of his books, it is worth looking into de Soto's background and connections, as Mitchell does, to understand the genesis of his thinking and analysis. De Soto is depicted as a Third World economist by his neo-liberal confreres, in an effort to give his work more authenticity. Who knows more about Peruvian economics than a Peruvian economist, after all? But de Soto's ties to First and neo-liberal worlds are extensive and long-standing. He studied, not in Latin America, but at the Graduate Institute of International Studies in Geneva, a stronghold of European neo-liberalism, whose faculty included Ludwig von Mises and Wilhelm Ropke, two founding members of the Mont Pelerin Society (MPS).[24]

On his return to Peru, de Soto invited Hayek to speak about democracy and the market economy at a conference in Lima. He was assisted in bringing Hayek to Peru by Guatemalan businessman Manuel Ayau, a Hayek disciple who was serving as MPS president and assisting in the neo-liberal colonization of Latin America. After the conference, Hayek put de Soto in touch with Antony Fisher, founder of three leading neo-liberal think tanks, including the Fraser Institute, as Chapter 2 notes. Fisher was putting the finishing touches on the Atlas Economic Research Foundation, whose purpose would be to help conservative businessmen, financiers and policy entrepreneurs set up think tanks in Third World, and later Eastern European, countries. Atlas assisted de Soto in setting up and funding his think tank, the Institute for Liberty and Democracy, as its first project. The bulk of the funding for de Soto's fledgling organization came from the Center for International Private Enterprise (CIPE), which was established jointly by officials in the Reagan administration and the U.S. Chamber of Commerce to promote private-property rights and free enterprise (capitalism) in Latin America and elsewhere. As with Atlas, de Soto's think tank was CIPE's first major project.[25] It didn't take long for de Soto to launch his property-rights project.

His work was packaged and heavily promoted by neo-liberal networks and quickly reached Canada's shores. Owen Lippert, a senior fellow at the Fraser Institute, reviewed *The Mystery of Capital* in the institute's monthly newsletter, *Fraser Forum*. He speculated as to how de Soto's methods could be applied to Canada's aboriginal experience, claiming that "aboriginals on Canadian reserves have even less than the poor in the Third World."[26] The Fraser Institute seemed to like the potential of de Soto's work for promoting private-property rights, because the next year it invited de Soto to explain the mystery of capital at a round-table luncheon in Vancouver. Institute executive director Michael Walker asked de Soto if he had "any comments about how we should deal with the native land claims issue here in Canada?" De Soto replied that he couldn't tell Walker what to do in Canada, but made the curious point that "human beings have established two basic concepts: sovereignty (which is very political) and property." Property is much more stable than sovereignty, he said. "If people have recognized rights to their property, the overarching political system doesn't seem to be as important."[27] It was the old neo-liberal dictum first enunciated by Milton Friedman, as Chapter 1 discusses: economic freedom is more important than political freedom. No wonder Friedman endorsed de Soto's book.

De Soto was back for another Fraser Institute round-table address the following year, this time to a Toronto audience. Tom Flanagan, the Fraser Institute senior fellow, had just published his controversial book *First Nations? Second Thoughts*, which argues that First Nations were merely the "first immigrants" in North America, preceding the French and British by a few thousand years. Consequently, there could be no indigenous entitlements. Aboriginals were simply a people conquered by Europeans with a higher degree of civilization. Reserves should be turned into private property and opened up to free-market exploitation, and aboriginals should simply be assimilated into mainstream Canadian society. Flanagan was concerned about dispelling the belief that aboriginal peoples had no conception of property. He claims that "while it is true that Indians did not have the specific notion of selling land, they understood other aspects of property, especially the right to exclude others from what they considered to be their own lands."[28] His source for this statement is Richard Pipes, an anti-communist expert on Russia. Pipes wrote a polemic claiming that private property ownership is essential not only for economic development, but also for liberty and the rule of law.[29] Flanagan informs his readers that "the discussion about Indian conceptions of property is both confused and ideologically charged."[30] Yet his own work adds materially to the ideologically charged confusion. Using a common neo-liberal rhetorical device, Flanagan sets up a fallacious debate. On one side, he says, are the "aboriginal advocates" who "portray Indians as proto-socialists and natural environmentalists." But since institutions of property are found in all civilizations, "native partisans cannot deny that Indians had property without making them seem like savages." He does not cite any of these aboriginal advocates, which leads to the suspicion he is creating a straw man he can use against his opponents. On the other side of the debate, Flanagan continues, are the "advocates of free-market capitalism," citing free-market environmental economists Terry Anderson and Bruce Benson, with whom he would later edit a volume of essays.[31] They believe "that Indians cannot make progress in the contemporary world without reliance on property and economic competition," a view Flanagan admits he shares. But Anderson and Benson "overemphasize the extent of property rights prior to contact with European civilization," again using that loaded word.[32]

Flanagan would set the record straight by guiding readers through "these swirling ideological cross-currents" to find "the historical truth about aboriginal institutions of property."[33] Yet the small clutch of experts he relies on to help navigate the currents all group together at one end of the ideological spectrum. They include the aforementioned Richard Pipes, and Harold Demsetz, a neo-liberal economist of the University of Chicago school, Mont Pelerin Society director, and creator of the theory of property rights. Flanagan also cites James DeLong, an analyst from the neo-liberal Competitive Enterprise Institute. All three repeat the mantra that prosperity and freedom depend on having a system of private-property rights.

Given the biased framework he provides for his inquiry into aboriginal property institutions, Flanagan's conclusion is unsurprising: First Nations cannot make progress in the contemporary world without relying on property rights. He bemoans the fact that "Canada's aboriginal people seem as far as ever from attaining a workable system of property rights," and concludes that "if there is anything for which Canadians should feel guilty, it is that our government, laws and courts have kept Indians outside the world of individual property rather than encouraging them to step inside."[34] Flanagan suggests that the way forward is to "think about making small steps in the right direction" (i.e., toward assimilation).[35] This must happen "if the goal is widespread individual independence and prosperity for aboriginal people."[36] One small step he recommends on the book's last page is "a regime of individual property rights."[37] Then along came de Soto's book, and the regime of individual property rights leapfrogged to the front page.

Several months after de Soto's first Fraser Institute address, Flanagan published a commentary in the *National Post*, praising the Peruvian economist's work, outlining the types of private property available on reserves, and making the unsupported claim that aboriginal leaders are "mainly capitalist in outlook" and want "to make profits."[38] He amplified the commentary in the Fraser Institute policy study written with his graduate student Chris Alcantara. They survey the range of ownership types that exist on First Nation reserves, such as customary rights, certificates of possession under the *Indian Act*, and lease agreements made possible by the recently enacted *First Nations Land Management Act*. They weren't yet ready to recommend fee-simple ownership. "We do not have a sweeping proposal for the privatization of the First Nations land base," they wrote. "First Nations . . . will have to decide what to do with it."[39]

On-the-ground research and advocacy for fee-simple ownership on reserves came from the Manny Jules–inspired First Nations Tax Commission. Over two decades and three governments, this government-financed organization transitioned seamlessly from assisting First Nations in collecting property taxes, to advocating for more certainty in how reserve lands are registered, to developing and promoting the *First Nations Property Ownership Act*. During the 1980s, Jules, as chief of the Kamloops First Nation, lobbied for changes to the *Indian Act*, so his band could collect property taxes from commercial developments on its reserve land. With support from First Nations across Canada, Jules was able to get the *Indian Act* amended by the Mulroney government in 1988 (Bill C-115). The so-called "Kamloops amendment" set up the Indian Taxation Advisory Board (ITAB) to promote and facilitate tax collection on reserves. With Jules as chairman, ITAB developed and delivered specialized education and training programs in property taxation, assessment, communication, and dispute resolution to

First Nations tax administrators. ITAB also helped Indian bands court potential investors, so they could improve the revenue potential of their tax base.[40]

ITAB was replaced by the First Nations Tax Commission (FNTC) in 2005 under legislation developed and passed by the Chrétien and Martin governments (the *First Nations Fiscal and Statistical Management Act*). But before it ceased operations, ITAB completed four research papers that looked at ways to improve the certainty of land titles on First Nation reserves. Papers by Diane Cragg, registrar of land titles for the Nisga'a Lisims government, and corporate law firm Lang Michener suggest that a Torrens-based land-registry system — the one used in Ontario and Western Canadian provinces — is superior to the existing First Nations registry, because, under Torrens, successful registration of a property is a legal guaranty of ownership. In contrast, the First Nations registry, the papers conclude, is "a limited deeds system with a limited legislative framework."[41] The other two papers were prepared by Fiscal Realities, a Kamloops-based economics firm led by André Le Dressay, a co-author of *Beyond the Indian Act*. Le Dressay set up shop in Kamloops in the early nineties, conducting economic studies for ITAB and other First Nation clients. His papers found that, because of the deficiencies and uncertainties in the existing registry system, "investors shy away from First Nation projects and First Nation persons are less able to earn equity from their land or use it as collateral for business start up loans."[42] In aggregate, the papers blast the existing system of land registration and argue vigorously for a Torrens-style system under First Nations administration.

As part of its legacy in training First Nations to become competent in tax issues, ITAB created the Tulo Centre of Indigenous Economics, "a not-for-profit institution dedicated to building capacity so markets work on First Nation lands."[43] It was then that ITAB was transformed into the First Nations Tax Commission (FNTC), with Jules as chief commissioner. It continued its taxation work by developing sample laws and legal standards so First Nations could issue bonds to investors and provide greater certainty to investors, taxpayers, and First Nations. The FNTC also entered into a partnership with the Tulo Centre and Thompson Rivers University (TRU) in Kamloops, B.C., to run certificate programs for indigenous people in "areas related to First Nation tax administration, public finance and economics."[44] Le Dressay became Tulo's director of education and taught the First Nation taxation courses at TRU.

The FNTC continued its efforts to improve certainty in First Nation land titles, with $737,000 in funding from Indian and Northern Affairs Canada (INAC) over the next two years.[45] In 2009, the tax commission convened an expert panel to review this research. Panelists included Maria del Carmen Delgado, from de Soto's Institute for Liberty and Democracy (ILD), Flanagan, and Terry Anderson from the Property and Environment Research Center in Montana, an advocate for free-market environmentalism. The FNTC reported it would continue to work with these experts as the initiative advanced.[46] But with the appearance of de Soto's ILD on the scene, a shift was occurring in this initiative's real purpose. Under the priority of "improving land title certainty," the 2008–09 annual report stated that

> *The FNTC will continue work to improve the*
> *First Nation business environment and revenue*
> *base through improvements to the land tenure*
> *system. This year, the FNTC will pursue a*
> *partnership with Hernando de Soto's Institute*
> *of Liberty and Democracy to advocate for an*
> *improved First Nation property rights system.*[47]

Land-title certainty had morphed into property-rights advocacy, and hardly anyone noticed. Jules went to Peru to sign a memorandum of understanding with de Soto "to promote, develop and implement market compatible indigenous property rights systems."[48] It was at this time Jules and Flanagan began coordinating their efforts. In Calgary in December 2008, they appeared together to discuss property rights and tax regimes on aboriginal lands during the final evening of the Fraser Institute's fall cocktail series, "Behind the Spin: Fraser@Centini," hosted by Flanagan's ex-student Danielle Smith.[49] The following year, property ownership became a top priority, and Jules revealed he was working on a legislative option that would enable First Nations to assume underlying title to their lands.[50] He had the support of the Harper government for this venture. INAC money for land-title certainty dried up, but the spigot was turned on for First Nations property ownership, with over four million dollars directed to this initiative by 2013.

The Conservative Party of Canada made no secret of its support for private ownership on reserves. Its 2006 election platform declared that "a Conservative government will support the development of individual property ownership on reserves, to encourage lending for private housing and businesses."[51] This statement was ambiguous enough to not raise red flags. Individual property ownership could mean ownership of one's house and not the underlying land, which could remain communally owned, a practice already being followed by several First Nations. Jim Prentice, Harper's first minister of Indian Affairs, removed the uncertainty several months after Harper's victory, when he said, during an interview, that "individuals should be able to buy and sell reserve land." The tradition of communal land ownership was denying First Nations their right to participate in the economy. "It's important for any citizen in Canada to have the ability in their own community to buy and invest in property, mortgage it, service the mortgage and move forward," he said. "It's the whole basis of wealth creation in our society."[52]

Prentice's comments caught native leaders off guard. "We've never talked about private land ownership," Assembly of First Nations chief, Phil Fontaine, responded. Privatizing reserve land has been resisted in the past by First Nations, because buying and selling reserve land by individuals could "result in the alienation of our lands," Fontaine explained. Guy Lonechild, vice-chief of the Federation of Saskatchewan Indian Nations, said parcelling out land to individuals would severely undermine the strength and traditions of First Nations. Academics at the University of Saskatchewan cautioned that the Conservatives would have a major fight on their hands if they tried to push the idea through. "It would cause them nothing but grief," said history professor Michael Cottrell. "This is their land. They have a right to decide how it is used. For hundreds of years, they have insisted on collective land ownership."[53] The Conservatives were already working their way around this roadblock. If First Nations were resisting this Conservative government initiative, then the initiative had to come from inside the tent, from First Nations sources themselves. And that meant Manny Jules.

Would Jules and Flanagan, with the Harper government's low-profile support, achieve what no one had been able to before? *Beyond the Indian Act* was published at the end of the 2009–10 fiscal year. The government gave Jules the task of recruiting bands willing to buy into the property-ownership program. To increase the salience of the scheme, INAC sent Jules to New York City to speak at Canada's side event — "Canada's Federal Framework for Aboriginal Economic Development" — at the ninth session of the United Nations Permanent Forum on Indigenous Issues. Back in Canada after a successful mission, Jules's work was made easier when Harper replaced Chuck Strahl as Minister of Indian Affairs with Vancouver Island North MP

John Duncan, described by the *Globe and Mail* as "a long-time advocate of private home ownership on reserves."[54] INAC then quietly launched a project to determine why some Indian reserves are doing well. Officials made a list of Canada's sixty-five most economically successful aboriginal communities.[55] INAC sent senior official Paul Fauteux to meet with thirty-three chiefs. The ostensible goal was "to uncover the secret to the reserves' success, and use this knowledge to help struggling communities, as a *National Post* editorial framed the quest."[56] But there was really no secret. As mentioned earlier, most prosperous reserves are in or near cities or resort locations and can lease and develop their lands and receive rents. The situation parallels de Soto's experiment in Peru, where Timothy Mitchell found hours worked was related to location and not ownership. Among the chiefs Fauteux would meet was Clarence Louie of the Osoyoos First Nation in the fertile Okanagan Valley, which employs hundreds of natives and non-natives at wineries and resorts and in construction. All of this was accomplished using leases, and not private ownership, Louie noted pointedly. Fauteux, who was INAC's land-branch director-general, would not be bringing back earth-shattering news. So why was he sent? Some chiefs remarked that Fauteux's letters inviting them to meet with him were copied to Jules, raising suspicions among some that the effort was merely a ploy to push the privatization effort among the most successful First Nations.[57] As the *National Post* saw it, "[the study] may even lead us to wholesale reform of the *Indian Act,* and the outdated, Soviet-style collective land-ownership model that goes with it."[58]

The next step on INAC's agenda was to support Jules in hosting a policy conference that could kick-start the process of drafting legislation. Holding conferences is a useful technique to advance the neo-liberal doctrine. Conferences bring together leading players in a policy area and expose them to the ideas conference sponsors want to promote.[59] If a conference addresses an issue of public concern, it may be reported in the news media. Frequently conference proceedings are published, with the resulting publications distributed to decision-makers and policy experts and to the general public by being deposited in public and academic libraries. The conference was held in Vancouver in October 2010. Flanagan didn't make a presentation, although he was reported as having been there,[60] creating an impression this was a First Nations' initiative co-hosted by Jules's First Nations Tax Commission and the Indigenous Bar Association. Along with a cross–Canada roster of aboriginal leaders, lawyers, economists, and academics, INAC brought in de Soto as keynote speaker. He repeated his trademark message that it's time to unleash the billions of dollars of "dead capital" on our lands.[61] This message had been adopted by conference organizers, who used it extensively in promotional materials.[62] Jules later echoed the point in a *National Post* commentary, complete with a picture of de Soto.[63] The day after the conference, the Tulo Centre for Indigenous Economics and de Soto's Institute for Liberty and Democracy signed a memorandum of understanding to work together "to support markets and property rights on indigenous lands."[64]

Discussion about private-property ownership legislation dropped from sight for more than a year, while Harper won a majority government and crafted his first budget. It emerged again in the House of Commons finance committee's pre-budget report at the end of 2011, which recommended that "the federal government examine the concept of a First Nations Property Ownership Act as proposed by the First Nations Tax Commission."[65] The following day Conservative MP Chris Warkentin, who chaired the House aboriginal-affairs committee, reported that his committee was already holding hearings on proposals to encourage private land ownership on reserves. Future witnesses could include Jules and Flanagan, as well as native leaders who oppose private land on reserves, he promised.[66]

The issue arose again in the Harper government budget at the end of March. "Some First Nations have expressed an interest in exploring the possibility of legislation that would allow private property ownership within current reserve boundaries," the budget document declared. "Economic Action Plan 2012 announces the Government's intent to explore with interested First Nations the option of moving forward with legislation that would allow for this."[67] Then, during the summer doldrums, when Ottawa was devoid of most MPs and senators, an unnamed official "speaking not for attribution because Aboriginal and Northern Affairs Minister John Duncan comments publicly for the government on native policy," told the *Globe and Mail's* John Ibbitson that a new act was coming.[68] Duncan wasn't commenting publicly, but that didn't stop the paper from putting the story on its front page and turning it into a three-day news event. "We intend to move on our commitment to implement legislation to allow on-reserve property rights," the unnamed official confirmed. "There is solid support from First Nations for this and we will work with them," the official continued, exaggerating the level of support for the initiative. Ibbitson didn't question this declaration, and the official didn't indicate when the government would introduce the bill.

The *Globe* followed the next day with a question-and-answer piece based on one primary source — Manny Jules — who repeated the de Soto mantra that the purpose of the law "is to free the dead capital that's here in our communities."[69] The next day, Ibbitson assured readers the legislation would happen: "The Conservative government will move slowly on the question of property rights on native reserves, but it will move." Jules had already drawn up a template for the legislation, he claimed.[70] (The First Nations Tax Commission's 2011–2012 annual report reveals that INAC contributed $550,000 "to prepare a FNPOA legislative outline."[71]) The *Globe* added an editorial welcoming the news, such as it was, as a "step forward," and suggesting that *Beyond the Indian Act* provides clues as to the bill's contents.[72]

John Ibbitson's unnamed official wasn't the only source for the story. Conservative Senator Patrick Brazeau told QMI Agency, the news service for Quebecor Media (Sun News, Sun TV, and Quebec-based media), that the Harper government had a plan to allow First Nations to opt into the same property rights that every other Canadian enjoys.[73] The next day, Jules told CTV News about the benefits of transferring land ownership to bands and allowing private ownership.[74] Disseminating a story through multiple sources without actually standing behind it was a typical Harper government manoeuvre, careful observers noted. The well-coordinated distribution of talking points led to a flurry of news stories and opinion pieces across the country. But how much substance did it contain? A spokesperson for Duncan told the media that legislation hadn't been drafted, despite *Globe* reports the legislation was coming.[75] "There are no plans — at this time — to introduce legislation. We will continue to work with First Nations on this initiative," Jason MacDonald, Duncan's communications director, said in an email.[76] In contrast, Jules said Ottawa was acting on his proposal which was needed "to free dead capital." Flanagan said he'd seen a draft of the act, and a working group was helping the government craft it. "They're far advanced in the drafting," he explained, saying the government was expected to have draft legislation ready soon, but cautioning the bill would be introduced only when the situation was politically opportune.

As the fall of 2012 unfolded, the politically opportune moment slipped away. Idle No More erupted into the political space as a reaction to provisions in the government's omnibus budget legislation. Bill C-45 was set to drastically reduce the number of waterways that would be federally regulated and would "have a disastrous effect [on] First Nations that are located in environmentally sensitive areas where development is taking place," *Saskatoon Star Phoenix* columnist Doug Cuthand concluded. The second provision of Bill C-45 that provoked Idle No More was an amendment to the *Indian Act* that made it easier for reserve lands to be surrendered and designated for other uses.[77] Idle No More spread quickly across the country, fuelled by Twitter and Facebook and outrage at the many moves of the Harper government to withdraw long-standing environmental protections. Then Chief Theresa Spence of the Attawapiskat First Nation went on a hunger strike she said would continue until she could meet with the prime minister and the governor general to discuss treaty negotiations.

These issues limited Harper's ability to press forward on the property-ownership front, at least in the short-term.[78] Many First Nation leaders were opposed to individual ownership of reserve land. Chief Darcy Bear of the prosperous Whitecap Dakota First Nation south of Saskatoon, told a reporter he didn't "think we have to sell off our lands to do business." He took the reporter on a tour of his reserve, pointing out the top-rated golf course, eighty-thousand-square-foot casino, for-profit water utility, new housing subdivision, and hotel under construction. "For me to privatize and sell off our reserves is not the way to go," Bear said.[79] His band prospered without private ownership, relying on long-term land leases for commercial and residential development. Bernd Christmas, a former executive of the Membertou First Nation in Nova Scotia, said that long-term leases were sufficient to produce eighty million dollars a year in revenues from a commercial fishing company, a licensed gambling facility, and a trade and convention centre. "I'm a believer that you can move forward on First Nations without changing to private ownership," he said. "This way you maintain your lands, and will never have them taken away."[80] A private-property system flew in the face of the desire of many First Nations to protect their aboriginal lands as a collective resource with cultural and spiritual significance.

Unlike Theresa Spence of remote Attawapiskat, Bear and Christmas are fortunate, because their reserves are located in prime locations. But they are typical of First Nations leaders who don't want private ownership on their reserves. The Assembly of First Nations (AFN), the major aboriginal lobby group, represents six hundred and thirty First Nations across the country. The chiefs met in Winnipeg for the AFN's annual general assembly less than a month after media reports that the Harper government was getting behind the Flanagan–Jules scheme. In Resolution 44/2010, the chiefs rejected the proposal — with just three chiefs opposed — mentioning the aboriginal "spiritual connection with our territories" and resolving to file a complaint at the United Nations, "outlining Canada's violations of our Nations' collective rights to our territories and resources."[81] Westbank First Nation chief Robert Louie warned the government it would face major opposition if it attempted to bring in the legislation. "There's going to be such a huge outcry against this."[82]

A few months after the chiefs rejected the Jules–Flanagan proposal, Conservative back-bencher Kelly Block introduced Bill C-575, *An Act Respecting the Accountability and Enhanced Financial Transparency of Elected Officials of First Nations Communities*. The bill would require each First Nation in Canada to disclose the remuneration paid to its chief and council. The information would be made available on the website of Aboriginal Affairs and Northern Development Canada (AANDC, the new name for INAC). "We trust First Nations leaders will welcome this act as an important tool in helping deliver transparency and accountability to their constituents," Block said on introducing the bill.[83] Coming so soon after the chiefs' strong stand, the bill could be seen as an act of retaliation designed to turn band members against their leaders. That the Harper government was behind the bill was evident from the fact it was fast-tracked through second reading and referred to the Aboriginal Affairs and Northern Development Committee.

An observer also has to wonder at the sudden prominence of Kelly Block on this issue. This Saskatoon–area MP and former small-town rural Saskatchewan mayor, had never uttered a word of concern about the lack of transparency in First Nation finances. In fact, she rarely spoke about First Nations at all. She had no reserves in her riding. And she admitted in her evidence to the AANDC committee that she didn't consult with any aboriginal organizations to help her prepare the bill. Nor did she specify who she did consult.[84] However, as with Conservative backbencher Russ Hiebert, who introduced Bill C-377 that would impose onerous reporting requirements on trade unions (see Chapter 3), Block's bill could not be tied directly to Harper's PMO.

The bill didn't come out of the blue, though. The Canadian Taxpayers Federation (CTF), an anti-tax advocacy group, had been on a crusade since the mid-nineties against alleged widespread corruption among aboriginal leaders, calling for audits of all First Nation books. It even set up a centre for aboriginal policy change in Calgary to promote an audit agenda. The campaign gained momentum in 2010, when the CTF claimed it was receiving information in brown envelopes from angry members of some bands about their leaders' excessive salaries. Around the time Block introduced her bill, the CTF received from the federal government, under the access to information law, a list of salaries and honoraria paid during fiscal year 2008–09 to the chiefs of more than five hundred bands across Canada?[85] It released one batch of salaries two days before the House of Commons commenced second reading, receiving widespread media attention and placing Block's bill in the spotlight.[86]

A careful look at the situation reveals that the PMO and the CTF seemed to be co-ordinating their efforts. Certainly the ties between the two organizations were close. Four former CTF staffers worked in the PMO during 2010: John Williamson, former CTF national director, was Harper's director of communications; Sara MacIntyre, former CTF B.C. director, was Harper's press secretary; Adam Taylor, former CTF national research director, was a PMO issues-management adviser; and Neil Desai, former CTF Ontario director, was a strategic-initiatives manager in the PMO.[87]

A brief battle of the numbers ensued, although it wasn't much of a battle. In terms of positive media coverage, the CTF campaign outgunned the Assembly of First Nations defence of its practices by a wide margin. The campaign kicked off with a front-page *National Post* column by John Ivison, who justified Kelly Block's private-member's bill, because of the "shocking salaries" of some First Nation leaders. Then the Fraser Institute's Mark Milke chimed in with a supportive piece on the CTF's release of salaries without revealing he once worked for the CTF as B.C. and Alberta director. The headlines tell the story: "Native Chiefs Make PM Look Like Pauper" (*National Post*); "Band Councillor Pulls in $1M" (*Winnipeg Free Press*); "Canada's 'Me-First' Nations" (*Calgary Herald*). The chiefs were placed in an untenable situation. When a chief criticized the numbers, the frame remained negative: "'Inaccurate' Report Upsets Chief" (*Regina Leader Post*).

It didn't take long for the media to make the connection that the antidote to such shocking salaries was Kelly Block's bill. The AFN issued a report debunking the CTF numbers, but the media weren't interested. After a two-month drubbing, the AFN passed a resolution requiring elected band officials to disclose their salaries and other funds to their members, but not to the general public, as the CTF, Kelly Block, and her backers demanded.[88]

Bill C-575 moved quickly forward, receiving second reading and referral to the Aboriginal Affairs Committee for detailed consideration, after fifteen Liberals supported the minority Conservatives. But the committee's work was cut short when Harper called the 2011 election and the bill died on the order paper. With a majority safely in his pocket, Harper reintroduced the bill, this time as a government measure, numbered C-27. This bill went further than Block's, requiring the publication on a website of not only the salaries and expenses of chiefs and councillors, but also detailed audited financial statements. If bands didn't provide the required documents, a member of the band or the minister of aboriginal affairs could go to court to obtain the information. The minister could even withdraw funding for bands that didn't publish the information. Bill C-27 barrelled through Parliament, clearing the House by the end of November 2012. Fuelled by suggestions of financial mismanagement in an audit of Attawapiskat First Nation books, the bill moved quickly through the Senate, and received Royal Assent by the end of March. The CTF's Colin Craig was "ecstatic" at the bill's passing. "A lot of chiefs and councillors are going to be looking at this bill and scaling back their pay," he warned, "because they know that, starting next year, they're going to have to start disclosing it."[89]

While chiefs and band councils prepared for the greater disclosure requirements of Bill C-27, the Harper government was readying its property-ownership legislation, Michael Den Tandt of Postmedia News reported in a budget preview: "Enabling greater access to private property on reserves, for bands that welcome such reforms" was framed as an aboriginal economic-development measure. Likely taking his lead from PMO talking points, Den Tandt referred to an emerging government aboriginal strategy: "to engage on a case-by-case basis with those among the country's 600-plus bands that express a clear desire to pursue economic growth,"[90] remaining true to the de Soto doctrine that economic growth occurs only with well-defined property rights.

* * *

Much has changed in aboriginal relations since Paul Martin proposed the Kelowna Accord in 2005. Two months before Harper became prime minister, Martin committed the federal government to spend an additional $5.1 billion over five years. The goal was to raise First Nations out of poverty by improving education, housing, and health services and promoting economic development. Phil Fontaine of the Assembly of First Nations called the meeting historic, because aboriginal leaders were present as equals at the table. It would be different this time, because there was a plan.[91] Harper must have looked on with chagrin as Martin, the premiers, and aboriginal leaders trooped into the media centre at the Grand Okanagan resort to sign a "transformative change accord" that locked the federal government into a new relationship with First Nations. Most disturbing to Harper and those who thought like him must have been the insistence that the agreement recognized aboriginal rights and title and were conducted on a "government-to-government" basis.[92] Collective rights involving hundreds of governments making long-term plans — these were serious violations of neo-liberal dogma.

During the election that followed, Harper said he "supports the principles and objectives" of Kelowna, but not the price tag.[93] His Speech from the Throne several months later made no mention of the accord. And his budget the following month explicitly scrapped the deal and suggested a radically different approach, one based not on grand plans and splashy nation-to-nation negotiations, but on incrementalism, the achievement of modest-but-concrete goals. Goals toward what end was hinted at but not spelled out until the *First Nations Property Ownership*

Act burst onto the scene with the Flanagan–Jules book.

An idea dreamed of by Canadian corporate and political elites — private ownership of First Nation reserves — moved into play after languishing in policy purgatory for over a century. Federal governments dating back to John A. Macdonald tried — and failed — to break reserve land into individually owned plots. In 1969, Pierre Trudeau and his Indian Affairs minister Jean Chrétien also failed to end the special legal relationship between aboriginal peoples and the Canadian state, and to dismantle the *Indian Act*. Trudeau's goal was a "just society" in which all citizens — aboriginals included — shared the same rights, opportunities, and responsibilities. But based on their concerns about aboriginal and treaty rights, title to the land, self-determination, and access to education and health care — the same concerns they expressed thirty-five years later in Kelowna — aboriginal leaders forcefully opposed the proposal, and it died. They also opposed the *First Nations Property Ownership Act*, but Harper had engineered a different process. Change is occurring despite the opposition of most bands. It's another illustration of Harperism in action.

A few, however, are onside. The first domino was in northwestern British Columbia, where three houses were turned over to their occupants by the Nisga'a Nation in November 2013. The Nisga'a differ from most First Nations, because the treaty the band negotiated with the federal and provincial governments in 2000 ceded two-thousand square kilometres of B.C.'s Nass Valley to the Nisga'a people; the *First Nations Property Ownership Act* isn't needed. But ideology isn't far beneath the surface. "We aspire to a market economy," Nisga'a Lisims chair Kevin McKay said, "and this is a key feature of any market economy."[94]

Meanwhile, with backing from unnamed sources, the Fraser Institute set up a centre for aboriginal policy studies to promote fee-simple ownership on reserves, with an associate director

fresh from the office of the minister of aboriginal affairs.[95] Its
network of fellows and scholars includes Jules and Flanagan. The
centre's first study was written by Flanagan and a Ph.D. student
and concludes, perhaps unsurprisingly, that "our findings are
consistent with comparative and international research that has
highlighted the importance of property rights and the rule of
law for economic growth."[96] Also, perhaps unsurprisingly, most
of the comparative and international research Flanagan and his
co-author cite emanate from neo-liberal sources. An introduction was written by Mike Lebourdais, chief of B.C.'s Whispering
Pines First Nation, who was already onside with the property-
ownership initiative as chair of the Tulo Centre for Indigenous
Economics.

***

The genie is out of the bottle — there's no going back. Harper
has set in motion a process that could eradicate, or at least compromise, collective ownership and integrate First Nations into the
market economy. He has put in place measures that will continue
to frame the myriad, intractable problems facing First Nations
as economic, not political or constitutional — and that will be
hard or impossible to undo. The atrocious living conditions on
remote First Nation reserves will be solved, not by more federal
money and programs, or by new constitutional or government-
to-government deals, but by economic development through
resource-revenue sharing, individual property ownership, and
education and skills training. After all, in the neo-liberal universe,
economic freedom comes before political freedom or even democracy. And it will proceed with the incremental approach, so the
aboriginal population won't be provoked enough to engage in
resistance. As Harper told the CBC's Peter Mansbridge in January
2012, a week before he was to have his first face-to-face meeting

with First Nation leaders, "significant change needs to happen. Aboriginal people in this country are not anywhere near where we want or need those communities to be," thus revealing an astonishing level of paternalism.[97] But it won't be "grand visions and declarations that achieve these things. It will be moving forward one step at a time."

The likely success of the *First Nations Property Ownership Act* demonstrates that the formula established by Hayek works. Neo-liberal think tanks can undertake research — in de Soto's case on a massive scale — to prove the neo-liberal doctrine that economic development is dependent on a secure system of property rights. The fact that economic development in Peru was related, not to property rights, but to government subsidies and property location, was elegantly demonstrated by Timothy Mitchell. But Mitchell's work lacks the support of a highly subsidized infrastructure of information dissemination and languishes in obscure academic journals. De Soto, in contrast, received worldwide publicity, as neo-liberal networks persuaded the media his work was groundbreaking and worthy of being reported.

Trudeau's goal of equality of citizenship may have been a noble one, but it was doomed to failure. Harper's goal is very different: equality in the market. Harperism for First Nations. Poverty will be relieved, not by expensive government programs, but by giving reserve residents a legal title, the possibility of a tiny pot of money, and access to education and trades training. Then they're on their own. Perhaps some will become millionaires. Most won't likely improve their lot at all. No matter: step-by-step, increment-by-increment, the idea that prosperity and economic development depend on individual property rights and not collective action is being imprinted on the minds of policy and media leaders. It will not be easily erased.

5

COUNTER THE ENVIRONMENTAL THREAT TO THE MARKET

In a speech to the 2008 general meeting of the Mont Pelerin Society in Tokyo, Czech Republic president Vaclav Klaus spoke bluntly to his friendly and supportive audience. "I consider environmentalism and its current strongest version — climate alarmism — to be . . . the most effective and . . . dangerous vehicle for advocating, drafting and implementing large-scale government intervention and for an unprecedented suppression of human freedom."[1] The dispute was "not about temperature or CO_2," he insisted, but instead was "another variant of the old, well-known debate: freedom and free markets versus *dirigisme* [state control], political control and regulation . . ." It was the same old story: the "anointed" — the alarmists — were here again to "restrict freedom and stop human prosperity" under the slogan of stopping the destruction of the planet.

Klaus didn't believe for a moment that the climate — or the planet — was endangered, despite almost-daily articles about "the movements of tenths of a degree of Celsius or Fahrenheit, pictures showing the retreat of glaciers, data about the increase of sea level, about the changes in the concentration of CO_2."[2] This isn't the issue, he told his audience. Missing from the coverage are "arguments about the role of the market, prices and property rights on the one hand and about the tragic consequences of the inevitable government failure connected with the ambitions to control global climate on the other." Climate change isn't a concern, he argued, because technological progress and properly functioning markets will take care of the problem, if there is a problem.

Efforts to control global warming are emblematic for the Mont Pelerin Society and its associated think tanks, academics, and media outlets, and go to the heart of Friedrich Hayek's critique of central planning. In *The Road to Serfdom*, he wrote that "[planning] would make the very men who are most anxious to plan society the most dangerous if they were allowed to do so . . . From the saintly and single-minded idealist to the fanatic is often but a step." The planner and coordinator, Hayek opined, was little more than an "omniscient dictator."[3] Global warming wasn't an issue when Hayek wrote *The Constitution of Liberty* in 1960. But in this classic neo-liberal text, he did apply his critique of central planning to the belief — mistaken in his view — in the need for central (i.e., government) direction in the conservation of natural resources, such as forestry and mineral extraction. How much should we use today, and how much should we save for future use? It would be a grievous error to rely on central direction for an answer to this question, he argued, because the market knows more than government ever can.

There will normally exist a potential sale price of the resource which will reflect opinion about all the factors likely to affect its future value, and a decision based on the comparison of its value as a

salable asset with what it would bring if exploited
now will probably take into account more of all
the relevant knowledge than could any decision of
a central authority.[4]

Hayek's comparison of market and government has been critiqued on the grounds he underestimates the information costs in the operation of the market and overestimates the information costs of detailed planning.[5] Writing before the advent of mass computing, but after Claude Shannon and Warren Weaver published their 1949 groundbreaking work about information,[6] *The Mathematical Theory of Communication,* Hayek should have known that the costs of information collection and analysis would be dropping dramatically, making it feasible for central authorities to have a more comprehensive grasp of relevant economic information. Nor does he recognize — or admit, since this seems to be a common neo-liberal blind spot — that major actors in the economy are not individuals, but large multinational corporations with the same information-gathering challenges as governments.

Hayek dismisses the possibility that members of a community might want to pool their resources (through taxation) to achieve outcomes, such as resource conservation, that they could not accomplish individually. This argument, he claims, "rests on an unreasoned prejudice."[7] In his view, "all resource conservation constitutes investment and should be judged by precisely the same criteria as all other investment."[8] The market sets the price for oil and, if it recognizes that climate change might affect future supply and prices, the current price will adjust accordingly. There is no need for government involvement.

Hayek does allow a role for government, however, "where the aim is the provision of amenities or of opportunities for recreation, or the preservation of natural beauty or of historical sites or places of scientific interest, etc."[9] In these situations "the individual beneficiary [may] derive advantages for which he cannot be charged a price," and very large tracts of land are usually required. Hayek would rather these amenities be provided by voluntary organizations, but he sees no objection to government provision, if government owns the land or even acquires it with government funds raised through taxation.

Exceptions aside, the neo-liberal analysis was music to the ears of fossil-fuel companies and wealthy conservatives, once global warming had become a threat to continued oil dependency. Their deep pockets fuelled a twenty-five-year campaign to manufacture uncertainty, a campaign that was astonishingly effective in confusing the public and politicians about the reality of global warming and delaying meaningful responses from governments, many of which were dependent on corporate interests in any case.[10]

Just how effective the campaign has been can be seen in a June 2012 Angus Reid poll of Canadian adults, which found only 41 per cent of Alberta, Saskatchewan, and Manitoba respondents believe global warming is a fact and is mostly caused by emissions from vehicles and industrial facilities. Fifty per cent of respondents in those three provinces believe global warming is an unproven theory or, if it is occurring, is caused by natural changes.[11] (Nine per cent were unsure.) In British Columbia, a bare majority — 51 per cent — and in Ontario a slightly larger majority — 56 per cent — believe global warming is a fact and is mostly caused by emissions from vehicles and industrial facilities. Only in Quebec (71 per cent) and Atlantic Canada (75 per cent) did a substantial majority of respondents believe in human-caused global warming. These results are striking given the overwhelming scientific consensus for anthropogenic (human-caused) global warming (AGW). One 2012 survey of peer-reviewed scientific articles published over a twenty-year period found that only twenty-four of 13,950 articles reject AGW. That's 0.17 per cent![12] A second and more nuanced survey of 11,944 peer-reviewed articles found that, among papers expressing a position on AGW, 97.2 per cent endorse the consensus. This analysis concludes "that the number of papers rejecting the consensus on AGW is a vanishingly small proportion of the published research."[13]

It's a mistake to claim that the success in creating such erroneous beliefs among Canadians is due solely to the corporate interests that backed their perpetuation. True, corporate money magnified the confusion, but Hayek's analysis and its adoption by neo-liberal networks provided the intellectual muscle for the denialist position. It was a natural partnership. Big Oil could continue to extract its sizeable profits, and intellectuals like Klaus could continue their crusade for a market society. Klaus was a frequent speaker at the the Chicago-based Heartland Institute, the leading think tank in global warming denial efforts. After leaving his position as president of the Czech Republic in 2013, Klaus became a distinguished senior fellow at the Cato Institute, another leading denialist think tank. Both think tanks and the deniers they support received tens of millions of dollars from Exxon Mobil and Koch industries, the second-largest private company in the United States, with vast oil and gas holdings. Charles Koch joined the Mont Pelerin Society in 1970 and founded Cato in 1974.[14]

Stephen Harper, the Hayek-trained economist, was certainly on board with the Klaus analysis. Harper was leader of the Canadian Alliance in October 2002, when the Chrétien government was preparing to ask Parliament to ratify the Kyoto Accord. He wrote a letter to Alliance members requesting funds to stop ratification. "Kyoto is essentially a socialist scheme to suck money out of wealth-producing nations," he wrote. "I'm talking about the 'battle of Kyoto' — our campaign to block the job-killing, economy-destroying Kyoto Accord."[15] When

Harper was Conservative Party leader, scrapping Canada's participation in Kyoto was adopted as official party policy before the 2006 election. Several months after his minority victory, Harper buried Canada's commitments to reduce CO_2 and other greenhouse-gas emissions within vague and contradictory policy pronouncements.

The stage was set for a vast scale-up of Canadian bitumen[16] production. The stage was also set for a scale-up in opposition to increased bitumen production, because of its profoundly negative environmental impact. Resistance to increased oil use and bitumen development is the latest and perhaps most effective challenge to the neo-liberal project, a threat recognized by Klaus in his address to the Mont Pelerin Society. To protect the expansion of bitumen extraction and transport, and to further progress towards the market state envisioned by Klaus and Hayek, this environmental opposition had to be neutralized.

Neo-liberals/libertarians and environmentalists share little in their views of the environment. Neo-liberals hold what Australian political scientist Robyn Eckersley calls an "anthropocentric or human-centred" world view. They believe "that the world was made for humans, that humans are the centre of value and meaning in the world, and that the rest of nature is merely raw material to be bent to human purpose."[17] Environmentalists, in sharp contrast, lean towards an "ecocentric" world view, she writes. They believe "in a respect for all life-forms (not just humans) and a recognition that all life-forms should be given the opportunity to pursue their own destinies."[18] The two world views clash most directly on the battleground of growth and development. Neo-liberals do not believe there are limits to growth, because human ingenuity and technological developments will solve any ecological problems that society may encounter. Environmentalists recognize both ecological and social limits to growth. Development must occur within the carrying capacity of ecosystems. Because humans have limited understanding of how such ecosystems operate, a cautious approach is mandatory.

The sides clashed head-on over three projects to export Alberta bitumen: the Northern Gateway pipeline to the British Columbia coast, the twinning of the Kinder Morgan pipeline to Burrard Inlet, and the Keystone XL pipeline to Nebraska and American refineries. To counter environmental opposition to these pipelines, Harper engaged in two reframing exercises, the first turning the environmentalists' redefining of Alberta bitumen as "dirty oil" into Harper government "ethical oil," and the second reframing environmentalists themselves as "radicals" who are outside the mainstream. Both exercises enjoyed some success.

***

On September 1, 2010, the term "ethical oil" didn't exist, except as the title of a soon-to-be-released book by conservative commentator and activist Ezra Levant. Four months later, ethical oil was Harper government policy, or at least an official government talking point. In his first day on the job in January 2011, newly appointed environment minister Peter Kent called oil from the Alberta bitumen deposits an "ethical" source of energy. Profits from this oil "are not used in undemocratic or unethical ways," he told an interviewer.[19] The story of how ethical oil moved from book title to government policy is extraordinary, given that ideas often take years to percolate through public-opinion filters before they end up on policy agendas. It followed by just six months the rise of the proposal for private ownership on First Nation reserves, described in Chapter 4.

Establishing ethical oil as a component of government rhetoric illustrates the growing success of a Canadian right-wing echo chamber, copying the tactics of the Republicans in the

United States.[20] A year before Levant's book was published, then-environment minister Jim Prentice was stunned to learn just how poorly foreigners regard oil from Canada's bitumen fields, according to a U.S. diplomatic cable released by WikiLeaks. "The public sentiment in Norway shocked him and has heightened his awareness of the negative consequences to Canada's historically 'green' standing on the world stage," a 2009 cable said, recounting a meeting between Prentice and U.S. ambassador to Canada David Jacobson.[21]

The environmentalist position is that oil from bitumen deposits is "dirty oil," considering that it poisons the environment and is a major contributor to global warming, because of the high levels of greenhouse gases required to extract the oil. This view had been largely accepted in Norway and other European nations, thanks to efforts by environmental groups to lobby for boycotts of Canada's dirty oil. The promotion of ethical oil was meant to counter this dirty-oil frame. It was a classic diversionary tactic, intended to redirect public attention away from dirty oil, a "bait-and-switch" device, as Ed Whittingham, executive director of the Pembina Institute, which promotes sustainable energy, called it.[22] Greenpeace and other "radical" groups may call oil from bitumen deposits "dirty," Levant counters, but they end up promoting unethical oil from tyrannies like Saudi Arabia and Nigeria. Is that what they want? If so, then what kind of organizations are they?[23]

But the argument for ethical oil is defective. The *National Post*'s energy-industry champion Claudia Cattaneo admitted that "many of the multinationals working in Canada's oil sands, from Total SA to Chevron Corp., are also players in Saudi Arabia. The kingdom is a big employer of Canadian oil workers and of Canadian energy expertise and technology."[24] Were Canadians working in Saudi Arabia unethical, while those in Alberta were blameless? What about those who transferred from Fort

McMurray to the Saudi oil fields? Were they transformed overnight? The promotion of ethical oil was roundly criticized, even
by some industry sources. The *Petroleum Economist*, an authoritative international journal that has monitored the oil industry
since the 1930s, found Levant's book to be filled with "strange
arguments that show little grasp of the global economy, or the
way its most important commodity is traded."[25] To counter
Levant's charge that Middle Eastern oil producers are guilty of
unethical conduct, the journal explained that these producing
countries "deployed their wealth to prop up Western financial institutions during the [2007–08] recession," preventing a
complete economic collapse. Hardly unethical behaviour, the
journal implied. And even if Canadian oil exports to the U.S.
double by 2020, as the Canadian Association of Petroleum Producers predicts, this will still account for less than a quarter of
American consumption. Most oil will still need to come from
somewhere else. The choice Levant poses — ethical Canadian
oil or unethical Saudi oil — is fallacious. Nor, according to the
journal, does Levant seem to understand that world oil prices
depend on the Organization of Petroleum Exporting Countries
(OPEC). With prices set at seventy-five dollars a barrel, oil from
Alberta's bitumen deposits is a viable operation. But if OPEC cut
prices by fifteen dollars — which it could do because of excess
capacity three times the amount of Canadian production —
the bitumen oil will look "dicey." It matters little what Canada
does. Any new developments depend on "OPEC's visible hand
on the market to remain plausible." As for what is truly ethical
oil, a quarter of the world's population does not have adequate
access to energy, according to the World Energy Council. That
is where energy must go, to help developing nations draw their
people out of poverty. Levant instead argues that more oil needs
to go to what the journal calls the "overfed consumers of the
U.S." The journal's definition of ethical oil is very different from

Levant's: ethical energy is energy "that reaches the starving, not the obese."[26] Unfortunately the *Petroleum Economist* is read by few outside the industry, so Levant had carte blanche to voice his opinion — and get a respectful hearing.

Initial support for ethical oil came from the newspapers in the conservative Sun Media chain, where Levant is a columnist. The *Ottawa Sun, Toronto Sun, London Free Press, Calgary Sun,* and *Edmonton Sun* published three excerpts on three successive days, giving the book national exposure. The excerpts cover a lot of ground, attacking Saudi Arabia, environmentalists, and proponents of green-energy jobs, while defending the Alberta government and the Canadian oil industry.[27] The papers next gave Levant a podium to attack Greenpeace, which had been critical of his thesis. Levant lambasted the environmental organization as "second only to PETA for outrageous stunts that erode their credibility but enhance their PR."[28] The Saudis don't have to attack Canada's bitumen deposits for stealing market share. They don't "have to say a word, with groups like Greenpeace out and about. They'll do all the oilsands-bashing for them." None of the papers gave space to Greenpeace to allow their readers to hear from the environmental organization itself. Anything readers learned about Greenpeace's concerns with bitumen deposits came from the organization's opponent, Levant.

The next day the papers reported favourably on a talk Levant gave at the Economic Club of Canada in Toronto. A week later, Levant's column attacked Hollywood director James Cameron, who was critical of bitumen extraction and was coming to Alberta to see for himself. Levant focused on Cameron's "extravagant projects with their vast energy consumption,"[29] utilizing an ad hominem attack against Cameron, a common technique.

Ethical oil was hyped in the pages of the *National Post*, where personal attacks on bitumen opponents continued unabated. The *Post*'s Peter Foster claimed the Pembina Institute had "never created a productive job in their lives" and "continued to unload factual garbage by the dump truck." Meanwhile, Ezra Levant "exposes the lies and hypocrisy of the media-coddled opponents of the vast resource."[30] The same day, the *Post* gave a lengthy and entirely positive report on Levant's Economic Club talk.[31] It was followed the next day by an editorial lauding Levant, who had once been a *Post* editorial board member. This editorial concluded that "far from marking Canada as a 'climate criminal,' the oil sands are an important and ethical resource that will serve the world's energy needs for generations."[32] Levant appeared at least four times on CBC radio and television, and was interviewed by conservative broadcasters Charles Adler and Michael Coren — who subsequently joined him on the new Sun TV channel — as well as on CTV and other mainstream media. He received positive coverage in columns and editorials in Postmedia papers, such as the *Calgary Herald* and *Montreal Gazette*.

A boost in establishing ethical oil as a viable concept came from the network of advocacy groups and neo-liberal think tanks that sponsored many of Levant's events. His presentation at the Economic Club, the one that received rave reviews in Sun papers and the *National Post*, was sponsored by the National Citizens Coalition. His lunch address at the Vancouver Club three days later was hosted by Leah Costello, a West Vancouver Conservative Party board member, who had worked at the Fraser Institute for nearly a decade. The Fraser Institute sponsored receptions and dinners for Levant in Toronto and Calgary. The Frontier Centre for Public Policy hosted breakfast or lunch receptions in Winnipeg, Calgary, and Regina.

On the Internet, the Blogging Tories, a network of 270 conservative bloggers, pumped the book and trashed its critics, with contributions from Dr. Roy's Thoughts, Small Dead Animals, Just Right, Spin Assassin and BC Blue, amplifying the ethical-oil meme around the blogosphere. Debating environmentalists was a key strategy in the Levant publicity campaign. Levant faced off against Satya Das (author of *Green Oil*), Andrew Nikiforuk (author of *Tar Sands*), Elizabeth May (leader of the Green Party), and Ben West (healthy-communities campaigner for the Wilderness Committee), as well as several representatives of Greenpeace. Levant is a seasoned debater, having won several national championships as a University of Calgary business-school student. But it didn't matter who won these debates, since the phrase "ethical oil" was repeated over and over again, giving Levant a publicity advantage, as ethical oil began to compete with dirty oil for credibility.

It didn't take long for ethical oil to move onto the political agenda. First to endorse it was Danielle Smith, leader of Alberta's Wildrose Party and a Levant associate since their days together as Fraser Institute interns in the 1990s. When Smith led the Canadian Property Rights Research Institute, Levant was on her board of advisers. When she hosted *Global Sunday*, the public-affairs show on Global TV, Levant was a regular contributor.

The Harper Tories moved quickly to get behind ethical oil. Six weeks after Levant's book went on sale, Senator Nicole Eaton, a Toronto Conservative Party fundraiser appointed by Harper, kicked off a Senate inquiry into "Canada's oil sands, the world's most ethical source of oil."[33] She was supported a week later by Senator Linda Frum, another Toronto Conservative fundraiser appointed by Harper. "By focusing on these . . . occasional and minor bird accidents in the oil sands instead of the massive, systematic, routine environmental devastation in OPEC or the shockingly common violation of human rights in OPEC countries, critics of the oil sands are no longer acting ethically," Frum opined.[34] A month later, Levant was invited to testify before the House of Commons Standing Committee on Natural Resources, which was studying Canada's energy policy. This committee was chaired by Conservative MP Leon Benoit, a farmer and original

Reform MP, whose Alberta Vegreville riding borders the Cold
Lake Oil Sands Area. NDP committee member Nathan Cullen
thought it more than coincidental that television cameras were
present for Levant's presentation, when requests for cameras in
the past had been sidelined by Benoit.[35]

The spin machine took a Christmas break, but the New
Year had barely started when Harper appointed long-time TV
news anchor Peter Kent as his new environment minister, perhaps because TV news anchors engender feelings of credibility
and trust, which is what Harper needed on this file. Another
reason for Kent's appointment may have been his stint as a vice-
president at public-relations giant Hill and Knowlton, where
he focused "on strategic client planning, leadership training
and senior media relations support." A major H&K client was
Enbridge, proponent of the Northern Gateway pipeline.[36] The
day after his appointment, Kent gave his first media interview,
saying that profits from Canadian bitumen deposits "are not
used in undemocratic or unethical ways." Later, on CBC's *Power
and Politics*, Kent used the term "ethical oil." Two days later,
Harper backed Kent with a rousing defence of bitumen. The
world should know Canada "is a very ethical society" and a "very
secure source of energy for the United States, compared to other
sources," Harper said.[37] The *Globe and Mail* ignored Levant's
ethical-oil campaign until Harper gave his blessing. Then the
paper made up for lost time, with four articles over the next
week, including a sympathetic profile by Jane Taber, complete
with a third-of-a-page photo of Levant.[38] Ethical oil had arrived
and it wasn't long before the Harper government took ownership.

Levant had set up a website — EthicalOil.org — to promote his
book. When he went to work for Sun TV, the site languished for
several months until it was relaunched under the management
of Levant's friend Alykhan Velshi. Velshi had been immigration

minister Jason Kenney's director of communications before he went into the Conservative Party war room for the 2011 election. He emerged with a reputation as a clever strategist in the Liberal Party's crushing defeat.[39] Velshi's first task for EthicalOil.org was the production of provocative Internet ads which contrasted "conflict oil" from Saudi Arabia, Venezuela, and Iran with "fair-trade oil" from Canada. One ad showed two men in a Middle Eastern country with nooses around their necks, waiting to be hanged for being homosexuals, with the word "persecution" stamped on the photo. Next to it was a photo of two men holding hands — in Canada, we assume — with rainbow bracelets and the word "pride." The ad received a front-page defence in the *Calgary Herald*.[40] By the fall Velshi had enough money — from where he wouldn't say — for television ads attacking the Saudi record on women's rights.[41] And when National Energy Board hearings on Enbridge's $5.5-billion Northern Gateway project got under way in northern British Columbia in January 2012, EthicalOil.org launched a series of radio and newspaper ads in local communities attacking environmental groups for taking money from U.S. foundations to fight the pipeline proposal.[42]

Meanwhile, Velshi had gone to work in the Prime Minister's Office as director of planning. His position at EthicalOil.org was taken by two part-timers, Jamie Ellerton, a former executive assistant in Kenney's office, and Kathryn Marshall, a University of Calgary law student who was married to Harper's former strategic-planning manager. In December 2012, a law firm representing EthicalOil.org filed a complaint with the Canada Revenue Agency, alleging that the Sierra Club Canada Foundation was in violation of tax rules, because it was spending more than 10 per cent of its revenues on political advocacy. Sierra Club executive director John Bennett had predicted this move a year earlier when he wrote that "discrediting the environmental movement at every turn while attacking its sources of funding and ability to communicate is not only a necessary measure — it's key to their strategy."[43] Ethical Oil's lawyers were the Calgary law firm JSS Barristers, led by managing partner Glenn Solomon, who had a long-time involvement in Conservative politics. He was an Alberta representative on the National Constitution Committee of the Conservative Party of Canada and also president of the Calgary Centre Conservative Association.[44]

Was the ethical-oil campaign successful? Not according to former U.S. vice-president Al Gore, who told an audience at Ryerson University in Toronto in May 2013 that "there is no such thing as ethical oil. There's only dirty oil and dirtier oil." But in a follow-up survey of 7,800 *Globe and Mail* readers who responded to an interview with Gore in the paper, a bare majority — 52 per cent — agreed with Gore, while 41 per cent disagreed, saying there was such a thing as ethical oil.[45] That's Harper's margin of victory in the next election. EthicalOil.org, meanwhile, faded away, but by then, Harper had moved on to his next attack on environmental resistance to the market state. Establishing the "radical environmentalist" frame brought together Mont Pelerin neo-liberals such as Vaclav Klaus and the Fraser Institute, and social conservatives such as Preston Manning. Both camps had reason to be profoundly disturbed by environmentalism.

***

Almost a year to the day after Peter Kent first uttered the word "ethical," Natural Resources Minister Joe Oliver released an open letter, accusing "radical" environmentalists and "jet-setting celebrities" of blocking efforts to open access to Asian markets for Canadian oil. "These groups threaten to hijack our regulatory system to achieve their radical ideological agenda," Oliver wrote.[46] "They seek to exploit any loophole they can find, stacking public hearings with bodies to ensure that delays kill good projects." Oliver was familiar with the oil business from his days as a banker when he raised money for companies.[47] In an interview on CBC News Network, Oliver explained that radicals are "a group of people who don't take into account the facts but are driven by an ideological imperative," without explaining what that might be.[48]

Radical environmentalism wasn't a new idea created by Joe Oliver and the Harper government. Its roots lie in the 1970s with groups like Greenpeace and Environmental Life Force (ELF) that took direct action in defence of the planet and all living beings. Greenpeace rammed whaling ships and confronted nuclear-weapons testers; ELF used explosive and incendiary devices to protest government policies and corporate activities. Greenpeace eventually rejected violence, in favour of non-violent, direct action, and grew into an international organization with offices in forty countries and 2.9-million donors.[49] ELF lasted just two years after its leader, John Hanna, was arrested and jailed for placing incendiary devices on crop-dusters at a California airport on May Day, 1977.[50] ELF was followed by Earth First!, Earth Liberation Front, People for the Ethical Treatment of Animals (PETA), and others that sometimes engaged in violent actions. Many were labelled "eco-terrorist."

Direct action can also take non-violent forms, such as marches, sit-ins, and strikes. These are still radical in Harper's world. Even organizations and individuals who make presentations to regulatory hearings opposing bitumen pipeline construction are radical, because they overload regulatory proceedings with submissions and slow down the approval process. In the final analysis, everyone is radical unless they welcome the development of Alberta's bitumen, because of the increased prosperity it will bring.

The current use of the term "radical environmentalist" comes from a decade-old Frank Luntz briefing memo for the

Republican Party. Luntz is a long-time Republican pollster and strategist whose specialty is using language to evoke feeling. In a 2003 interview on PBS's *Frontline*, he said: "My job is to look for the words that trigger the emotion. Words alone can be found in a dictionary or a telephone book, but words with emotion can change destiny, can change life as we know it."[51] Luntz was a Ronald Reagan adviser and a major force behind Newt Gingrich's 1994 Contract with America. He helped George W. Bush win re-election in 2004 by portraying opponent John Kerry as a flip-flopper.

Luntz's sixteen-page 2002 memo, "The Environment: A Cleaner, Safer, Healthier America," crafted the words Republicans used in debates over the environment for the next decade. His first rule was to never use the term "global warming," which suggests something more cataclysmic, while the term "climate change" suggests something more gradual — something that takes place over time, and that is "a more controllable and less emotional challenge," like "going from Pittsburgh to Fort Lauderdale," as one Luntz focus group participant observed.[52] He advised Republicans "to continue to make the lack of scientific certainty a primary issue."[53] Luntz's second rule was never to call yourself an environmentalist, which has "the connotation of extremism." Instead, he said, use the word "conservationist," which is more positive and "conveys a moderate, reasoned, common sense position between replenishing the earth's natural resources and the human need to make use of those resources."[54]

Luntz travelled to Ottawa in the spring of 2006 to help Preston Manning promote his new project, the Manning Centre for Building Democracy, which was intended to advance conservative ideas and politicians. His connection to Manning went back to the 1993 federal election, when Luntz was the Reform Party's official election pollster and strategic adviser.[55] With Luntz's help, the Progressive Conservatives under Kim Campbell were annihilated — Luntz watched the election results from Manning's suite — and Reform emerged as the party of the right. Thirteen years later, along with helping Manning, Luntz met with Harper for a photo-op session and to provide advice for Harper's new minority government. Luntz was impressed with Harper, whom he called "a genuine intellectual, brilliant in his understanding of issues."[56]

Luntz also spoke at the tenth annual conference of the Civitas Society. Some of Harper's key aides — then-chief of staff Ian Brodie and political advisor and former national campaign chair Tom Flanagan — attended Luntz's talk. Preston Manning introduced Luntz.[57] Harper himself dropped by unannounced for the opening reception, which featured a speech by then-Treasury Board president, John Baird. Harper soon became adept at Luntz-speak. Luntz advised the Civitas audience to tap into national symbols like hockey. "If there is some way to link hockey to what you all do, I would try to do it." Before long Harper was writing a book about hockey. He successfully framed Stéphane Dion as a "flip-flopper," echoing Luntz's portrayal of John Kerry, and the proposed coalition of Liberals and New Democrats, with Bloc Québécois support, as a "reckless coalition of losers." Stephen Guilbeault of Greenpeace Canada saw Luntz's hand in Harper's messaging about global warming: "If you look at the advice [Luntz] gave to the Republicans some time ago and compare it with how the Conservatives are talking about these things [environmentalism], it's just cut-and-paste, basically," Guilbeault charged.[58] Some examples he put forward:

- Luntz advised his American clients to stress common sense and accountability. Several days after Luntz came to town, Environment Minister Rona Ambrose told the House of Commons that "my mandate is to have accountability on the

environment and show real results and action on the
environment for Canadians."[59]

- Luntz advised depicting the cost of regulation in
  human terms, emphasizing how specific activities
  will cost more, from "pumping gas to turning on
  the light." During the same session of the House,
  Ambrose claimed that "we would have to pull
  every truck and car off the street, shut down every
  train and ground every plane to reach the Kyoto
  target. Or we could shut off all the lights in Canada
  tomorrow, but that still would not be enough."[60]
- Luntz advised that technology and innovation
  are the keys to curbing climate change. Echoed
  Ambrose, we will be investing "in Canadian
  solutions, Canadian technology, and Canadian
  communities."[61]

As in his other successful framing exercises, Harper's "radical environmentalists" message came from multiple sources inside and outside government. In Parliament, Fort McMurray–Athabasca Conservative MP Brian Jean called for legislation that would block foreign funding of the "radical" Canadian environmental movement.[62] In Washington, D.C., John Baird, now foreign affairs minister, told an interviewer "there's a great deal of frustration . . . that the future prosperity of our country could lie in the hands of some radical environmentalists and special interests."[63] Outside government, Marco Navarro-Genie, research director at the Frontier Centre for Public Policy, a regional neo-liberal think tank, wrote in the *Calgary Herald* that the "real aim [of] . . . radical environmentalists is eventually to stop production of all hydrocarbons."[64] The targets of these assaults — David Suzuki, Elizabeth May, Tides Canada, which provides financial support for Forest Ethics, and other opponents of bitumen development — likely made things worse by denying they were radicals, giving the "radical environmentalist" frame a longer shelf life than it might otherwise have enjoyed.[65]

Did it work? Later in the year, the Montreal Economic Institute, another regional neo-liberal think tank, released a survey suggesting that a majority of Canadians — 52 per cent — think "several environmental lobbies are too radical," compared with 27 per cent who disagree with this statement.[66] The survey also found that 72 per cent of Canadians are in favour of developing the bitumen deposits, "while maintaining a continuous effort to limit the environmental impact."[67]

***

But if every effort to limit the impact of projects that threaten the environment is labelled as radical, what is the alternative? Preston Manning has the answer. Younger Canadians in particular, the former Reform Party leader argues in a 2010 *Globe and Mail* commentary, believe strongly in environmental protection and conservation, "but they have become disillusioned by the ineffectiveness of the political debate on the subject."[68] Manning presents no evidence for this claim, but nonetheless asserts that it gives Canadians "a starting point for a new dialogue on how to reduce the negative environmental consequences of hydrocarbon use." We need to blend regulatory action and market-based initiatives, he writes. This is a reasonable approach, but Manning's "new dialogue" — perhaps unsurprisingly — is almost all on the market-based side: bring full-cost accounting into environmental assessments; improve the ability to move scientific innovations into the marketplace; harness markets to meet our demands for clean water and air; create public–private utility partnerships. As for regulatory action, his single recommendation is to push government to focus on macro-regulation, not explaining what that means. Hands off?

Manning expanded on his comments several months later: "If you zero in on the under-40 crowd, for example, for whom economy and ecology are seen as one, you've got fertile ground there," once again providing no evidence for this claim. But if Canadians do accept it, then they might also accept his assertion that conservative solutions can be employed. "You attach a price to pollution, or a price to a resource, which then brings it into a market which will allocate it more efficiently," he explains. "Because Conservatives profess to believe in markets and have done a lot of work on how do you make markets work, I think the harnessing of that horse to the environmental-conservation cart could be a signature contribution of conservative people."[69] Manning's horse is a private sector "think-tank/do-tank," dedicated to devising business strategies and public policies to move discoveries from the laboratory to the marketplace. Coincidentally, such a horse existed, and Manning was riding it. Sustainable Prosperity (SP) is based in the University of Ottawa's Faculty of Law, calls itself a "green-economy think-tank" and has as its motto, "making markets work for the environment." Manning joined SP's board of advisers in 2009.

Sustainable Prosperity burst out of the gate in 2007, supporting the B.C. government's carbon tax as "smart public policy."[70] Promoting carbon taxes and reframing the environment as a series of markets are SP's major projects. With funding from the McConnell Family Foundation ($725,000), the Social Sciences and Humanities Research Council ($1.8 million), and the Dalton McGuinty government ($5 million), SP is not a neo-liberal think tank in the Fraser Institute mold. It accepts government funding and maintains close ties with government departments, especially Environment Canada, activities that are verboten for the neo-liberal think tank. But SP is certainly neo-liberal in mission and spirit. In the "What We Do" section of its website, for instance, the organization claims that:

> *The operating system of our modern world — the*
> *capitalist market — is an incredible tool. It links*
> *billions of producers and consumers every day,*
> *generating price signals that help people around*
> *the world decide what to make and what to buy.*
> *But when it comes to conserving Earth's natural*
> *environment, our markets are badly broken: we*
> *don't pay the true environmental costs of making,*
> *using, and getting rid of stuff.*[71]

Friedrich Hayek couldn't have said it better. But something is left unsaid in SP's quest to make markets work for the environment, especially in regard to SP's program to "create markets for nature's environmental services, services that we now treat as free." The organization says nothing about the most fundamental component of a market: private-property rights. SP's 2011 report, "Advancing the Economics of Ecosystems and Biodiversity in Canada," purports to put a value on natural ecosystems (ecosystem "services," in the new jargon), to create economic incentives to conserve Canada's "natural capital" and use it more productively.[72] The report cites approvingly programs that are already doing this: Ducks Unlimited pays landowners to restore wetlands in their fields and pastures; the Alberta government helps pay landowners to manage their farms to store additional carbon; the federal government provides tax credits to landowners who donate ecologically sensitive lands to environmental charities.[73] In these examples, benefits accrue to existing landowners; those who don't own land get nothing. In SP's world, prosperity, evidently, is for the already-prosperous. Australian political scientist Robyn Eckersley observes that the "consequence of . . . the privatisation of environmental resources . . . is likely to be the intensification of the already wide gap between the propertied and the propertyless, and the rich and the poor."[74]

SP's first annual survey of environmental markets in Canada[75] follows the well-trodden path blazed by neo-liberal think tanks to promote particular tenets of neo-liberal dogma, such as the Fraser Institute's school report cards, hospital waiting lists, and economic freedom of the world (EFW) indexes. Producing a survey of a particular phenomenon year after year helps domesticate the beast. "For a lot of people, just the fact that these markets exist is news," claims Alex Wood, SP's director of policy and markets and a former adviser to TD Bank Financial Group.[76] But do these markets really exist, or are they being constructed, as is the case with the EFW index discussed in Chapter 1? The Fraser Institute says that, if it matters, measure it. The true task for neo-liberal think tanks, though, is that if you can measure it, it matters. So get busy.

Preston Manning is the most prominent member of SP's board of advisers. He joins the former CEO of the Canadian Gas Association; a former senior vice-president of Alcan; a business analyst from Manitoba Hydro; a lobbyist, with clients such as Nova Chemicals, General Motors of Canada, Nexen, and Spectra Energy Transmission; a former policy adviser to Stephen Harper; a former deputy minister of Environment Canada; two academics; and several others. SP has no environmentalists on its board of advisers and none on its research network committee or staff. The organization may say its mandate is to make markets work for the environment, but there are no voices speaking for environmental values within the organization. This task is left to business executives, consultants, economists, and lawyers.

Through his political and media cachet, Manning is bringing from the sidelines into the mainstream a variant of free-market environmentalism (FME), a Hayek-inspired effort to replace government regulation and oversight with market transactions.

It's then an easy step from the Manning–SP version of market-based environmentalism to full-blown FME. All that's missing is private-property rights. If you can put a value on a resource or service, then someone can own it. And if someone can own it, then it can be used to borrow money for investment through environmental bonds or other securitization instruments. It's perhaps relevant to note that the president of the U.S.–based Nature Conservancy, one of the largest players in the "ecosystem services market," is a long-time Goldman Sachs investment banker.[77]

As FME founders Terry Anderson and Donald Leal explain, "at the heart of free market environmentalism is a system of well-specified property rights to natural resources." No matter who owns these property rights, "a discipline is imposed on resource users because the wealth of the owner of the property right is at stake if bad decisions are made."[78] Only the owner's wealth matters; the wealth of the community is of little relevance, while government's role is to define and enforce the rights. Following Hayek, Anderson and Leal claim that individual property rights and well-functioning markets will always lead to better decisions than those made by political or centralized authorities. FME as a coherent philosophy was developed at the Pacific Research Institute (PRI) in San Francisco where Anderson worked in the 1980s. (PRI is a sister organization to the Fraser Institute, both established by Antony Fisher in the seventies to bring the neoliberal revolution to North America. Hayek was an adviser to both organizations. Anderson's book on private-property rights won the 2005 Antony Fisher Prize.) Anderson was a participant on the panel organized by Manny Jules of the First Nations Tax Commission to discuss property rights on First Nation reserves, as described in Chapter 4.

The Political Economy Research Center (later the Property and Environment Research Center, or PERC) was spun off as a single-issue advocacy organization in Bozeman, Montana, to promote FME. Its co-founder is Mont Pelerin Society member John Baden, who, like Anderson, is an environmental economist. The remote Bozeman was selected as the location for PERC, perhaps because Anderson, PERC's senior associate, was a professor at nearby Montana State University. Bozeman is also Baden's home base. PERC leads the charge for FME, but other American multi-issue think tanks, such as PRI, the Cato Institute, and the Reason Foundation, support FME research and dissemination. In Canada, the Fraser Institute has been beating the drum for FME since the 1990s. Now Preston Manning and Sustainable Prosperity are putting market-based environmentalism on the political agenda, and it's being adopted by federal government departments with environmental mandates (DEMs) — Environment Canada (EC), Fisheries and Oceans Canada (DFO), Parks Canada, Natural Resources Canada (NRC), and Agriculture and Agri-Foods Canada.

The DEMs' retreat from scientific research and environmental regulation is well-documented: nearly a third of Parks Canada's entire scientific complement — including fifty ecosystem scientists — declared surplus or "affected"; EC losing its ability to stay current with advances in science and technology; the closing or disbanding of DFO's Habitat Management Program, DFO's teams of experts, EC's Polar Environment Atmospheric Research Lab, and the Canadian Foundation for Climate and Atmospheric Sciences; the closing of science and environmental libraries at NRC and Parks Canada. Also well-publicized are the many examples of federal scientists being censored in their efforts to communicate their research to the media and the public, which will be explored further in Chapter 6.[79]

Less well-known is the DEMs' embrace of market-based environmentalism. While they were losing their ability to monitor ecosystems, they were ramping up their ability to put a price on them. Shortly after Harper won his majority government, the DEMs commenced a two-year interdepartmental collaboration — led by Statistics Canada — to produce "a compendium of interdisciplinary research initiatives focused on improving our understanding of the value of ecosystem goods and services through ecosystem accounting," as the 2013 Statistics Canada report "Measuring Ecosystem Goods and Services in Canada" frames their quest.[80]

With its central role in government environmental activity, Environment Canada is ground zero in the transition from over-sight to markets. The department launched a strategy in 2010 "to better engage policy and economic academic experts." This strat-egy combines sixty million dollars in budget cuts — including scientific research activities — with an expansion of the depart-ment's capacity to tally the economic value of environmental goods and services. EC commissioned Sustainable Prosperity's 2011 report that surveyed the economic tools available to place a value on ecosystem services. The following year, EC launched an economics and environmental policy research network, com-prising seventy researchers and co-sponsored by the University of Ottawa — Sustainable Prosperity provides management and support — and the University of Calgary.[81] (See Chapter 2 for Calgary's interest in promoting the oil and gas industry.) The strategy was revealed in briefing notes prepared for the depart-ment's new deputy minister Bob Hamilton and reported by Postmedia News.[82] Hamilton is the right person for this job. Like Harper, Hamilton has a Master's degree in economics. He rose through the ranks of the Finance Department and Treasury Board, where he oversaw Harper's tax cuts, the establishment of Tax-Free Savings Accounts, and deregulation measures. Harper appointed Hamilton to head the Canadian delegation to the Regulatory Cooperation Council, which was responsible for "har-monizing" Canadian and American regulatory regimes, another exercise in deregulation. Hamilton then moved to Environment Canada to oversee the transition from science and regulation to markets and property rights.[83] Like everything Harper does, this transition is occurring quietly and incrementally, but it is occurring. It's another example of Harperism.

Ecosystem guardians outside government — the environmentalists so demonized by Levant and Harper — are being forced to make an unhappy choice: oppose everything, be called radical and a supporter of oil imports from tyrannies like Saudi Arabia and Venezuela, and become irrelevant; or line up behind a version of market-based environmentalism, as many are already doing through their support of carbon taxes and cap-and-trade programs. Most environmental problems occur because industry is able to externalize its costs onto the environment by emitting pollutants via land, air and water and by not paying the full social and economic costs of resource extraction. One purpose of regulation is to limit pollution to socially acceptable levels. Neo-liberals counter that creating markets for pollution is more efficient than regulation: let the market decide the cost of pollution. Of course governments will have to get pollution markets up and running, as they've already done with emissions-trading systems. The European Union, for instance, has established a limit on overall greenhouse gas emissions for high-emitting industry sectors. Within the limit, which is gradually reduced, companies can buy and sell emission allowances as needed.[84]

As Vaclav Klaus insisted, environmental science is suspect because it is tied to central planning, which will always result in inferior decisions. Harper follows this principle by attacking environmentalists and hobbling his government's ability to do science. But this is far from a done deal. EC retains a large complement of scientists who are doing what they've always done, albeit under more restrictive conditions. Their research still informs EC decision-making, but for how long? Just as free-trade deals are largely irreversible, so the changes at EC and the other DEMs cannot easily be undone. Some courageous future government may attempt to boost public spending on scientists, but for what purpose? The government's institutional memory is fast disappearing — libraries are shuttered, research stations are abandoned, research is scattered to the four winds, as we will see in Chapter 6. Meanwhile, government's capacity to promote the economic perspective on ecosystems is being bulked up. And once the economic perspective takes hold, property rights for the environment cannot be far behind. That would be Harperism on a grand scale.

6

UNDERMINE SCIENTIFIC KNOWLEDGE

Canada Gazette is the Canadian government's official news-paper, publishing formal public notices, official appointments, and regulations and acts of parliament in three parts. Part 1 lists notices and proposed regulations. Sharp-eyed observers noticed something amiss in the June 26, 2010, issue. Statistics Canada was prescribing the questions to be asked on the Census of Population that would be taken in May 2011. These observers remarked that the form was only eight pages long, whereas the form for the 2006 population census was thirty pages in length. The earlier census asked questions about where a person was born, what languages were spoken, citizenship and immigration status, ethnic or cultural origins and status, aboriginal status, places where the person had lived one and five years earlier, education details, unpaid household activities, employment status and occupation, business or industry worked in, method of transportation to work, income from self- or paid employment, government and investments, and housing status and costs.[1] These questions were asked in a long-form census sent to 20 per cent of Canadians, while the other 80 per cent — plus the 20 per cent who were given the long census — received a short census form that required them to answer questions about their address, age, gender, marital status, first language learned, and the relationships among those living at their address. The long-form census had been "disappeared." In the past, completing both forms was mandatory. For 2011, the long-form census would be replaced by a voluntary national household survey sent to a third of households.

Statistics Canada had been blindsided by the Harper government. "Officials from [the agency] say the 2011 census went through the usual consultation process, with citizens invited to provide feedback online," CanWest News reported, "but there was no indication this change was under consideration." Stats-Can, which falls under the purview of Industry Canada, knew nothing about it. A spokesperson for industry minister Tony Clement confirmed the decision to change the census came from the government and not from the ministry or Statistics Canada.[2] StatsCan's head, Munir Sheikh, resigned. A voluntary survey could not "become a substitute for a mandatory census," he said defiantly. "Under the circumstances, I have tendered my resignation to the prime minister."[3]

The elimination of the long-form census came under fire from many sides. A lengthy list of social-work organizations, social- and immigrant-services agencies, and planning and municipal organizations signed on to the opposition.[4] They needed the information, they claimed, to tailor services such as day care, schools, hospitals, seniors' homes, recreation services, police and fire protection, and public transit.[5] Just weeks before the elimination of the long-form census became public knowledge, the *Ottawa Citizen* editorialized that "the Census is a source of invaluable up-to-date data about who we are and how we live, providing a framework for public policy, public

debate and a better understanding of the changing Canada . . .
Census information is essential to governments and agencies in
shaping economic and social programs."[6] Even organizations like
the C.D. Howe Institute, the Canada West Foundation, and the
Institute for Research on Public Policy, as well as several organizations of business economists, were opposed.

These organizations were proved right two years later when
StatsCan started releasing National Household Survey (NHS)
results. The overall response rate for the voluntary survey was 68
per cent, well below the 94-percent rate expected for the mandatory census. The low response means results are less reliable,
especially in communities with fewer than twenty-five thousand
residents. As a result, StatsCan withheld data on a quarter of
all Canadian communities, mostly rural or First Nations. That
makes it problematic to set policies in small communities and,
at a provincial level, to set social policy, Regina Sadlikova, a
development services director in rural British Columbia, commented. "It puts more guesswork into local government planning
policy."[7] These governments would have to pay private consultants to gather the needed data, she said, but few municipalities
can afford to do so. Other provinces experienced similar gaps.
Manitoba's chief statistician, Wilf Falk, says that one-third of his
province's municipalities have no data published from the NHS,
because not enough people in those communities filled out the
questionnaires. That makes it tougher to figure out population
shifts and gaps in housing, education, or health care.[8] Across the
country, groups most likely to need more and specialized services
— new immigrants, aboriginals, the poor — are most likely not
to fill out surveys.

Why would the Harper government move forward with such
an obviously dysfunctional policy? University of Ottawa political
scientist Paul Saurette suggests that the use of StatsCan information by an infrastructure of organizations to discover inequalities

in society "and then to lobby the government and Canadian society to reduce these inequalities through social programs" fostered a climate of opinion that legitimized a government role in helping people. But if the data are not credible, as Munir Sheikh maintains, then the issues will become less credible, and advocacy groups less able to persuade Canadians that government programs are necessary. "The less government programs seem necessary, the less government itself seems valuable," Saurette writes, and "the more likely it is that conservative market-oriented values and principles can flourish."[9] In a nutshell, that's the Harper agenda.

Munir Sheikh wasn't the only senior StatsCan official to leave the agency. Philip Cross, StatsCan's chief economic analyst, left two years later, citing a clamp-down on the free exchange of ideas within the organization.[10] But while Sheikh took an academic position in the School of Policy Studies at Queen's University, Cross moved across town to the neo-liberal Macdonald–Laurier Institute, transferring from an organization that collects data for public policy and planning to one that uses data selectively to further neo-liberal ideology, as Chapter 2 explains. Writing in the *National Post*, Cross pooh-poohed criticisms that the NHS couldn't provide statistics for thousands of smaller communities. People in Tinytown, Manitoba, don't need this information anyway, he countered. They "only have to drive down the main street to see what the problems are as well as emerging new trends." And the census is passé in any case, because computerized health, tax, and other record sets are more readily available. Meanwhile, "private sector firms are increasingly producing their own data."[11]

The termination of the long-form census was a Mont Pelerin moment: a pre-emptive strike at the government's ability to make certain kinds of decisions by starving it of the quality information it needs. As Sheikh points out, the information provided by a voluntary survey is of lesser quality and reliability. Government can no longer plan for or provide carefully targeted services for the poor, new immigrants, and aboriginals, because these groups didn't fill out the forms in sufficient numbers. In the neoliberal world, planning equals socialism or centralized control by faceless bureaucrats who will always make wrong decisions. Only the market — decisions made by millions of individuals acting in their own self-interest — can get prices and almost everything else right. Of course, the market doesn't consist only of millions of individuals. Giant multinational corporations also make decisions in their own self-interest, but neo-liberal analysis seems to forget that these large, market-distorting companies exist.

In fact big business didn't care about the long-form census. The Retail Council of Canada, Canadian Chamber of Commerce, and Canadian Manufacturers and Exporters, all claimed the move to a voluntary survey wasn't an issue for them. Ross Laver, vice-president of policy and communication at the Canadian Council of Chief Executives and a former editor and writer at *Maclean's*, stated "we don't have a dog in this hunt."[12] A poll of business leaders by COMPAS, an opinion research firm, found that 62 per cent of respondents said they use neither long-form nor short-form data and only 21 per cent used long-form data.[13] They were likely getting the information, data, and statistics they need from their own proprietary sources.

The Fraser Institute admitted it used long-form census data in its school report-card rankings, but still claimed the mandatory census was a "truly intrusive instrument" that "requires Canadians to complete 40 burdensome pages of intrusive personal questions." Why is this census necessary, the institute asked. Because it has "simply become a cheap way for academics, economists, and social scientists" — who are vociferous critics of removing the long census — "to get information that should be acquired using market surveys of the kind that are routinely collected on a voluntary basis."[14] They should pay for their data like business does. Evidently there's no need for Canadians to "have access to timely, relevant, and quality statistical information on Canada's changing economy and society for informed debate, research, and decision making on social and economic issues," as the Treasury Board frames StatsCan's mission.[15]

The 2011–12 federal budget indicated the assault on reliable statistical information was not over. StatsCan learned it would need to cut $34 million, or about 7 per cent, from its budget by 2014–15. Nearly half the agency's 5,700 staff members received layoff notices, although the final job cuts were fewer. Soon the agency discovered the news was even worse. The cuts were deeper, because government departments that pay StatsCan for surveys also had their budgets cut, resulting in an additional $20-million loss for the statistical agency. "Everything that is going to be cut is going to hurt a lot," complained Ivan Fellegi, StatsCan's former chief statistician.[16]

The budget also revealed the termination of three institutions that provide statistics and advice to government. The National Round Table on the Environment and the Economy provided information on sustainable development, the First Nations Statistical Institute provided data on First Nations communities that the census may have missed, and the National Council on Welfare provided information on poverty in Canada.[17] As Harper asked a reporter on a European tour, why should his government fund these agencies, when they offer solutions that run counter to government policy?[18]

Harper asked the same question about scientists who worked for his government, especially those in departments with environmental mandates, as discussed in Chapter 5. Are they, too, creating information that runs counter to government policy? Then they, too, must be silenced. Early in 2008, Postmedia News science reporter Margaret Munro obtained a

PowerPoint presentation from Environment Canada's executive management committee detailing a new policy to control the department's media message. "Just as we have 'one department, one website,'" the presentation declares, "we should have 'one department, one voice.'"[19] All media queries were henceforth to be routed through the government. The presentation lays out the process: the media office asks reporters to submit their questions in writing; researchers are asked to respond in writing to the media office, which sends the answers to senior management for approval. If a researcher is eventually cleared to do an interview, he or she will be instructed to stick to the "approved lines," Munro reports. Scientific explanations will come from the Harper government, not from the scientists who do the research.

Using the *Access to Information Act*, Munro obtained documents detailing the new communications policy for Natural Resources Canada, another government department with a large complement of scientists. A summary of the media-relations process stresses in bold type that "Approval from the minister's director of communication must always be sought — no exceptions."[20] The government's goal is to operate in an environment of "no surprises." Everyone needs to be on message, no matter what the science says. In the past, media requests were handled by scientists and communications staff across the country. Scientists would often discuss their research directly with reporters. Under the new regime, a small army of "subject-matter experts" — media officers, senior bureaucrats, and political staff — craft and approve responses, if a response is even permitted.

When the annual conference of the American Academy for the Advancement of Science was held in Vancouver in 2012, Munro told scientists and science writers about the numerous examples of government interference and of reporters being denied timely access to scientists.[21] Conference attendees wrote to Harper, calling on his government to stop muzzling federal researchers.

"Despite promises that your majority government would follow principles of accountability and transparency, federal scientists in Canada are still not allowed to speak to reporters without the 'consent' of media relations officers," the letter read.[22] It was followed by an editorial in the British journal *Nature*, decrying the Harper government's "startlingly poor behaviour" regarding its media policies.[23]

But just like users of StatsCan's long-form census data, science writers and scientists were wasting their breath. Quality taxpayer-financed census information was becoming a thing of the past, and government-sponsored science would be pressed into the service of the neo-liberal agenda or be silenced. As for scientists who didn't work for government, Gordon McBean, a University of Western Ontario geographer and internationally respected climate-change scientist, expressed their frustration. "I think there is a significant problem — unwillingness to entertain, or invite, or listen to, people who are experts in their fields and want to provide advice and guidance to the government."[24] Simon Fraser University criminologist Neil Boyd agrees. "They have a very strange antipathy to science and to evidence-based policy making," he comments.[25]

***

To understand the Harper government's suspicion of scientists and experts we need to refer, once again, to Hayek's *The Road to Serfdom*. Hayek lauded science for the "great strides [it made] which in the last hundred and fifty years have changed the face of the world."[26] But scientists go too far, he argued — passionately — when they are "agitating for a 'scientific' organization of society."[27] He denigrated this view by associating it with German scientists who fell in line with the National Socialism (Nazi) movement in Germany. His main target, though, was scientific planning in Britain, during the Second World War and after.[28] As the war raged on, the market system was more or less abandoned, and many parts of the economy were placed under central control. Decisions about what to produce had to be made centrally, as resources were reallocated away from the production of peacetime consumer goods and towards the production of war materials. With fewer consumer goods available, the prospect of inflation loomed. To avoid inflation, further intervention was necessary, and the standard policy response was to fix prices and institute a system of rationing. Hayek's fear was that socialists would want to continue such controls in peacetime. He needed only to point to an editorial in the weekly magazine *Nature*, which was advocating for scientific planning. This is the same *Nature* that seventy-two years later berated Harper for muzzling scientists:

> *The contribution of science to the war effort should be a major one . . . Moreover the work must not cease with the end of the War . . . the principle of the immediate concern of science in formulating policy and in other ways exerting a direct and sufficient influence on the course of government is one to which we must hold fast. Science must seize the opportunity to show that it can lead mankind onward to a better form of society.[29]*

Scientists leading "mankind onward to a better form of society." Such a declaration set off alarm bells that echoed through the decades. Hayek's suspicion that scientists have a political and ideological agenda they are surreptitiously imposing on mankind became embedded within the neo-liberal thought collective. Philip Cross, StatsCan's former chief economic analyst, who moved to the neo-liberal Macdonald–Laurier Institute, took direct aim at government scientists who "really want . . . to use their department (or agency) of the Government of Canada, and all of the profile and credibility attached to it, as a platform to leverage their own political or ideological agenda," he wrote in the *National Post*.[30] It also became a predominant frame in corporate-media depictions of science. The Vancouver *Province*'s libertarian columnist Jon Ferry said it well: "I am getting quite used to the fact that much of what passes for science these days is essentially eco-propaganda."[31]

***

If climate and environmental scientists top the Harper government's list of enemies, because they provide evidence of global warming and other reasons for government to take action on environmental problems, criminologists and sociologists, who provide evidence on crime and punishment, run a close second. "Get tough on crime" was a core Reform Party policy, going back to the party's 1991 Blue Book, which was written by Harper. By the time of the 2004 election, Harper was leader of the newly united Conservative Party and put forward a tough-on-crime agenda that included strict parole qualifications, immediate deportation of illegal residents, and "three-strikes-and-you're-out" legislation for violent offenders.[32] It didn't get him elected prime minister, but it did force the Liberals to minority status.

Two years later, in the run-up to the 2006 election, the Boxing Day shooting of a fifteen-year-old girl in downtown Toronto by a stray bullet fired in a turf war between rival drug gangs vindicated his tough-on-crime stance and gave him a wedge issue he exploited effectively.[33] Four days after the tragic shooting, Harper claimed in an opinion piece in the *National Post* that "the brutal end to a promising young life should be a wake-up call . . .

to crack down on gun crime and gang violence." He blamed the situation on "years of government lassitude and neglect."[34]

Harper had barely put the election victory behind him, when criminologists and sociologists began their criticism. Neil Boyd was a persistent critic. He called the Conservatives' election platform "an extremely expensive agenda of prison building." He asked the new government to provide evidence that keeping people in jail longer is a deterrent to crime. "There's no evidence it will make us a safer society" for such "an enormous expenditure of funds."[35]

Evidence was the neo-liberal *bête noire*. Sociologists and criminologists keep coming up with all kinds of evidence that building more prisons, imposing mandatory minimum sentences, or making conditions of incarceration harsher and more punitive do not reduce the rates or severity of crime. To neo-liberals, such evidence is irrelevant — but, strangely, welcome. Ian Brodie, Harper's former chief of staff, explained why during a candid talk on Conservative strategy at Montreal's McGill University a year after he left the PMO. "Every time we proposed amendments to the *Criminal Code*, sociologists, criminologists, defence lawyers and Liberals attacked us for proposing measures that the evidence apparently showed did not work. That was a good thing for us politically," he told his audience, "in that sociologists, criminologists, and defence lawyers were and are held in lower repute than Conservative politicians by the voting public. Politically, it helped us tremendously to be attacked by this coalition of university types."[36]

Harper iced the cake several years later. The day after the Boston Marathon bombings killed two and maimed and wounded dozens, and soon after a failed attack on a Via Rail passenger train, new Liberal leader Justin Trudeau said it was essential to look at the "root causes" that might lead someone to plot such attacks. Here was Trudeau sounding like a social scientist, and Harper pounced. "This is not the time to commit sociology, if I can use an expression," he told a news conference. "I don't think we want to convey any view to the Canadian public other than our utter condemnation of this kind of violence . . . and our utter determination through our laws and through our activities to do everything we can to prevent it and counter it."[37]

Sociologists seemed not to understand what Harper was doing and why he was doing it, so they resorted to name-calling. University of Regina's John Conway declared that "Harper has put his foot in his mouth once again and looks completely ridiculous,"[38] while Ottawa sociologist Wayne MacDonald accused Harper of exhibiting a "narrow-minded intellectual immaturity and misunderstanding of important social issues," attacking the messenger and not being attentive to the message.[39] A letter written to the *Vancouver Sun* accused Harper of "committing ideology," but didn't follow up on this promising line of inquiry.[40] If he had, he might have solved the puzzle by following sociologist antipathy back to its neo-liberal roots.

Gary Becker's influential 1968 article, "Crime and Punishment: An Economic Approach,"[41] brought neo-liberalism into the criminal-justice arena, as neo-liberalism was extending its reach into more and more areas of social and cultural life. Becker, a University of Chicago economist who later served as president of the Mont Pelerin Society and won the Nobel Prize in economics, posits that criminals, like all individuals, are rational maximizers of expected utility. Criminal acts generate benefits — material gain, revenge — and are subject to costs imposed by the state. The "Beckerian rational calculator weighs the expected costs against the expected benefits, and if the first are lower than the second, the person commits the crime," Stanford Law School's John Donohue explains.[42] Society can reduce the amount of crime by either lowering the benefits criminals gain from their illegal activities or raising the costs that will befall them, or both. Becker suggests two possible tools to raise the cost of crime: increase the probability of apprehension or increase the severity of punishment for those who are caught.

Becker's basic model favours monetary fines over incarceration as a more efficient means of deterring crime, but this distinction was lost in the stampede to get tough on crime that followed. Worse, his model was fatally flawed, because it relies on criminals being "fully rational, well informed, sufficiently solvent to be responsive to high monetary sanctions, and risk neutral. Unfortunately, none of these conditions are true," Donohue writes.[43] Donohue's observation is most poignant in the case of individuals with mental illnesses and other disorders, such as fetal alcohol spectrum disorder (FASD). About a third of a million Canadians — 1 per cent — are considered to have this disability.[44] They are born with a variety of brain and central nervous system dysfunctions. Children with FASD "exhibit poor judgement, impulsivity and had difficulty thinking rationally," Kwadwo Asante, a pediatrician who practised in northern British Columbia and first noted the disorder, reported of some of his patients.[45] "They couldn't learn from their experiences, couldn't understand consequences of their actions, and had learning disabilities. They failed at school." They develop substance-abuse problems and many end up in jail. A recent literature review estimates that youths with FASD are nineteen times more likely to be in prison than youths without FASD.[46] But putting those with FASD in prison is futile if the purpose of incarceration is deterrence. They are unlikely to make the connection between what is happening to them today and something they did months before. Nor can they foresee the consequences of their actions. They just don't get it, and tend to reoffend. They exhibit none of the characteristics of the Beckerian rational calculator.

Inadequacies aside, "Becker's message started to powerfully influence criminal justice policy in the 1970s and provided the intellectual support for the . . . increasing harshness of the American criminal justice system over the last 30 years," Donohue wrote in 2007.[47] The hardening of criminal law soon spread to Britain and other countries — Canada included — where neo-liberalism was taking hold.[48] Becker went further with his model, supporting the view that the death penalty has a substantial deterrent impact and therefore should be used to reduce crime. Donohue notes, though, that the most recent work on this issue "has shown that solid empirical support for this proposition is virtually nonexistent."[49] The lack of such evidence, once again, is irrelevant to the expansion of neo-liberal ideology.

***

But it was the mounting evidence of global warming and other environmental threats that proved more of a challenge for Harper. He prepared for his second year as prime minister with a preview of his government's priorities, making the case for why voters should give him another mandate. In a speech to the Canadian Club in Ottawa in February 2007, he vowed to cut taxes, control spending, and eliminate debt, a strategy designed to differentiate his government from the opposition. But he spent most of the time emphasizing the importance his government placed on protecting and improving the environment,[50] a claim that likely took his critics by surprise, since he had already cancelled twenty federal programs meant to reduce greenhouse-gas emissions.[51] "The fundamental challenge of our time is to make real progress on environmental protection while preserving jobs and standards of living," he said. "Finding that balance will require sound science, rational debate, and political will over a long period of time."[52]

"Rational debate" and "political will" seem common enough terms for his audience, but "sound science" is an unusual turn of phrase for Canadian ears. It flew under the media's radar, except for the *Globe and Mail's* Rick Salutin. "Hmmm, why *sound* science?" he asked. "Wouldn't you normally just say, science? Sound as opposed to what — aha, *junk* science. The kind that Harper allies at the Fraser Institute — egged on, we now know, by lots of money from oil and energy companies — have always railed against for being alarmist about global warming."[53] Fraser Institute to be sure, but there's also the Frank Luntz factor to consider. In his memo to Republicans before the 2002 congressional election, discussed in Chapter 5, Luntz advised them that, on environmental policy and global warming, "Sound science must be our guide in choosing which problems to tackle and how to approach them."[54] American science writer Chris Mooney, observed in 2005 that "on global warming, perhaps the most pressing science-based issue today, conservatives follow the Frank Luntz 'sound science' strategy to a T."[55] A year after Mooney's assessment, Luntz was in Ottawa with the newly elected prime minister for a photo-op session and with advice on how to run a minority government. Harper followed the Luntz sound-science strategy to a T in his speech to the Canadian Club.

Harper used sound science again in the run-up to the 2011 election. He was on a farm in southwestern Ontario, asking voters for a majority so he could finally kill the federal long-gun registry. (His efforts to do so in the past were stymied by the combined opposition that voted to keep the registry.) "A re-elected majority Conservative government will scrap the wasteful and inefficient long-gun registry once and for all," Harper promised. He also promised to create a hunting and wildlife advisory panel "to ensure that government decisions are based on sound science and balanced advice." Hunters and anglers, and not scientists, will advise government on endangered-species laws, conservation, and wetland protection.[56]

Harper won his majority, and a year later spoke at the National Fish and Wildlife Conservation Congress in Ottawa.

The long-gun registry was gone. "Promise made, ladies and gentlemen, promise kept," he said. He kept his second promise, too, by announcing the members of the Hunting and Angling Advisory Panel, whose wisdom, he said, will ensure "our Government's decisions are based on sound science and balanced advice,"[57] using the same wording as in the previous year. Sound science will be delivered by representatives of provincial wildlife associations, the Fur Institute, the Canadian Shooting Sports Association, and other hunters and anglers, although the panel did contain two scientists.[58]

If Harper was playing chess, this was a move inspired by Hayek, who argued that "scientific knowledge is not the sum of all knowledge," because there is a body of "very important but unorganized knowledge," not of "general rules," as science attempts to discover, but of "the particular circumstances of time and place."[59] Anglers and hunters know about local conditions. Their expertise consists of practical knowledge beyond what science can provide, with its quest to understand underlying principles and to use that understanding for political ends. Practical knowledge, Hayek maintained, is coordinated, not through scientific research, but by the price system. It's a short trip from sound science to the market.

Frank Luntz packaged sound science for Newt Gingrich, George W. Bush, and Stephen Harper, but he didn't invent the term. That honour belongs to the Tobacco Institute, Big Tobacco's powerful PR and lobbying outfit. In 1992, a U.S. Environmental Protection Agency report estimated that second-hand smoke causes three thousand lung cancer deaths a year. This is a fraction of the 125,000 deaths a year from smoking, but it raised panic within the ranks of Big Tobacco.[60] After decades of denial, the industry had crafted a successful defence by arguing that it's unfortunate people die from smoking, but after all, it's their choice to smoke. Second-hand smoke — even with fewer victims — is different, because someone can die from exposure to tobacco smoke even though they don't smoke. Consequently, the EPA might impose regulations that could include bans on smoking in public places. Such an outcome would pose a serious risk to tobacco-industry profits and had to be stopped. The Tobacco Institute called the EPA's conclusions "another step in a long process characterized by a preference for political correctness over sound science."[61]

Philip Morris launched The Advancement of Sound Science Coalition (TASSC) to stimulate criticism of the EPA report, but kept its financial backing secret.[62] The project proved so successful in alerting policy-makers and the public to the dangers of "junk science" — the new name for political correctness — that it expanded its scope to include asbestos, pesticides, ozone depletion, global warming — make that climate change — and water quality. As for what sound science really means, one reporter had it right: "shorthand for the notion that anti-pollution laws have gone to extremes, spending huge amounts of money to protect people from miniscule risks."[63] Sound science is code for deregulation, while junk science means regulatory overkill. For a decade, TASSC covertly set the ground rules for public discourse regarding pollution and other health, safety, and environmental threats. It even came to Canada in 2002 to organize a conference of global-warming deniers in an unsuccessful last-ditch effort to derail parliamentary ratification of the Kyoto Accord.[64]

TASSC faded away after George W. Bush became president and made "sound science" fundamental to his administration. In Canada, the Harper Conservatives became staunch advocates. They never explained what they mean by sound science, but are consistent in its use, supporting the interests of industry and downplaying the results of scientific research. Joe Oliver, then natural resources minister, was a frequent user, as he made the case for Alberta's bitumen. He worried that

California's low-carbon-fuel standards discriminated against Alberta producers, because the standards "needed to be based on sound science [and] . . . be fair and non-discriminatory."[65] A larger concern was the European Commission's proposed Fuel Quality Directive (FQD) which, Oliver claimed, "unfairly singles out Canadian oil sands crude" for excessive greenhouse-gas emissions, compared to other dirty oil producers. "We ask only that the FQD be fair and effective to everyone and based on sound science,"[66] he told an audience at Canada House in London. He made the same point in Kuwait City at the 2012 International Energy Forum, where he reinforced Canada's position on the FQD and the need to ensure that "it is non-discriminatory and based on sound science."[67] Later in the year, he was at Port Metro Vancouver to assure British Columbians that "the federal government has put in place strict rules and regulations governing the development and shipment of products like oil to safeguard public health and the environment. And we are determined to raise the bar even higher," he said, "based on sound science and world-class standards."[68]

Other departments used this convenient shorthand to defend corporate interests. When Health Canada announced new rules banning the use of Bisphenol A (BPA), an endocrine-disrupting chemical associated with obesity, attention deficit disorder (ADD), various cancers, immune-system dysfunctions, early puberty in females, higher rates of miscarriage, and a wide range of developmental problems,[69] the rules applied only to baby bottles and sippy cups, a tiny fraction of overall BPA use. The chemical is found far more frequently in resins that line metal food and drink cans, keeping out metallic flavours and creating an airtight seal to prevent spoilage. Hundreds of products on supermarket shelves were exempted from the regulations, a decision no doubt of great relief to food processors and can manufacturers. "This government is taking action to protect

Canadians, and our decisions are based on sound science," Health Minister Tony Clement's press secretary wrote. "We will continue to study BPA among many other chemicals."[70]

When China vowed to uphold its ban on Alberta pork entering the country, because of suspected H1N1 virus, Agriculture Minister Gerry Ritz complained to parliament that China was "operating outside of sound science," and Canada might take the matter to the World Trade Organization.[71] Harper's first fisheries minister, Loyola Hearn, said his decision to reopen Newfoundland's northern cod fishery was based on sound science, but fisheries scientists said the move would stunt the growth of future populations of the fish — junk science, presumably.[72] And a later fisheries minister, Gail Shea, wanted to open up fisheries in the North as Arctic ice melts. The Canadian government was working with the other Arctic Ocean coastal states, she announced, "to determine, on the basis of sound science, the next steps regarding fisheries in the North."[73]

If sound science is ubiquitous, so is junk science, which the *Oxford Advanced Learner's Dictionary* defines as "ideas and theories that seem to be well researched and scientific but in fact have little evidence to support them."[74] At first, junk science was used correctly. A 1988 study by the George C. Marshall Institute — copiously funded by ExxonMobil, it was later discovered — claims the earth's temperature is driven by sunspot activity, and the twenty-first century will be colder than the twentieth. Jerry Mahlman of the U.S. National Oceanic and Atmospheric Administration called the study "noisy, junk science."[75] The first use of the phrase — in the TASSC–Philip Morris sense — in Canadian newspapers was a 1994 piece by Terence Corcoran, just as TASSC was ramping up its operations. Corcoran, then writing for the *Globe and Mail*, attacked a water-quality report by the International Joint Commission outlining threats to Great Lakes water quality and calling for greater regulation of discharges

into the lakes. Such findings are based on "attention-grabbing
. . . scaremongering" junk science, Corcoran harrumphed,[76] as
he commenced his crusade to ferret out this scaremongering
wherever it occurred. But it wasn't until Conrad Black launched
the *National Post* and brought Corcoran in to run the business
section, that junk science leapt to the forefront. Media mentions
tripled between 1998 and 1999, the first full year of *National Post*
publication. In the years since, the *Post* has been the source of 39
per cent of the nearly 1,400 mentions of junk science in major
Canadian newspapers.[77]

One reason for the big jump in mentions was Corcoran's
launch of Junk-Science Week to "examine some of the issues
surrounding the spread of junk science as a vehicle for spooking
people into believing that their food, environment and virtually every man-made product pose health and environmental
risks."[78] Corcoran was still at it in 2013, celebrating the paper's
fifteenth annual Junk-Science Week issue. His definition of
junk science had shifted somewhat; junk science "occurs when
scientific facts are distorted, risk is exaggerated and the science
adapted and warped by politics and ideology to serve another
agenda."[79] During this week, the paper:

- Attacked studies demonstrating significant
  statistical correlations between increased numbers
  of women on corporate boards and stronger
  financial performance, claiming these studies draw
  on fallacies of statistical significance to promote a
  political objective;
- Attacked the position that polar-bear populations
  are declining because of reduced sea ice due to
  global warming, claiming biologists cannot tell if
  this is really happening;
- Attacked biodiversity as a "happy anti-hunting

ground for those who oppose development, seek
to bring the corporate sector to heel, or simply like
scaring schoolchildren";

- Attacked the Intergovernmental Panel on Climate
Change for ignoring actual observations in its
"expensive climate modelling enterprise" as part of
the "'humans-cause-everything-bad-that-happens'
juggernaut";

- Attacked the Millennium Alliance for Humanity
and the Biosphere for its report arguing that "the
evidence that humans are damaging their ecological
life-support systems is overwhelming." This claim,
the *Post* argues, sees "a world in which mankind is a
cancer that can only be kept in check by the tyranny
of big government";

- Attacked the claim that the Harper government
is muzzling its scientists, because some of these
"scientists really want . . . to use their department . . .
and all the profile and credibility attached to it, as
a platform to leverage their political or ideological
agenda" (the piece was written by Macdonald–
Laurier's Philip Cross).[80]

With the Harper government lauding sound science and the
National Post trashing junk science, the scientific quest to better
understand our world and society was being undermined. How
can we trust science to help us make good policy decisions if it's
driven by politics and ideology?

***

Hayek's knowledge problem infused many Harper initiatives. Why
use scientific knowledge to guide policy, when local, individual

knowledge is more accurate, especially when it can be tied to prices and markets? Harper took this approach when he created the Red Tape Reduction Commission in 2011 "to identify irritants to business stemming from federal regulatory requirements" that "have a clear detrimental effect on growth, competitiveness, and innovation." At the same time, the commission was supposed to ensure "that the environment and the health and safety of Canadians are not compromised in the process,"[81] suggesting a role for scientific research. No commission members, though, had expertise on health, safety, or environmental matters; instead they were rural Conservative MPs or owners of small or medium-sized businesses in the rail-line construction, trucking, mechanical-contracting, uniform-manufacturing, and industrial-equipment industries. Clearly they had a vested interest in getting rid of "detrimental" regulation. Consideration of health, safety, and environmental factors as inputs to decisions about regulatory oversight was missing by design. Scientific knowledge would not be consulted in the exercise to reduce red tape.

Was Harper following another Frank Luntz playbook, one written in 2010 to help derail American financial regulatory reform? Luntz's seventeen-page memo, "The Language of Financial Reform," urges Republicans to reject the final legislative product, because it is filled with bank bailouts, lobbyist loopholes, and additional layers of complicated government bureaucracy.[82] Red tape, along with accountability and bloated bureaucracy, are among the eighteen terms to use in this ultimately successful exercise to fend off regulation of the financial industry. New laws just add layers of red tape, regulations, and bureaucracy,[83] is the argument Luntz told opponents of financial reform to repeat. By framing regulation as red tape and layers of bureaucracy, Luntz, Harper, and their allies diverted attention away from the true purpose of regulation — public oversight. The fact that governments create regulations to protect the environment and public health and safety gets lost in the shuffle.

Harper's Red Tape Reduction Commission was headed by the minister of state for small business and tourism, Rob Moore, and included Maxime Bernier, a founder of the Montreal Economic Institute and a strident anti-regulation crusader. Catherine Swift, president of the Canadian Federation of Independent Business (CFIB) — a public-relations and lobbying organization for small-business owners — was also on the commission, and seemed to be the guiding light behind the commission's work. Harper timed the announcement of the commission to coincide with CFIB's Red Tape Awareness Week, the goal of which is to make the public aware that regulation "is a huge hidden tax that frustrates entrepreneurship," as Laura Jones, CFIB's vice-president for Western Canada, explained in a *Globe and Mail* interview.[84] Jones is a former director of regulatory studies (i.e., deregulation) at the Fraser Institute. With such a pro-business agenda, concerns about health and safety and environmental factors in government decisions to impose and enforce regulations — junk science? — were unwelcome.

Commissioner Gord Peters, who owns Cando Contracting in Brandon, Manitoba, provides a case in point. Six months before Harper created the commission, Peters's company built a rail-car storage yard on Canadian National right-of-way outside Edmonton to store 225 Imperial Oil petroleum tank cars. According to residents who live nearby, it is a classic exercise in skirting and ignoring government regulations. They claim the yard was built without notifying them. No environmental or socio-economic impact assessments were undertaken. Nor were there any opportunities for residents to comment on the project, because it is governed by federal regulations and does not require approval. The federal regulations, though, do not permit rail yards within three hundred metres of homes. This yard is 68 and 163 metres from the closest houses, while two protected wildlife-conserva-tion areas are about thirty metres away. Residents say they are stuck with the noise, smell, health and visual impacts, devalued properties, and ruined quality of life. Many laws, policies, and guidelines "have been breached in the building and operation of this rail yard," they wrote on their Railroaded blog.[85] Red tape didn't hold up this project.

Gord Peters and his fellow commissioners received 2,300 ideas "about red tape irritants that get in the way of business pro-ductivity."[86] They fashioned a report proposing fifteen systemic changes, such as a "one-for-one" rule, which requires regulators either to remove a regulation each time they introduce a new regulation with an administrative burden, or else cut adminis-trative costs from existing regulations equal to additional costs due to new or amended regulations. The rule says nothing about the relative importance of the regulations. The commission pro-posed ninety changes to specific departmental regulations. Some of these are:

- Health Canada should consult with food manufacturers about regulations, policies, and standards;
- Fisheries and Oceans Canada should work with provinces and the aquaculture industry to minimize the number of applications for permits, authorizations, and licences;
- The Canadian Food Inspection Agency should "modernize" and "streamline" its operations, such as introducing new regulatory approaches for low-risk fertilizers;
- Transport Canada should work to reduce the number of projects subject to the *Navigable Waters Transportation Act*.[87]

The commission then packed up and went home. Later in the year, the Treasury Board released its Red Tape Reduction Action Plan, detailing the government's enthusiastic support for virtually all commission recommendations.[88] At the beginning of the 2013 Red Tape Awareness Week, Treasury Board president Tony Clement was in Toronto to announce the government's first modest moves to cut red tape.[89] The next day, CFIB released its Red Tape Report Card, awarding the federal government a B+ for reforming the regulatory weight on Canadian small businesses, an improvement over 2012's B- and 2011's C+. "The Prime Minister and his government 'get' this issue, and deserve credit for their work that will make Canada more competitive in the long run," Laura Jones enthused.[90] The federal government maintained its B+ rating in 2014.

*　*　*

A common theme links Harper's actions on the long-form census, his budgets, his shuttering of scientific activities, and his Red Tape Reduction Action Plan. It's not simply about shrinking government, but redefining its role. The census initiative is intended to reduce government's — or anyone else's — ability to make decisions based on centralized knowledge — the data, information, and statistics collected and processed by Statistics Canada. Harper's budgets are not just about downsizing — although they do that — but seem to be deliberate attempts to obliterate the use of research and evidence as the basis for making policy decisions and to handicap those who might use scientific facts and evidence to challenge government policies. The deregulation initiative is intended to shrink centralized oversight of the market. The Harper government doesn't want to know about problems in society unless they impact the economy or have direct political consequences for the government or the party. Without such knowledge, the problems — poverty, housing conditions, pollution, the ruined quality of life for Gord Peters's rail-yard neighbours — may as well not exist, at least for the government. It's up to the market to decide if there's a problem and if there's a profitable solution to the problem. Harper doesn't need scientists or criminologists to tell him what to do. They're just purveyors of junk science, who give advice that runs counter to the new role. Nor should government second-guess how businesses intend to provide their goods and services. As Hayek warned, centralized government can never make the best decisions, because it can't amass and digest all the necessary information, as can the market with its dispersed information-processing capacity. Knowledge of local conditions coordinated by the price system will always produce results superior to those of centralized knowledge and political agendas.

The changes envisioned by Stephen Harper and the Mont Pelerin Society and its associated networks are not as dramatic as the bloody and protracted transformation of society from feudalism to capitalism. After all, Keynesianism, social democracy, and neo-liberalism are variants of capitalism. But the changes will nonetheless have profound impacts on how we organize our world. It will be a long journey indeed to create a society in which science plays little role in shaping public policy. Many of Harper's changes can be undone. The long-form census can be reinstated, policy networks reconstituted, and funding for scientific research re-established. But the credibility of scientific knowledge is on the table for our consideration, and some of us are interested. Under Harperism, scientific knowledge and planning will have to compete with local knowledge and the market for predominance. Science would certainly win today. But tomorrow?

7

DENY INCOME INEQUALITY

The Fraser Institute released its 2011 *Economic Freedom of the World* (EFW) index at a gala dinner at Hong Kong's Harbour Grand Hotel, with partner Lion Rock Institute, a local neo-liberal think tank. The news was not earth-shattering for the assembled dignitaries and tycoons. Hong Kong was judged the freest economy in the world for the fifteenth consecutive year, driven by its low level of government spending, smallest state-backed company sector, and lowest marginal tax rates. Hong Kong chief executive Donald Tsang was full of self-congratulations, but all was not well, economic-freedom-wise, in the Special Administrative Region (SAR). The Fraser Institute issued a warning to Tsang and his administration, which had recently introduced minimum-wage and competition laws, developments anathema to the neo-liberal thought collective. "Hong Kong's score is almost certain to drop in the future," Fred McMahon, the Fraser Institute's vice-president of research, predicted.[1] He cautioned that "Hong Kong will remain a relatively free economy, but with these two pieces of legislation, it well might be that Hong Kong will lose its No. 1 position."

The Hong Kong government brought in the legislation to address — at least minimally — another feature of life in the free-market paradise. There's no question economic freedom has been good for some — Hong Kong boasts more billionaires per capita than any other jurisdiction. But it fails many residents. The Hong Kong SAR has the highest level of income inequality in the developed world, and the gap increased under Tsang's leadership (2005–2012). In the first decade of the twenty-first century, income grew 60 per cent for the city's top 10 per cent of earners and dropped 20 per cent for those in the bottom 10 per cent. The Gini coefficient measures inequality from 0 (all incomes equal) to 1 (one person earning all income) in an economy. Hong Kong's Gini coefficient rose from 0.525 in 2001 to 0.537 in 2011.[2] To respond to such growing disparity and to the outcry that accompanied it, Tsang brought in a minimum-wage law that was set low, but did raise salaries in the poorly paying security, cleaning, and hospitality industries.[3] For those at the top, the government passed a competition law that would make anti-competitive behaviour — price-fixing and agreements to limit production — illegal. Hong Kong was the last developed economy to introduce such a law,[4] one reason, perhaps, for the city's stellar performance on the economic-freedom rankings.

Fred McMahon didn't like it. "The minimum-wage law interferes with voluntary arrangements between hirers and employees," he protested, ignoring how voluntary the arrangements between wealthy, powerful employers and desperately poor, powerless workers could really be. As for the competition law, it "has the potential to limit economic freedom."[5] The Heritage Foundation, the leading American neo-liberal think tank, had put its own spin on these unwelcome developments when it issued its economic-freedom rankings eight months earlier.

Hong Kong still topped its charts, but the minimum-wage law had "moved Hong Kong modestly in the direction of a more bureaucratic and politicized economy."[6] For its part, the *South China Morning Post* called the minimum-wage law "a dent in our crown."[7]

Achieving a high ranking on the Fraser Institute's economic-freedom index, while also experiencing a high level of income inequality (II), is not an aberration found just in Hong Kong. Singapore always ranks second on the index, and its II is second only to that of Hong Kong.[8] The most comprehensive studies on II are done by the Organisation for Economic Co-operation and Development (OECD), the Paris-based organization of thirty-four highly developed and developing countries. (Hong Kong and Singapore are not members.) The OECD's landmark 2011 study, *Divided We Stand: Why Inequality Keeps Rising*, confirms that inequality has increased dramatically in most OECD countries over the past thirty years.[9] OECD secretary-general Angel Gurria seemed troubled by the dire situation facing the developed world. "Income inequality in OECD countries is at its highest level for the past half century," he reported at OECD headquarters.[10] "The average income of the richest 10 per cent of the population is about nine times that of the poorest 10 per cent across the OECD, up from seven times twenty-five years ago." The OECD defines the income gap as the ratio of average income of the bottom 10 per cent to average income of the top 10 per cent,[11] providing a somewhat different measure than the Gini coefficient.

The average II for OECD countries masks huge differences among member nations. The gap between rich and poor widened in the early eighties in the United Kingdom and the United States, the countries where neo-liberalism first took root under Margaret Thatcher and Ronald Reagan. By the late eighties, inequality became widespread, as neo-liberalism spread to other

European countries and to the OECD bureaucracy itself.[12] Even in traditionally egalitarian countries, such as Denmark, Norway, Finland, and Sweden — countries that still perform well on the EFW index — the gap between rich and poor expanded from five to one in the 1980s to six to one in the late 2000s. It's ten to one in EFW leaders New Zealand, Australia, Canada, and the United Kingdom, and fourteen to one in the United States.[13] Hong Kong and Singapore would come in at about thirty to one. Canada's II grew 13 per cent between 1980 and 2009. As measured by the Gini coefficient (using income after taxes and government transfers), inequality was moderate during the Mulroney years of the eighties and early nineties, reaching a low of 0.281 in 1989. It took off in the mid-nineties, after the Canada–U.S. Free Trade Agreement began to bite, Liberal finance minister Paul Martin brought down his 1995 budget that slashed federal transfers for social programs (and launched Canada's climb up the EFW ranks), and provincial governments cut social assistance and other benefits. The Gini plateaued at 0.32 in 2000, and remained there.[14]

What causes inequality? One set of factors that leaps to the forefront of OECD research is "labour market institutions, policies, and regulations."[15] Trends such as declining union membership, minimum wages not keeping up with inflation, weakening employment-protection laws, and decreasing unemployment-benefit duration and generosity, have all contributed to increasing divergence in wages over the past thirty years. (These trends, not coincidentally, boost a country's ranking on the EFW index.) The OECD estimates that changes in these factors account for 44 per cent of increased II across all OECD countries between the early 1980s and the late 2000s.[16]

In Canada, as in other OECD countries, declining minimum-wage laws and union membership, as Chapter 3 documents, have increased inequality. Countries with high minimum wages, such as many European countries, tend to have less inequality than

Canada. However, most provinces boosted minimum wages after the 2008 economic meltdown, contributing to large wage increases for men and women at the lower end of the wage pyramid,[17] and preventing inequality from rising even further. Unions also affect the wage structure. A 2004 study of the relationship between unions and wage inequality in Canada, the United States, and the United Kingdom over two to three decades suggests that unionization declined in all three countries, with the greatest drop occurring in the U.K. and the smallest in Canada. At the same time, wage inequality rose in all three countries, with the largest rise in the U.K. and the smallest in Canada. The study concludes that "unions systematically reduce the variance of wages for men in all three countries" and reinforces the point that the correlation is not coincidental.[18]

A second set of factors that increase inequality is what the OECD calls "technological progress," although this reveals an organizational bias. What is progress?[19] Nonetheless, the OECD estimates that business spending on research and development accounts for about 33 per cent of increased II.[20] Tech change — the increasing adoption of information and communication technologies — increases inequality, because the demand for well-educated workers pulls up their wages and reduces the demand for the less-skilled. At the same time, though, tech change often simply means the adoption of computers in the workplace, which are especially suited to "carrying out 'routine tasks' based on well-defined rules and procedures."[21] These jobs do not command high wages, and are easily sent offshore to countries with low wages. They are located in the middle of the wage-distribution pyramid, "resulting in a 'polarization' of the workforce, with fewer jobs paying a 'middle-class wage' and greater employment at the top and bottom of the distribution."[22]

In contrast to these trends, one factor that reduces inequality significantly is a country's taxation and transfer system. How progressive is the tax system? What benefits and social programs redistribute income to those less well off? How generous are they? In all countries in the OECD study, in the late 2000s taxes and transfers reduced inequality by about one-quarter, being higher in Nordic countries and lower in the United States and Switzerland.[23] Prior to the mid-nineties, Canada's tax and benefit system was as effective in stabilizing inequality as that in the Nordic countries, but redistribution's impact has declined since then, as federal and provincial governments cut social transfers to lower earners and taxes on higher earners,[24] boosting Canada's EFW ranking — but ratcheting up inequality.

One problem with the Gini coefficient is that it doesn't do a good job of explaining changes at the extremes, including the top 1 per cent of earners, because it "places disproportionate weight on movements in inequality in the centre of the distribution and less at the extreme ends."[25] The Occupy movement, with its slogan "We are the 99 per cent," focused attention on the top-earning 1 per cent, exposing adulation of the rich in the pages of *Forbes*, *Canadian Business*, and the corporate press to the scorn and critical glare of the public sphere. In Canada, the top 1 per cent brought in 8 per cent of total income in the late seventies. By 2009, the top income share nearly doubled, to 14 per cent.[26] An analysis by the Canadian Centre for Policy Alternatives (CCPA) and the Edmonton-based Parkland Institute, two progressive think tanks, reveals how great the disparity has become. Using new Statistics Canada data, the organizations calculated that, in 2010, the richest 1 per cent of Canadians made an average of $180,000 more than it did in 1982 (adjusted for inflation). The results for major cities were even more dramatic. In Vancouver, the top 1 per cent saw its pay increase by $189,000, while the bottom 90 per cent actually lost money over the twenty-eight-year period, dropping by $4,300. Not surprisingly, Calgary led the field as the most unequal city in Canada. The top 1 per cent of Calgarians experienced a phenomenal $570,000 increase since 1982, while the bottom 90 per cent saw an increase of just $2,000.[27] These astounding gains are explained mainly by the fact that the 1 per cent increased its share of income growth after each recession. In the most recent growth spurt (2009–10), the 1 per cent captured 28.2 per cent of income growth, while the bottom 50 per cent took home just 3.0 per cent of the new income.[28]

Inequality seems here to stay, perhaps because of media reluctance to discuss the issue — except to deny its importance. The CCPA–Parkland study was reported only in Postmedia Network's two Alberta papers, a short 287-word article in the *Edmonton Journal*, and a longer piece in the *Calgary Herald* that was followed the next day with an editorial attacking the study.[29] The *Globe and Mail* ignored this study and commented instead on the Statistics Canada report that provided the data. Under the provocative headline "Hug the 1 per cent,"[30] the *Globe's* editorial board — whose employer is Canada's wealthiest family, the Thomsons — applauded the 1 per cent for contributing 21.2 per cent of federal and provincial income tax while earning just 10.6 per cent of the country's income (a low estimate). The Occupy movement failed, the editorial argued, because "the top 1 per cent of earners is not really a problem in Canada." These good folk are "doing their part to pay" for reducing child poverty and creating good schools. This claim is deceptive, because the *Globe* ignores all other sources of taxation. (Even the Fraser Institute doesn't ignore these when it does its calculations for tax-freedom day.) An earlier CCPA study tabulated all taxes and charges — sales, corporate, CPP premiums, EI premiums, property tax, and other provincial taxes and fees — and found that, in 2005, the bottom 10 per cent of earners paid a combined rate of 30.7 per cent, while the top 1 per cent paid slightly less, 30.5 per cent.[31]

***

Writing in 1960, at the height of the Keynesian era that was propelled by principles abhorrent to him, Friedrich Hayek argued that inequality is essential for economic progress. "The rapid economic advance that we have come to expect seems in a large measure to be the result of this inequality and to be impossible without it," Hayek observed in *The Constitution of Liberty*. Progress and growth are not possible without inequality. "Progress at such a fast rate cannot proceed on a uniform front but must take place in echelon fashion, with some far ahead of the rest."[32] In contrast to what socialists believe, rich capitalists are not exploiting anyone. In fact, they are in the front echelons, leading the way so the poor can follow behind. "A large part of the expenditure of the rich, though not intended for that end, thus serves to defray the cost of the experimentation with the new things that, as a result, can later be made available to the poor."[33] The relatively poor can have a car or a refrigerator or take an airplane trip "at the cost of a reasonable part of their income" because in the past "others with larger incomes were able to spend on what was then a luxury. The path of advance is greatly eased by the fact that it has been trodden before. It is because scouts have found the goal that the road can be built for the less lucky or less energetic."[34] It was a spirited defence of wealth.

For Hayek, liberty depends fundamentally on equality before the law. This is the only kind of equality he accepts, because other forms — equality of treatment, or outcome, or even opportunity — will eventually destroy liberty. In fact, he writes, "liberty . . . is bound to produce inequality in many respects . . . if the result of individual liberty did not demonstrate that some manners of living are more successful than others, much of the case for it would van-ish."[35] Consequently, Hayek asserts, we must live with inequality, because government intervention to reduce it will make things worse. "At any given moment we could improve the position of the poorest by giving them what we took from the wealthy. But, while such an equalizing of the positions in the column of progress would temporarily quicken the closing-up of the ranks, it would, before long, slow down the movement of the whole and in the long run hold back those in the rear."[36] Hayek tries to prove this point by referring to recent (i.e., pre-1960) European experience. Rich societies, such as the advanced welfare states of Great Britain and Scandinavia, "have become static, if not stagnant," he argues, because of their "egalitarian policies."[37] He contrasts the declining performance of these countries with dynamic and progressive countries like West Germany, Belgium, and Italy. Hayek gets this quite wrong though. Many Scandinavian countries, for instance, were able to advance economically while maintaining their egalitarian policies. Italy, with paltry social programs, fell behind.

By 1960, the demand for social justice was in the air, and Hayek was appalled. The idea "that all must be assured an equal start and the same prospects," Hayek saw as "the opposite of freedom," and questioned the motivations of the promoters. "When we inquire into the justification of these demands, we find that they rest on the discontent that the success of some people often produces in those that are less successful, or, to put it bluntly, on envy," he writes, launching an attack on the critique of inequality as "the politics of envy." "The modern tendency to gratify this passion and to disguise it in the respectable garment of social justice is developing into a serious threat to freedom."[38] Such ideas moved from the fringe to the mainstream after they were given the seal of approval by Britain's newly elected Conservative Party leader Margaret Thatcher, a Hayek disciple. Inequality soon ratcheted up to unprecedented levels in the United Kingdom.

***

With inequality as a core tenet of the neo-liberal project — inequality is crucial for an efficiently operating market — it's not surprising the thought collective and its support groups went to great lengths to obscure the relationship after the 2009 publication of *The Spirit Level: Why Equality is Better for Everyone*. British epidemiologists Richard Wilkinson and Kate Pickett link income inequality to a variety of health and social problems across the rich countries of the OECD and the states of the United States. They develop an index of health and social problems for each country and state. It combines a variety of factors: level of trust, mental illness, life expectancy, obesity, children's educational performance, teenage births, homicides, imprisonment rates, and social mobility (the Y-axis). They then match the index against the level of income inequality in the country or state (the X-axis). The result is a striking graph, rising from low income inequality/better index of health and social problems on the lower left, to high income inequality/worse index of health and social problems on the upper right. Clustered at the lower end are Scandinavian and some other European countries; in the middle are Canada, Spain, France, and Ireland; tending to the upper end are Australia, New Zealand, the United Kingdom, and Portugal. The United States is in a category of its own, with the worst ranking for health and social problems and the highest income inequality.[39] (Hong Kong and Singapore are not included in the study.)

It didn't take long for attacks on the epidemiologists to begin. It was a neo-liberal slugfest. Most skirmishes occurred in the U.K., where Wilkinson and Pickett are based. Emanating from seemingly disparate quarters and within a few days of each other, the attacks seemed coordinated, although Christopher Snowdon, who participated in many of the sorties, assures his readers "it was a coincidence."[40] Snowdon describes himself as "an independent writer and researcher," but he's also director of "lifestyle economics" at the Institute of Economic Affairs, the think tank set up by Antony Fisher in the mid-1950s at Friedrich Hayek's urging.

The Taxpayers' Alliance (TA), which campaigns for lower taxes and lower spending, and which is funded by wealthy Conservative donors,[41] launched the first missive. It narrowed its target to one correlation in the book — life expectancy and income inequality — and discovered it is "at best so flimsy that it disappears under the slightest scrutiny."[42] This study was undertaken by researchers at Captus, a neo-liberal think tank in Sweden. The authors are also officers in the Swedish Taxpayers' Association, which espouses the same goals as TA. The following day, the Policy Exchange, a neo-liberal think tank based in London, released its report. This was written by researcher Peter Saunders, who had recently returned to England from his position as social research director at the Centre for Independent Studies, which was modelled on the Institute of Economic Affairs. Saunders worries that *The Spirit Level* "threatens to contaminate an important area of political debate with wonky statistics and spurious correlations."[43] He concludes that his "careful evaluation and analysis shows that very little of Wilkinson and Pickett's statistical evidence actually stands up, and their causal argument is full of holes."[44] The day after that, Snowdon and the Captus researchers blasted the book in the pages of the *Wall Street Journal*. Their message is that the book's "conclusion sounds promising to socialist ideologues, but finds little support in the scientific literature,"[45] but they don't back up this charge. Later, through the neo-liberal Democracy Institute based in London and Washington, D.C., Snowdon published his own book, *The Spirit Level Delusion*, which makes similar attacks. Snowdon and Saunders co-wrote a defence of their attacks in *The Guardian*.[46] Wilkinson and Pickett responded to every barb thrown their way on the website of The Equality Trust, a non-profit website set up "to educate and campaign on the benefits of a more equal society,"[47] and as a chapter in the paperback edition of the book. But doubt had been cast on the veracity of *The Spirit Level*, at least in the U.K.

***

Long before *The Spirit Level* appeared on the scene, neo-liberals set out to challenge the idea that poverty is widespread in rich countries. In 1992, just as inequality in Canada was set to take off, the Fraser Institute published a study by economist Chris Sarlo of Nipissing University in North Bay, Ontario. Sarlo attacks Statistics Canada's use of the low-income cut-off (LICO) as the measure for determining the poverty line. StatsCan defines LICO as "an income threshold below which a family will likely devote a larger share of its income on the necessities of food, shelter and clothing than the average family."[48] Sarlo, in contrast, developed a basket of basic necessities that turned out to cost about half of StatsCan's LICO. Someone is poor, Sarlo says, if they can "afford, at best, only the basic physical necessities (food, shelter, clothing, health care, personal hygiene, transportation, telephone and other household necessities) at a standard of quality considered minimally decent in the community." He rejects the inclusion of amenities such as, but "not limited to, color TVs, VCRs, alcohol, tobacco, recreation equipment and fees, and a one-week vacation."[49] Nor does he demonstrate interest in issues such as reduced educational opportunities or poorer health status for low-income Canadians. StatsCan estimated that, in 1992, 3.8-million Canadians spent more than 56 per cent of their incomes on food, clothing, and shelter. In contrast, Sarlo estimates that fewer than one million Canadians lived below his poverty line.

His report was controversial — the *Edmonton Journal* claimed his definition of poverty was "indeed applicable — by Third World standards"[50] — but it received widespread coverage, including front-page stories in the *Globe and Mail* and *Vancouver Sun*.[51] His study even caught the eye of a young Stephen Harper, then senior policy adviser to the Reform Party. "There's absolutely no doubt that there's an agenda in some circles to

maximize poverty as an issue," Harper said. "There is an element of self-interest in the way that some social agencies and
professions evaluate our social problems. They're talking about
income inequality. But the public has never thought of poverty
in relative terms, and they [sic] would be shocked to find out
that that is how poverty has been defined by policy-makers for a
long time."[52] It was an early indication of Harper's contempt for
the way StatsCan collects and analyzes data and how advocacy
groups use it, as Chapter 6 explains.

Sarlo repeated his study in 1996. This time the LICO for a
family of four was $30,000, while Sarlo's poverty line was half
that — $15,400. Instead of a LICO-based poverty rate of 17.6
per cent, the Fraser Institute's rate was 3.3 per cent, hardly anything worth worrying about.[53] Andrew Coyne, recently brought
into Southam News by Conrad Black, joined the fray, repeating
Sarlo's message frequently over the next few years: "Poverty
Levels Will Remain in Doubt as Long as Statisticians Use a
Moving Target," "Statistics Show the Poverty Rate Is an Elusive
Creature," "Income Inequality Is Not the Same as Poverty: Poor
Canadians Only Relatively Deprived," "A Better Measure of Poverty," "A Tisket, a Tasket, a Basic Needs Basket," ran the Coyne
headlines.[54] Through such repetition, Coyne helped establish
the frame that the definition of poverty is controversial. The
Fraser Institute produced even more Sarlo studies in 2001, 2006,
and 2008. By 2006, Sarlo's basic-needs definition of poverty was
accepted as a legitimate contender for consideration by policy-
makers. The real level of poverty in Canada is very low according
to Sarlo, and the LICO measures inequality, not poverty — a
point Coyne hammered home.

The definition of poverty had been blurred — was it poverty
or was it inequality? Now it was time to do the same for inequality. Just as the basic-needs basket confused our understanding of
poverty, so the concept of income mobility would be exploited

to confuse our understanding of inequality. This campaign kicked off in the U.S. in the early nineties, after the Reagan years blew open the gap between rich and poor. The Gini coefficient barely budged between 1967, the first year it was fully measured (0.358), and 1980 (0.365). In 1990, after the Reagan era, it soared to 0.396[55] and needed defending. Glenn Hubbard, a Columbia University economist, who would later chair George W. Bush's Council of Economic Advisers, was a senior Treasury Department official in the George H.W. Bush administration. Hubbard was not a Mont Pelerin Society member, but, as a fellow at the Hoover Institution and a visiting scholar at the American Enterprise Institute, he was certainly a fellow-traveller. Hubbard was the author of a 1992 study purporting to deny the income gap was growing. Significant upward mobility during the Reagan years made inequality irrelevant, the study claimed.[56] Eighty-six per cent of individuals who started in the bottom quintile in 1979 had moved out by 1988. Like a Fraser Institute study twenty years later, Hubbard compared individuals in the sample, not with each other, but with the larger population. More individuals moved up the income scale than down, because the bottom ranks were always being replenished with younger wage earners. And like the Fraser Institute study would do, Hubbard "treated the normal tendency of earnings to rise with age as representing social mobility," liberal economist Paul Krugman noted in a highly cited critique.[57] *Washington Post* writer Steven Mufson drove this point home. He asked readers to "consider the advancement of the student who in 1979 spent part of his last year of college working for a newspaper for $5 an hour. By 1988, firmly established as a journalist, he could earn as much in a day as he did in a week nine years earlier."[58] As Hubbard would have it, Mufson wrote, this person "clawed his way out of 'poverty,' even though both his parents were professionals and he entered the job market with an elite college degree and no debts." But these criticisms were drowned out by the chorus of supporters in the media and think tanks.

Income mobility didn't cross the Canadian border until the Fraser Institute's most senior of senior fellows and former Reform MP, Herbert Grubel, one of the small handful of Canadian Mont Pelerin Society members, wrote about it shortly after Sarlo's 2006 study reinforced the message that the problem was inequality, not poverty. In a *Montreal Gazette* column, Grubel laid out the bait-and-switch strategy that would predominate in subsequent Fraser Institute work. He begins by referring to the "spate of news stories in recent months dealing with the suggestion the gap between the rich and the poor in Canada is at a 30-year high."[59] We shouldn't take these stories too seriously, he counters, because "claims like these make good headlines, but the cliché about the rich getting richer and the data supporting the claim are both highly misleading." He then switches tack. "At issue is the failure of this train of thought to consider income mobility — the extent to which the poor remain poor and remain in the 'poverty trap.'" Point made.

The Fraser Institute quietly developed its mobility-trumps-inequality theme over the next few years. A Conference Board of Canada (CBOC) report in September 2011 provoked the institute to respond. The CBOC, "hardly a bastion of far-left thinking," as the *Globe and Mail's* Jeffrey Simpson put it,[60] reported on the growing income inequalities in Canadian society after the OECD released its landmark study *Divided We Stand: Why Inequality Keeps Rising,* discussed earlier in this chapter. Inequality in Canada increased since the late eighties, the CBOC reported, as the richest quintile scooped up most of the increases in income. The poorest quintile did increase its average income modestly, the report noted, but the gap between rich and poor opened up dramatically over the period.[61] The Fraser Institute would have none of it, and lambasted the "hysteria" evident in media coverage of the CBOC report. Following Grubel's lead, it then shifted into bait-and-switch mode. "By examining the share of national income going to the 'richest 20%' and 'poorest 20%' of Canadians, the Conference Board continues to perpetuate the myth that most Canadians are born into, live, and die within certain income groups," the Fraser's Amala Karabegovic and Charles Lammam charged in the *National Post*. "But in reality, with some hard work, young Canadians can and will live better than their parents."[62] The institute authors didn't disclose just how much hard work would be necessary or where that work might be found.

The think tank must have decided it was time to do its own study on income mobility to counter the "hysteria." It followed the formula laid down by Hayek: package neo-liberal doctrine in "research" and deliver it to second-hand dealers in ideas in the media. The doctrine derives from the same source as the phrase "economic freedom trumps political freedom": Milton Friedman's 1962 polemic, *Capitalism and Freedom*. Friedman asks us to imagine "two societies that have the same distribution of annual income."[63] We have to imagine further that "in one there is great mobility and change so that the position of particular families in the income hierarchy varies widely from year to year." The other society, we are also asked to imagine, is rigid, and families stay in the same position year after year. This second society is clearly more unequal, Friedman proposes. The first society is driven by "competitive free-market capitalism." Its inequality, rather than being unhealthy, is "a sign of dynamic change, social mobility, equality of opportunity." Friedman's unequal-but-dynamic society was imaginary. The Fraser Institute set out to make it real by "proving" that inequality under capitalism is healthy.[64]

The institute had already made its position on inequality very clear. "Taking more money from successful Canadians and redistributing it to lower income Canadians will only decrease the incentives for lower income Canadians to become successful," institute staffers wrote in the *National Post* several years earlier.[65] Its study was released in November 2012 with major coverage from its most reliable second-hand dealer, the *National Post*, with an op-ed and front-page story. "Thankfully, the story of stagnating incomes in Canada is just that, a great fictional tale," Niels Veldhuis and Lammam write. "The reality is that most Canadians, including those initially in the poorest group, have experienced marked increases in their incomes over the past two decades."[66] It was Glenn Hubbard's study — flaws and all — all over again. The Fraser's study had no predictive value, because it didn't identify change in income mobility over time. So when Lammam told the *National Post*'s Kathryn Blaze Carlson that "where you are today is not where you're going to be in five, 10 or 20 years down the road,"[67] this may be true, but is not based on his study, which covers one specific time period and which could have been unique. The study contains little information to indicate whether social mobility is increasing or declining. But the fact that some — even many — individuals move from lower to higher income levels has little to do with the increase in inequality over the same period. If the gap is growing, then individuals in the lowest quintile in subsequent periods will have more difficulty moving up. The proper study would be to compare income mobility, say, between 1971–1991 and 1991–2011. The study does look at mobility over two five-year periods, 1997 to 2002 and 2003 to 2007, and reports that the results for the latter period "are virtually identical to those of the first five-year period." In fact, there is a slight downward trend in mobility in the two lowest quintiles in the latter period — 7 per cent fewer earners moved up — a trend that could have been explored.[68] Lammam provides one particularly misleading statistic in an effort to prove that "income inequality is actually on the wane." In 1990, the average income of people in the top 20 per cent was thirteen times that of the bottom 20 per cent, but nineteen years later, the people in the top 20 per cent were earning only twice as much as those who were initially in the bottom 20 per cent. It's an apples-and-oranges comparison. Those in higher brackets initially were likely already in their peak earning years, while those at the bottom were mostly just starting out, as Paul Krugman noted of the Hubbard study twenty years earlier.

The study has other problems. The researchers locate their investigation as a response to the Occupy movement, which re-energized the II debate. But the research doesn't mention the 1 per cent, or provide statistics relevant to it; instead it focuses on quintiles. The data set supplied to the Fraser Institute by Statistics Canada could have been segmented in a wide variety of ways,[69] but the think tank chose to utilize the least-revealing approach — quintiles. Even the OECD uses the more telling top-10-to-bottom-10-per-cent ratio. Of course the 1 per cent is part of the top 20 per cent, but it is very different in terms of wealth and income, a difference that is obscured.

The study claims that "too often, an underlying assumption in this debate is that low- and high-income Canadians are the same people year in and year out."[70] Because it doesn't indicate where the underlying assumption can be found, this claim is little more than a straw man that accuses the opposition of something it never claimed and then sets out to demolish the fabricated accusation, thus discrediting the opposition. Little information is provided on the detailed upward and downward mobility of individuals beyond their initial and final positions, ignoring possible income volatility. An individual might start in the fifth quintile and end up in the third nineteen years later, but which other quintiles did the individual pass through during that period? Was the change a slow and steady ascent, or was it volatile and unpredictable because the individual lost jobs, spent time on unemployment insurance, or took a series of temporary positions?

The study also takes a stab at what it calls absolute income, the average income earned by individuals through wages and salaries compared to those same individuals nineteen years later. This is the most dramatic number in the study. The income of a Canadian in the lowest quintile increased from $6,000 to $44,000 (in 2009 dollars), "an impressive 635-per-cent increase,"[71] the study boasts. But people making $6,000 a year — the average for the bottom 20 per cent — cannot be working full-time, as David Macdonald, senior economist at the CCPA, notes. They are "unemployed either forcibly (because they were laid off), voluntarily (students or parents home with children), or people working part-time."[72] Nor does the bottom 20 per cent include many seniors on low income who remained on low income, because they had to be alive nineteen years later to be included in the study. "It shouldn't come as a big surprise that someone who was a student in 1990 or who was unemployed is making more, sometimes much more, 20 years later," Macdonald writes.

Macdonald also raises some methodological shortcomings. The study looks only at wages and salaries for its measure of income, and excludes capital gains and dividends, which accrue mainly to the wealthy. The study does not deal with the significance of this additional income because it provides an average figure for all Canadians. Since most individuals in the bottom two or three quintiles likely collect little in the way of capital gains and dividends, providing a global average hides the importance of these forms of earnings for the rich, even though today's wealthy receive most of their income as wages and salaries. Similarly, the study ignores government transfers to individuals and families, such as the Canada Pension Plan, Old Age Security, the Guaranteed Income Supplement, social assistance, and

Employment Insurance, which provide a significant boost to the income of the lower quintiles, thus reducing inequality.[73]

Curiously, four years earlier the institute accused StatsCan of the same crime — ignoring government transfers — in a study that finds earnings for those in the lowest quintile declined by 20.6 per cent between 1980 and 2005. Not so, the think tank researchers argued then. When you include government transfers, the income of the poor actually increased (by 15.4 per cent). This analysis provides evidence for the importance of government programs to the well-being of lower-income Canadians, but the Fraser didn't draw this conclusion, preferring to focus instead on the "fantasy" of a "large and permanent underclass that is getting poorer."[74] It was government enhancing their well-being though, a point the institute didn't make.

By not looking at family income, since most people live in families, and by not including other sources of income for the well-off and the poor, the Fraser researchers provide a distorted and misleading picture of income mobility. As Paul Krugman noted twenty years earlier, nobody denies that income mobility exists. The question is, does it compensate for growing inequality? The work that started with Glenn Hubbard and continues with the Fraser Institute, renders the answer to that question elusive, just like the definition of poverty.

***

If income mobility didn't create enough confusion over the state of inequality, a second line of argument was pressed into service. This initiative came, not from figures in the neo-liberal establishment, but from the fringes of the Tea Party and right-wing Republicanism. Since the ranks of the lower quintiles are populated largely, but not exclusively, by young people, a discourse could be fashioned that blamed older people — an entire generation — for the predicament facing the young. American conservative blogger Michelle Malkin created the generational theft trope in a post in early 2009, after president-elect Barack Obama introduced his massive fiscal stimulus plan to attempt to save the economy from sliding into depression.

Titled the *American Recovery and Reinvestment Act*, Obama's legislation was intended to save jobs and create new ones. It would accomplish these goals by boosting spending on low-income workers and the unemployed, on infrastructure improvements, on education, on the prevention of teacher lay-offs, and on energy efficiency. Malkin didn't seem to think these were useful activities, because they weren't market-driven, so she renamed the act "The Generational Theft Act of 2009."[75] The stimulus — "Obama's prescription for economic pain" — was "useless in encouraging short-term growth, while ensuring anemic longer-term growth for the next decade (and beyond) at the expense of Obama's kids and my kids and yours," Malkin wrote. It was "more of the same old, same old mortgaging of our children's future for the sake of present political crisis management." She had deftly diverted attention from the real reason for the stimulus — preventing a major economic collapse that occurred because of the greed and corruption of Wall Street financiers — to a more nebulous discussion about our children's children, many of whom had not yet been born. Malkin transformed the victims of the financial meltdown — the millions of people who lost their jobs, homes, or life-savings — into criminals prepared to rob their grandchildren. Meanwhile, bankers slipped out the back door.

Such brilliant attention-diversion didn't go unnoticed in senior Republican ranks.[76] Within weeks House Republican leader John Boehner offered that the "hundreds of billions of dollars Washington is borrowing to finance this pork-barrel monstrosity will come from our children and grandchildren. This is not 'stimulus' — it's generational theft."[77] In the Senate, Tom Coburn of Oklahoma and John McCain of Arizona took up the cudgels. "The bill represents . . . the failed interventionist policies of the 1930s," Coburn complained. "As currently written, this bill represents the worst act of generational theft in our nation's history."[78] McCain brought generational theft to the audiences of CBS's *Face the Nation* and NBC's *Meet the Press*. He spoke about generational theft at the Heritage Foundation a month after that.[79] The folks at Heritage liked the idea so much they set out to write a book called *The Debt-Paying Generation*. Heritage didn't produce the book, but tried to turn "the debt-paying generation" into "a term that all Americans should become familiar with," as Dustin Siggins, a blogger with the conservative Tea Party Patriots, wrote. "It is the financial future of America, and not a pretty one at that."[80] Generational theft had arrived, Boomers became the target, and bankers were off the hook. Believers could even buy "Generational Theft" bumper stickers, T-shirts, aprons, hoodies, track suits, and infant bodysuits at Crusader Patriot store.[81]

Generational theft didn't carry the same urgency north of the border as it did in the United States, despite the efforts of McCain's 2008 vice-presidential running mate Sarah Palin, when she spoke to a sold-out crowd in Calgary in 2010 as part of the Fraser Institute's influential speakers' program. There she repeated the Tea Party message that the extent of the debt being incurred in America was "immoral generational theft."[82] It didn't catch on. Canadian political rhetoric isn't as hysterical as American, despite the efforts of Sun TV to ape the Fox News format of blind over-the-top partisanship. Nonetheless, generational conflict had to become an issue because Canada's income inequality, while not at American levels, had risen significantly over the previous decade. The generational-conflict frame had some heavy lifting to do here, too.

In Quebec, Eric Duhaime, avowed libertarian polemicist, *Sun* newspaper columnist, and co-founder of the Quebec Freedom Network, published a book titled *L'État Contre les Jeunes: Comment les Baby-Boomers ont Détourné le Système* (*The State Against the Young: How Baby-Boomers are Hijacking the System*). Duhaime, who attended Fraser Institute student programs in the nineties, wrote the book, he told a *Montreal Gazette* columnist, because he detected a growing problem of "generational inequity" in Quebec.[83] He "accuses Quebec's baby-boom generation of off-loading the cost of its own comfortable lifestyle on future generations." In a luncheon speech hosted by the Fraser Institute in Montreal, Duhaime approached Malkin–level rhetoric when he labelled Quebec's "irresponsible and insatiable spending" an "intergenerational holdup."

But it's in British Columbia where generational conflict achieved its greatest impact, thanks to a partnership between the *Vancouver Sun* and an academic at the University of British Columbia. Paul Kershaw, a professor of human early learning, was given a regular column by editorial-page editor and former Fraser Institute staffer, Fazil Mihlar, to "start a public dialogue about how we can distribute/invest tax dollars in a more equitable and efficient manner so that all Canadians can aim for the stars."[84] This is necessary, Mihlar explains, "because boomers are hogging a lot of public dollars with potentially disastrous consequences for society," and particularly for young families with children who "are being deprived of a chance at a good life." Boomers-versus-young-families-with-children replaced the 99-per-cent-versus-1-per-cent frame in the pages of the *Vancouver Sun*, whose editorial policy regarding the Occupy movement was hostile.[85]

The appearance of the column, just as the Occupy Wall Street movement was settling in to its Zuccotti Park digs in Lower Manhattan, seems more than coincidental. When Kershaw advocates for a new deal for young families — a national child-care strategy, more generous federally funded parental leave provisions — progressives agree. But when he engages in what Trent University history professor Robert Wright terms "silly pseudo-demography about competing generations," Kershaw diverts attention from the real issue — the growing gap between the rich and the rest — and advances, by diversion, the neo-liberal agenda.

A flaw in the generational-conflict frame, Wright argues, is that "the basic social unit . . . is not the birth cohort [but] the family . . . In most families generations are not at war [but] work together . . . Parents are supporting their children and even their grandchildren well into adulthood."[86] And families occupy all quintiles, from rich to poor, with the growing gap between them. At the bottom, some female boomer divorcees face a bleak future, as the number of "financially vulnerable older women in Canada is about to jump dramatically." Many boomer women are leaving the workforce to care for elderly parents and grand-children, evidence that social services, once underwritten by the state, are quietly being privatized within families. Nor are boom-ers spending their family fortunes and leaving crumbs for their children and grandchildren. Boomers are "keenly interested" in inheritance tax planning, Wright maintains, so they can give a leg up to their children.

It is true that government spending is biased towards older Canadians. Spending on health care goes disproportionately to the elderly, while government's modest tax benefits and spend-ing on child care is consumed by younger families. In contrast, though, Canada's long run of very low interest rates "amounts to a transfer of wealth from the old to the young," Bank of Canada governor Stephen Poloz claims.[87] As a result of such low interest rates, the investments of (older) Canadians produce poor returns, while younger Canadians benefit from inexpensive loans. Cheaper money keeps consumers buying and more workers on the job than might otherwise have been the case. Kershaw ignores this factor.

Kershaw wrote twenty-six columns hammering home his theme that the younger generation is being "squeezed" by the older one. His most supportive headline appeared, not in the *Sun*, but in the *Globe and Mail*, after his run of *Sun* columns ended: "Forget Occupy, the Real Divide is Generational."[88] This theme was fleshed out in a *Sun* piece titled "Movement Should Change Focus: Occupy Wall Street Zeros in on 'Fat Cats,' but This Thinking Overlooks Important Generational Realities."[89] This column appeared three days after Occupy Vancouver set up its Vancouver Art Gallery camp. Kershaw admits that "the richest 1 per cent of Canadians make 14 per cent of total income, and took home more than a third of the growth in incomes since 1998." But there is a problem, Kershaw warns. "'We're the 99 per cent' frames the issue as a select few fat cats gorging themselves on cream produced by many little mice churning the milk," he explains. "The story of Mouseland governed by cats is a metaphor that worked well for Tommy Douglas back in the day. It is less likely to move public opinion in Canada now," suggesting Canadians don't care as much about inequality as they used to. Kershaw continues: "Occupy Wall Street may signal a growing concern about inequity between the rich and the rest, but we can only address these pressures by tackling the intergenerational tension." Once again, Kershaw ignores the real causes of inequality, discussed earlier in this chapter, and sidesteps remedies such as re-establishing a progressive tax system in which corporations and individuals are taxed on their ability to pay or reinforcing the rights of workers to be represented by a union.

***

Despite multiple efforts to divert attention from inequality — obscuring the definition of poverty, focusing on income mobility or intergenerational conflict — pressure is mounting for governments to do something. In late 2013, the Roman Catholic Church's new pontiff, Pope Francis, issued his first apostolic exhortation, a kind of mission statement for his papacy. In the 224-page document, Francis pressed governments to stand up to the wealthy and regulate markets, because income inequality "eventually engenders a violence which recourse to arms cannot and never will be able to resolve," he said. "Money must serve, not rule."[90]

Barack Obama responded quickly. A week after the Pope's statement, Obama delivered a major speech to the Center for American Progress, a Washington-based think tank that supports Democratic centrists such as Bill Clinton and Obama himself. Titled "Remarks by the President on Income Mobility," the speech didn't seem to be about inequality.[91] But Obama wasn't resurrecting the Glenn Hubbard study of twenty years earlier, faulty logic and all. He acknowledged the Pope's eloquent speech and its references to inequality. He used the word "inequality" twenty-five times as he made the case that the mobility of the 1970s, when "the guy on the factory floor could picture his kid running the company some day . . . because of upward mobility," was long gone. Today, "a child born into the bottom 20 per cent has a less than 1-in-20 shot at making it to the top," Obama said. He then laid out an ambitious plan to lessen inequality: empower Americans with skills and education; empower workers, and ensure collective-bargaining laws are working as intended; raise minimum-wage laws; and support hard-hit communities, workers, and seniors with improved income-transfer programs. In typical centrist fashion he then undid much of this program by asserting that the U.S. had to "relentlessly push a growth agenda," while admitting this would not guarantee higher wages and incomes. Was this a nod to the neo-liberals? Obama focused on competitiveness and productivity — code words for cutting employment and wages — and recommended that corporate taxes need to be cut and regulations "streamlined."

At least Obama said something. Stephen Harper, in contrast, had nothing to say about the Pope's exhortation. In fact, there's no indication he's ever said anything about inequality. Instead, his minister of industry, James Moore, asked at a Vancouver event several weeks later if it's "always the government's job to be there to serve people their breakfast" in response to a discussion of British Columbia's burgeoning child poverty. "Is it my job to feed my neighbour's child? I don't think so," he responded.[92] Ironically, the Harper government may have contributed to this dire situation. Over his seven years as prime minister, Harper cut federal-government tax revenues to their lowest level in fifty years, constraining the government's ability to address inequality through taxation and transfer programs that go a long way to reduce inequality, as the OECD study discussed earlier demonstrates. Former Liberal staffer Eugene Lang estimates the cuts to be worth $45 billion a year in foregone revenue, or almost one-fifth of current spending on programs.[93] Friedrich Hayek's caution that government transfers to reduce inequality would impede economic freedom and block economic progress was being taken seriously in Stephen Harper's Canada.

Maintaining the Harper government's do-nothing approach to inequality, just before parliament adjourned for the eight-week Christmas 2013 recess, James Rajotte, chair of the House of Commons finance committee, tabled a report entitled "Income Inequality in Canada: An Overview." The Conservative majority had finally responded to a private member's motion of a year and a half earlier "to identify solutions to Canada's growing problem of income inequality."[94] The report, though, was little more than a reaffirmation of the status quo. Twenty of the twenty-four recommendations urged the federal government to continue doing what it was already doing: creating conditions for economic growth, helping First Nations build infrastructure, promoting skills training, keeping taxes low, encouraging youth to complete high school, creating a sustainable resource sector. Only four recommendations urged the government to do something new, and only two of these could be expected to have a positive impact on inequality: expand the Working Income Tax Benefit and boost early-childhood education. The other two recommendations could just as easily increase inequality: remove barriers to interprovincial trade and implement the *First Nations Property Ownership Act*, as Chapter 4 explains.

∗∗∗

Economic freedom is a core value in the neo-liberal pantheon, ranking above political freedom, which neo-liberals see as depending on economic freedom. But economic freedom inevitably leads to, and requires, inequality. From Hayek, to the Heritage Foundation, to the Fraser Institute, neo-liberals have considered inequality a fundamental prerequisite for the proper functioning of markets. Hayek's view that inequality is necessary for economic progress was outlined in his 1960 work, *The Constitution of Liberty*. The positive correlation between income inequality and higher ranking on the Economic Freedom of the World index suggests this is how today's neo-liberals see their world.

But inequality could be neo-liberalism's Achilles heel. When both the Pope and the President of the United States raise inequality, it becomes a salient political issue. Even in Canada, with the Conservatives lack of interest in the subject, inequality has risen up the political agenda, as indicated by mentions in major Canadian daily newspapers. In each of 2009 and 2010, income inequality was mentioned in just over sixty stories. In 2013, the number of mentions skyrocketed to 379, a six-fold increase.

Neo-liberals fear that governments will take measures to lessen inequality through political means, thus undermining economic freedom and moving neo-liberalism's Utopian dream of a society governed by market transactions farther away. But who in Canada is going to do something about it? Strengthening the tax-and-transfer system is the most direct way of reducing inequality. But given that all major Canadian political parties are neo-liberal-ish, not much is likely to change. Neither Liberals nor New Democrats have made inequality a major issue for their parties. The parties talk about the suffering middle class, but who will have the courage to propose significant divergences from the current direction? Who will recoup the $45 billion a year Harper carved from federal books, raise taxes on the rich and corporations, boost spending on health and social transfers, improve the fortunes of organized labour (although this is mainly a provincial responsibility), bring back high-paying jobs that were sent offshore to lower-pay jurisdictions or re-regulate the oil and gas industry? Until the narrative changes about why we have an economy, inequality is here to stay.

8

FASHION CANADA AS
A GREAT NATION

Beginning in March 2010, the some 170,000 immigrants who become Canadian citizens each year were required to learn their facts about Canada from a new citizenship guide.[1] The sixty-two-page *Discover Canada: The Rights and Responsibilities of Citizenship* was the culmination of a decade of concerted effort by a coalition of big business and conservative ideologues to remake Canada as a more traditional and compliant nation that favours military might and economic progress over peacekeeping and environmental protection.[2] The effort to remake our understanding of Canada did not yield results until Stephen Harper was installed as prime minister. It conformed with his plan to forge a permanent Conservative majority by imagining Canada as a "great nation," strong in its military and foreign-policy initiatives, forceful in its trade policies, confident on the international stage, unconditionally committed to defending the state of Israel as the outpost of Western values in a hostile land. Creating the narrative of a great nation populated by patriotic citizens is a priority for

Harper since he became prime minister and fashioned "The True North Strong and Free" theme on government websites. A great nation is a warrior nation: celebrating Canada's real and imagined military accomplishments continues non-stop under the Harper government. It is a key component of Harperism.

Most of Harper's attention is focused on the economy and his efforts to remove roadblocks from the market state, as earlier chapters argue. But to transform Canada into a conservative and Conservative nation, he needs to fashion a natural governing majority, and has exerted great efforts in this quest. He outlined his project to meld economic and social conservatives into a ruling majority in his talk to the seventh annual Civitas conference in Toronto in 2003,[3] as was described in the Introduction. Key to the success of his program is an incremental approach.

Discover Canada was the next increment. It replaced *A Look at Canada*, first published by the Chrétien government in 1997 and updated in 2005 by the Paul Martin government, which presented a more progressive, social-democratic view of the nation.[4] The picture of Canada painted in the new document would not be recognizable to Canadians who grew up in a country of peacekeepers, of equal rights and opportunities for all, of the cultural mosaic, of a country shaped by collective experiences and a respect for a social safety net. In answer to the question "What does citizenship mean?" the Chrétien–Martin guide includes "a commitment to social justice."[5] The Harper version doesn't contain this concept. The word "war" doesn't appear in the Chrétien–Martin guide, but is used fifty-five times in the Harper version. "All Canadians need to understand the enormity of sacrifices made by our men and women in uniform," Citizenship and Immigration Minister Jason Kenney declared when introducing *Discover Canada* on Remembrance Day, 2009. "You can't understand Canada without understanding our defining moments at Dieppe, at Juno Beach, at Vimy, at Passchendaele."[6]

In the new guide, the War of 1812 and the rebellions of 1837 and 1838 together earn over a page, the First World War and Remembrance Day, half a page each. The period between 1919 and 1939, which includes the 1920s boom, the Great Depression, and the birth of important social programs, is titled simply "Between the Wars," and is allocated a mere half-page, while the six years of the Second World War gets an entire page. Later in the guide, the Victoria Cross and its recipients merit a half-page.

In the Chrétien–Martin *A Look at Canada,* peace is one of four main democratic values. "We are proud of the fact that we are a peaceful nation and that we are accepted in many places around the world as peacekeepers," the booklet tells us.[7] "Peace" does appear seven times in *Discover Canada,* but four of these refer to the Peace Arch at Blaine, Washington, or the Peace Tower in Ottawa, while the other three occur in historical or legal contexts. The old guide contains two pages on "Protecting the environment — sustainable development." It says:

> *The Canadian government is committed to sustainable development. Economic growth is crucial for the future of Canada, but it cannot come at the expense of the environment. A healthy environment is important to the quality of life. We want our children to live in a country that is green and prosperous. Citizens must begin now to act in a responsible manner toward the environment.*[8]

The new guide doesn't contain the word "sustainable." The word "environment" is used nine times, but never in relation to environmental issues. There are no concerns about climate change or global warming in the fair "Dominion" (this word is used nineteen times in *Discover Canada,* but not at all in

A Look at Canada). Mention of same-sex rights was excised from the first edition of *Discover Canada*, but later re-entered, after considerable controversy, along with an expanded section on the War of 1812.[9]

Discover Canada's version of Canada was given a rousing thumbs-up by the corporate press. The *Globe and Mail* called the booklet "a welcome move that places a new and appropriate emphasis on Canada's history and personalities."[10] The *Globe* had waited a long time for this day. An editorial written nearly a decade earlier lamented the fact that "[s]choolchildren learn all about the story of women, the story of natives, the story of the labour movement, but little about the story of the country as a whole."[11] The *Winnipeg Free Press* opined that "all Canadians will benefit from its pages,"[12] while the *Ottawa Citizen* offered that "all Canadians, whether born here or not, could probably learn a thing or two from this guide."[13] The *Calgary Herald*, located deep in the Harper heartland, went over the top. It "teaches Canada's key values and history that are a crucial part of Canada's identity as a nation," the paper lectured, and warned darkly that "those of us who love this place intend to keep it that way."[14]

The conservative turn in Canadian political culture didn't emerge fully formed from Harper's brain. It occurred at least in part because of the efforts of well-funded advocacy organizations like the Dominion Institute and Historica Foundation. For a decade they beat the drum for a more traditional rendition of Canadian history, one devoid of special interests and devoted to the story of "the country as a whole," meaning the lives of the prime ministers, the wars, the great events, and the great men who shaped them. About half the individuals acknowledged as sources in *Discover Canada* are connected to these two organizations.

The Dominion Institute was set up in 1997 by some young conservatives, including Mike Chong, who became a Conservative MP in 2004, and Duncan Jackman, who runs the family's multi-billion-dollar insurance and investment empire. The Donner Canadian Foundation contributed $300,000.[15] Dominion's goal was to challenge the prevailing social-history approach taught in most schools, which emphasizes race, ethnicity, gender, and class, subjects which so irritated the *Globe's* editorial board, and to replace it with the story of great men and important wars and events.[16] A battle being played out in Canada was also taking place in most of the Western world; the Dominion Institute was the Canadian vanguard. Social history, which concentrates on the social, economic and cultural institutions of a people, burst onto the academic scene in the 1950s and expanded into educational curricula by the 1980s. It deals with "the structures of society and social change, social movements, groups and classes, conditions of work and ways of life, families, households, local communities, urbanization, mobility, ethnic groups, etc."[17] Social history challenged dominant traditional narratives constructed around the history of politics and the state, and the traditionalists were fighting back.

Like many Donner–backed projects, the Dominion Institute's propaganda function was central. "Everything we do at the Institute," executive director Rudyard Griffiths — also acknowledged as a source in *Discover Canada* — explained to the *National Post's* John Fraser, "is done with an idea to how it will play in the media. We measure success in hundreds of media hits for each project."[18] Fraser judged the Institute, then just four years old, as "wildly successful" in accomplishing its mission.

For about eight years, on the day before Canada Day — the Dominion people wished it was still called Dominion Day — the institute released a survey measuring how little Canadians know about important dates and events. And every Canada Day, the *Globe* and other papers ran headline stories decrying the abysmal state of Canadians' historical knowledge:

- "Test: Recite Canada's Constitutional Slogan" (1998);
- "Our Young Show Dismal Ignorance of History" (2000);
- "For Most Canadians, Our History Is a Mystery" (2001);
- "The Latest Canada Day Quiz Shows Many of Us Are in the Dark about War and Peace" (2003).

A second organization promoting a traditional view of Canadian history — the Historica Foundation — was started two years after Dominion. Lynton (Red) Wilson, chairman of telecommunications giant BCE, contributed $500,000 of his own money. Wilson was inspired by Jack Granatstein's book, *Who Killed Canadian History?* This polemic savages most Canadian historians for not sticking to the "Canadian story," an approach Carleton University historian Brian McKillop claims misrepresents and distorts Canadian historians and their scholarship.[19] But the money was on Granatstein's side. Corporate Canada jumped on board, pledging a further $10 million.[20] Charles Bronfman, whose CRB Foundation was producing "Heritage Minutes" television mini-documentaries, promised to match every dollar raised.

Two months before Kenney introduced *Discover Canada,* Dominion and Historica merged, bringing ideology and big business together into one powerful organization promoting history based on "the Canadian story." Historica had the money, but lacked ideological focus. Dominion had the strategic vision to take down social history. Andrew Cohen, then a journalism professor at Carleton University, was installed as president of the new organization, which was named the Historica–Dominion Institute and later, Historica Canada, making it sound like a government department, which it almost was. Cohen was an ideal candidate for the position, because he — apparently — espoused the organizations' traditional values but, more importantly, was not associated with either group, so that neither could be seen as taking over the other. Cohen engaged in a bit of Orwellian doublespeak when he explained the merged organization's mission: "to become . . . the future of the past in Canada." As for the new citizenship guide, "[it] . . . deserves the warm applause of our unconscious nation," Cohen wrote in the *Ottawa Citizen*. "It marks the first serious attempt in decades on the part of the federal government to tell our story."[21] But whose story did the Chrétien–Martin guide tell?

The lineup of Historica and Dominion people acknowledged in *Discover Canada* indicates the close ties with the federal government. Dominion's ties were forged early, when it persuaded the Chrétien government to sponsor programs like Passages to Canada, stories told by prominent immigrants to Canada, shifting the immigration focus from collective to individual experience, and the Memory Project, in which war veterans visit schools. Historica's association is a Harper government development. Harper had barely taken office in 2006 when he cut funding to organizations in his bad books: either they were connected to the Liberals or they represented "special interests." One of the first to go was the Canadian Unity Council (CUC), a Pearson-era, Liberal-friendly, Quebec-based federalist organization, which lost its $13-million federal funding.[22] One CUC program, Encounters with Canada (EWC), brings three thousand teenagers to Ottawa every year to stay for a week at the Terry Fox Canadian Youth Centre and learn about government and civic issues. This program was revived after a well-organized coast-to-coast outcry from alumni. But along the way it was turned into a vehicle for Harper government purposes.

Historica won the contract to administer EWC under controversial circumstances, even receiving a million-dollar-a-year

boost to its budget.[23] Royal Canadian Legion secretary Duane
Daly, whose organization lost out for the EWC contract, questioned Historica's suitability for the job. "Their business is
history, not citizenship and youth development."[24] Perhaps
that's the point. As George Orwell so brilliantly put it, "who controls the past controls the future." To ensure EWC meshed with
the Harper government's developing strategy of remaking Canada as a more conservative, militaristic nation, career bureaucrat
Colin Robertson was dispatched for a two-year stint as Historica
president.

Robertson was well-placed in the Ottawa power structure. He
had been a member of the team that negotiated the Canada–U.S.
Trade Agreement in the eighties. He helped draft the NAFTA–
implementing legislation in 1993, and became the first Canadian
NAFTA communications coordinator. Robertson's terms of
reference were to integrate EWC into Historica and review
all Historica programs and practices.[25] After the makeover,
Encounters with Canada presented a government-sanctioned
version of Canada. Student visits to Ottawa are organized around
theme weeks. Many themes, such as law, politics in Canada,
and medicine and health, are EWC's traditional offerings. But
several are tinged with Harper's militaristic orientation. "Canada Remembers" week features Remembrance Day, visits to the
Canadian War Museum, and talks by generals. "Vimy: Canada's
Coming of Age" teaches participants about the legacy of Vimy
and challenges them to take up the torch of remembrance. Other
students can spend their week encountering the RCMP and perhaps deciding to join the force after graduation.[26]

On paper, Historica was a non-profit organization with an
independent board of governors. By the end of Robertson's
tenure, the organization had been shaped into little more than a
collection of government-financed programs, but at arm's-length
from government and seemingly independent from it. This

relationship continued after Historica merged with Dominion. Government funds comprise about half of Historica Canada's $13-million budget, originating mostly with Heritage Canada.[27] Corporate funds supplement the government money. Nickel giant Vale and pipeline company Enbridge together donated one million dollars to support the Canadian Aboriginal Writing and Arts Challenge. This is not surprising, perhaps, given the mining and pipeline companies' efforts to woo First Nations' support for their projects.

The Harper government seems to be getting good value for its investment in Historica. During a three-week period in October and November 2012, for instance, Historica sponsored three events featuring government ministers: Heritage Minister James Moore hosted an interactive quiz show based on Heritage Minutes at a private Vancouver school; Veterans Affairs Minister Steven Blaney led a Remembrance Day ceremony, featuring a Memory Project speaker, at a private Ottawa school; and Immigration Minister Kenney led local students in a Citizenship Challenge with CBC journalists at an Ottawa Catholic school — public, non-sectarian schools were not included. Historica cheered the Harper government's decision to remake the Canadian Museum of Civilization into the Canadian Museum of History, where it would pay "tribute to the big events, ideas, and people that shaped Canada," and move away from aboriginal and international culture.[28] It was another illustration of the Harper government–Historica promotion of traditional over social history. Historica revived its Heritage Minutes series of mini-documentaries to tell the stories the Harper government wants told. The first two episodes are about the War of 1812, plus a new series commemorating the life of Sir John A. Macdonald — with $360,000 from Canadian Heritage — timed for the two hundredth anniversary of Macdonald's birthday in 2015.[29] Harper must like what Historica was doing. When Encounters with Canada's five-year funding ran out in 2012, his government provided increased funding for another three years.[30] Then it's only two years to Canada's hundred and fiftieth anniversary and the centennial of Vimy Ridge. Historica is going to be very busy.

In keeping with its hawkish agenda, the Dominion Institute had earlier urged the Harper government to hold a state funeral and declare a national day of commemoration when the last veteran of the First World War died.[31] Ninety thousand people signed an online petition and parliament unanimously consented. That event occurred when John Babcock died in 2010 at the age of 109. It turned out to be anti-climactic. Babcock never saw battle, because he was too young. The war ended before he turned eighteen. The only conflict Babcock witnessed came on Armistice Day, 1918, when a fight broke out between British and Canadian soldiers.[32] Moreover, Babcock lived most of his life outside Canada, in Spokane, Washington. Babcock didn't want a state funeral, nor did his family, and it didn't happen.

***

John Babcock didn't buy into the scenario that was being choreographed for him, but militarism was central to the Great Nation doctrine Harper was fashioning. He came into office with an agenda that had both partisan and ideological objectives: to make the Conservatives Canada's natural governing party and to make Canada more conservative. He was barely on the job as prime minister in 2006 when he served notice that Canada's military adventure in Afghanistan, initiated by the Liberals, would continue. "Canadians don't cut and run at the first sign of trouble," he announced. "That's the nature of this country. And when we send troops into the field, I expect Canadians to support those troops," he warned sternly.[33] If any members of parliament on Liberal, New Democrat, or Bloc Québécois benches want to pull out, can they be anything more than cowards? Harper repeated the message a week later during a surprise visit to Kandahar Airfield — signalling support for the Afghanistan mission was a top priority — where he told a thousand Canadian troops "there may be some who want to cut and run, but cutting and running is not your way. It's not my way, and it's not the Canadian way. We don't make a commitment and then run away at the first sign of trouble. We don't and we will not, as long as I'm leading this country."[34] Both stories received coast-to-coast coverage and "cut and run" became a hotly discussed item. It was an early triumph for the Prime Minister's Office. And it wasn't over. A month later, Harper was at Canadian Forces Base Wainwright, Alberta, to praise army graduates. "Leaders don't cut and run at the first sign of trouble," he told them. "Leaders stand up for values, leaders see the mission through, and leaders succeed."[35] Harper invoked Canadian military history from Vimy Ridge to Normandy to inspire the graduates, many of whom would be heading to Afghanistan.

Harper used Afghanistan deftly to establish the narrative that Canada was a country with a long and proud military history, populated by patriotic citizens who would never support a government that cut and ran. Critics saw this project as the rebranding of Canada as a warrior nation, a concept one-hundred-and-eighty degrees from Canada as the peaceable kingdom. If he was to succeed in transforming the Conservatives into Canada's natural governing party, Harper and his PMO would have to undo the symbols of Liberal hegemony and replace them with Conservative symbols. Peacekeeping was central to the Liberal identity,[36] and the Harper government engaged in a no-holds-barred assault on the idea that peacekeeping was a key component of the Canadian identity. After Afghanistan came the fifty-five mentions of war in the new citizenship guide, lionizing Canadian Forces efforts in Libya, restoring the "Royal" prefix to the navy and air force, spending $28 million on a year-long celebration of the War of 1812, and commemorating each of the four years in the run-up to the centenary of Vimy Ridge, whose memorial graces the back of the Canadian twenty-dollar bill. Marketing expert Patrick Muttart, who helped create the new narrative as Harper's deputy chief of staff, later explained that "what we're seeing is the emergence of a new patriotism or at the very least a small-conservative alternative to the established Liberal narrative about Canada."[37]

But how to keep the citizens patriotic? After five years of holding off the Taliban at a cost of 161 lives and $11.3 billion, Canada closed down its Kandahar military hub and shipped its tanks, vehicles, and equipment back to Canada. What would be next? The military scrambled to answer that question by looking for new hubs around the world — not on the scale of Kandahar, but rather operational support outposts as part of a plan to deploy the military on more overseas missions that include combat and security. It had seven such hubs in its crosshairs: Germany, Jamaica, Kuwait, Singapore, Senegal, South Korea, and possibly Kenya. In 2010, before Canada left Afghanistan, Chief of Defence Staff Walter Natynczyk signed a directive designed to improve Canadian Forces' "ability to project combat power/security assistance and Canadian influence rapidly and flexibly anywhere in the world."[38] The Harper government subsequently established operational support hubs in Germany and Kuwait and in September 2013 signed an agreement to establish a hub in Japan. Was Canada preparing for perpetual war? And why?

***

Rick Salutin didn't ask those questions, but gave a good answer nonetheless. In the second-last column he wrote for the *Globe and Mail* before being fired after twenty years as a weekly columnist,

Salutin asked what might explain Harper's "buttheaded" behaviour?[39] He was referring to Harper "firing decent people, lashing out, raising the partisan rhetoric, proroguing Parliament haughtily, bringing on military toys, mauling the census." Salutin had an answer: "Straussianism," which was exemplified by Harper's secretiveness, emphasis on religion and nationalism, populism and democracy, and contempt for opponents. These are Straussian characteristics to be sure. Leo Strauss (1899–1973) was a German–Jewish philosopher who fled Nazi Germany in 1938 and taught at the University of Chicago for several decades. He developed a following of students and disciples, called variously Straussians and neo-conservatives, who achieved enormous influence in academia and government in recent years. Straussians are those who follow in the Straussian intellectual tradition; neo-conservatives are those who apply — sometimes erroneously — Strauss's ideas to political and economic life. They don't have to be the same people, but often are.

Strauss believed in the inherent inequality of humanity. He agreed with Edward Bernays, the founder of public relations, that most people are too ill-educated to make informed decisions about their political affairs. Bernays's solution was to create a cadre of "invisible wire-pullers" who would move public opinion in the desired direction.[40] Strauss had a different solution. Allowing people to govern themselves will lead inevitably to terror and tyranny, as Germany's Weimar Republic succumbed to Nazi dictatorship, an event Strauss witnessed first-hand. (This is the same event that led Hayek to begin organizing neo-liberalism.) A ruling elite of political philosophers must make the decisions, Straus argued, because only it is knowledgeable enough; it must resort to deception to protect citizens from themselves. The "superior few" — Strauss's students — must rule over the ordinary people, "not honestly or with candid veracity," Shadia Drury, Strauss's foremost

Canadian critic, wryly observes, "but by duping, deceiving, and manipulating them."[41]

Liberal secular society was untenable for Strauss, because it led to the "isms" — individualism, liberalism, and relativism — traits that encourage dissent, which in turn could weaken society's ability to cope with external threats. What the people need most, Strauss believed, are religion and perpetual war. Strauss regarded religion as a political tool intended for the masses, but not for the superior few. He agreed with Karl Marx that religion is the opiate of the masses, but, unlike Marx, believed that the people need their opium.[42] Religion was necessary to provide society with moral order and stability. So Strauss's neo-conservative followers allied themselves with the religious right to promote a traditional religious agenda. Neo-conservatives "encourage family values and the praise of older forms of family life, where women occupy themselves with children, cooking, and the church and men take on the burden of manliness," ex-Straussian Anne Norton writes in her critique of Straussianism.[43]

Strauss taught further that a political order can be stable only if it is united by an external threat. Following political theorist Niccolo Machiavelli, Strauss maintained that, if no external threat exists, one has to be manufactured. "You have to fight all the time [to survive]," explains Drury. "Peace leads to decadence. Perpetual war, not perpetual peace, is what Straussians believe in." Such a view inevitably leads to an "aggressive, belligerent foreign policy," Drury adds.[44] Strauss died in 1973, so he didn't help with setting up the most prominent neo-conservative think tank, the American Enterprise Institute, as Hayek did with the neo-liberal ones. Nor would he likely have agreed to this project, given his preoccupation with secrecy. But some of his followers exploited his ideas for their own ends, pressed them into the service of the business elite, and promoted a reactionary agenda at home and abroad. Had Strauss lived to see the collapse of the Soviet Union, he might have been troubled, because the disintegration of the "evil empire" posed a threat to America's inner stability. For a decade neo-conservatives worked quietly to replace the Soviet Union with an enhanced threat of Islamic terrorism. Perpetual war could continue.

Strauss's teachings grabbed attention after the United States invaded Iraq. The U.S. had to invade Iraq, Straussians in the Bush administration told the people, because Iraq had weapons of mass destruction (WMDs). Strauss student Abram Shulsky, the director of the Office of Special Plans in the Department of Defense, "was responsible for finding intelligence that would help to make the case for the war on Iraq," writes Drury.[45] Strauss student Paul Wolfowitz was deputy secretary of defense and the number-two official at the Pentagon, from which perch he orchestrated the "invade Iraq" lobby.

When no such weapons were found, the American government said instead it had to go to war to depose a ruthless dictator and bring democracy and freedom to the Iraqi people. It was also discovered that the Bush administration knew that Saddam Hussein had no WMDs. Many Americans concluded that their leaders had lied. Thanks to Strauss, though, lies were no longer just a regrettable part of political life, but instead "virtuous and noble instruments of wise policy," social critic Earl Shorris explains.[46] Straussians knew that gaining control of Iraq's oil fields and privatizing the Iraqi economy were in the best interests of American business. But the American people would never agree to invade Iraq merely to enrich corporate coffers. They needed to be lied to.

In answer to Rick Salutin's question, what explains Harper's "buttheaded" behaviour, Straussianism and neo-conservatism are both appropriate responses. Harper isn't a genuine Straussian because he didn't study under Strauss or Strauss's students. Besides, Harper's area of study was economics and not political science, philosophy, or history, the typical Straussian disciplines. But Harper did associate with Straussians, and certainly learned from them. Straussians Ted Morton and Rainer Knopff — who studied under Strauss student Walter Berns at the University of Toronto — were teaching at the University of Calgary when Harper started his studies there. They were present at meetings later in the decade to help Preston Manning and Harper craft the fledgling Reform Party's policies, which were infused with Straussian deception.[47] And Harper did hire Straussian Ian Brodie — Ted Morton's student — to be his first chief of staff. And he did appoint two Straussians, Knopff and McGill University political scientist Christopher Manfredi — who studied under Strauss student Ralph Rossum at Claremont Graduate University, a Straussian stronghold on the west coast — along with a social conservative and three protocol experts, to advise him on who the next governor general should be. Stephen Harper is explained mostly by Friedrich Hayek and neo-liberalism, as this book documents. But there is an irreducible element of Straussianism and neo-conservatism in his agenda.

***

In a controversial essay, "The Neoconservative Persuasion," Irving Kristol, who studied under Strauss and was the first intellectual to call himself a neo-conservative, summed up the neo-conservative agenda: "to convert the Republican Party, and American conservatism in general, against their respective wills, into a new kind of conservative politics suitable to governing a modern democracy."[48] That was also Stephen Harper's agenda for Canadian conservatism and the Conservative Party. While neo-conservatives in the American Enterprise Institute and Bush administration were escalating pro-war rhetoric, Harper had become head of the Canadian Alliance and leader of the official Opposition. In the weeks around the invasion,

Harper rose almost daily in the House of Commons to ask the prime minister why Canada was not standing with its friends. Canada would not participate in the looming war "without a new resolution of the [United Nations] Security Council," Chrétien told the House to a rousing ovation from Liberal, Bloc Québécois, and New Democratic MPs.[49] Harper was undaunted. "Is the government now prepared to stand with our American and British friends for the end of the rule of Saddam Hussein?" he asked after the invasion commenced. The next day he chastised the government for "its failure to stand by our friends and allies." Harper used the word "friends" nineteen times during the four weeks surrounding the invasion, mostly about standing with or supporting the Americans and British. In Irving Kristol's essay, a principle of foreign policy is that "statesmen should, above all, have the ability to distinguish friends from enemies."

The day after the invasion, Harper gave a major speech in parliament. He accepted as proven that Iraq possessed WMDs. Harper was making them do similar work in Canada as in the United States. He brought up WMDs three times in his speech:

> It is inherently dangerous to allow a country, such as Iraq, to retain weapons of mass destruction, particularly in light of its past aggressive behaviour . . .
>
> As the possession of weapons of mass destruction spreads, the danger of such weapons coming into the hands of terrorist groups will multiply . . .
>
> We cannot walk away from the threat that Iraq's continued possession of weapons of mass destruction constitutes to its region and to the wider world.[50]

Harper also anticipated the importance of war for a Harper–led government:

> *However, to have the future once again of a great country, we must do more than stand with our friends in the United States. We must rediscover our own values. We must remember that this country was forged in large part by war, terrible war, but not because it was terrible and not because it was easy, but because at the time it was right.*

This speech raised criticism — not at the time Harper gave it, but five years later. During the 2008 election, a Liberal Party researcher discovered that about half the speech — including the references to weapons of mass destruction — was taken word-for-word from a speech Australian Prime Minister John Howard gave to the Australian parliament two days before Harper.[51] Owen Lippert, a Conservative policy adviser, former Fraser Institute staffer, and an expert on intellectual property, took the fall for the apparent plagiarism and resigned, but the speculation was that the Bush administration's neo-conservative advisers sent out talking points to all potential members of the "coalition of the willing."

***

The disintegration of the Soviet Union and the search for a new enemy was marked by the creation of a new American magazine, *The Weekly Standard*. It signalled the birth of a third age of neo-conservatism[52] and a new generation of foreign-policy hawks, Brookings Institution historian Justin Vaisse reports.[53] Started by Straussian William Kristol — Irving Kristol's son and a student of Strauss student Harvey Mansbridge — with the financial backing of Rupert Murdoch, the *Standard,* whose office of which is in the American Enterprise Institute (AEI) building, came to represent the quest for national greatness, the concept that defines the third age, Vaisse argues. The very first issue of this magazine set the agenda for the new neo-conservatism by applauding the NATO bombing of Serbia and berating the U.S. for being a "timid superpower" that "poses a greater danger to the present world order than ten Serbias."[54] America must be strong and ready to act in order to shape the world according to its political and security interests.[55] This muscular foreign-policy doctrine was formalized two years later with the creation of the Project for the New American Century, also with an office in the AEI building — by Kristol and his allies, with the support of neo-conservatives in the corporate media. Kristol was a Fox News regular, while Charles Krauthammer beat the drum for aggressive militarism in the pages of the *Washington Post* and David Brooks performed similar duties for the *New York Times.*

Stephen Harper didn't meet William Kristol and the neo-conservatives for several years after becoming prime minister. The Canadian Press broke the story about Harper and communications director, Kory Teneycke, meeting for lunch on March 30, 2009, in Washington D.C., with Murdoch and Fox News president Roger Ailes.[56] That meeting caused a storm of controversy in Canada and speculation about a "Fox News North" cable channel modelled on Fox. But the night before, Harper hosted a dinner with eight prominent conservative media personalities, including five leading neo-conservatives. Sitting down with Harper were Kristol and Fred Barnes of the *Standard,* Charles Krauthammer, David Brooks, and David Frum. No longer a Canadian citizen but still an AEI fellow, Frum had worked as a special assistant to President Bush for economic speechwriting and was one of the most vociferous voices in government calling for war in Iraq. Frum claimed credit for the expression "axis of evil" (Iraq, Iran, North Korea). Also at the dinner were three women: Peggy Noonan, former Ronald Reagan speechwriter and *Wall Street Journal* columnist; Anne Applebaum, anti-communist columnist for the *Washington Post* and *Slate*; and conservative talk-radio host Laura Ingraham, a frequent commentator on Fox News. They would, according to Bush's ambassador to Canada, David Wilkins, help Harper "share [his] opinions with opinion-makers in the United States."[57]

After Harper's 2011 victory, *Standard* editor Fred Barnes wrote that Harper was an "elected dictator," who "led the Conservatives to become the natural governing party of Canada." Harper was without doubt "the most powerful conservative leader in the Americas, north and south," Barnes opined.[58] That was followed three weeks later by an admiring piece by Kristol, comparing the "electoral and governing successes of conservative prime ministers Stephen Harper in Canada and Benjamin Netanyahu in Israel" with the achievements of Margaret Thatcher.[59]

It was an interesting comparison. Harper and Netanyahu certainly hit it off when the Israeli prime minister visited Canada in 2010. Netanyahu "received a welcome fit for a rock star," as the *Jerusalem Post* framed his visit to Toronto's Ricoh Coliseum before the start of the United Jewish Appeal's annual Walk for Israel. "The ties between Israel and Canada have never been stronger," he said to resounding applause from a supportive audience of seven thousand.[60] Then it was off to the nation's capital for talks with Harper. Netanyahu had barely arrived in Ottawa when Israel became embroiled in another crisis. Israeli commandos boarded a ship headed for Gaza loaded with humanitarian aid — it was in international waters — and killed nine crew members and passengers. Netanyahu defended his country's deadly military attack during a photo opportunity with Harper. He then cut short his visit to Ottawa and cancelled meetings scheduled with U.S. President Barack Obama. "Prime Minister," Harper said, "as I told you, Canada deeply regrets this action, the loss of life and the injuries that occurred and obviously we'll be looking in the days that follow to get all the information we can get to find out exactly what has transpired." Harper was sorry his meetings with Netanyahu were "coloured by this." Navi Pillay, the UN High Commissioner for Human Rights, saw it differently. She condemned Israel's use of military force as "disproportionate . . . nothing can justify the appalling outcome of this operation, which reportedly took place in international waters."[61] But Netanyahu didn't rush to the airport for several hours. During the photo session, Harper made clear Netanyahu's welcome was undiminished and wished him well. "Thank you, Prime Minister," he said. "God speed on your return."[62] Netanyahu praised Harper for being "an unwavering friend of Israel. He's been a great champion of Israel's right to defend itself and he stands against all the efforts to delegitimize the Jewish state," Netanyahu declared. The Israeli prime minister had ample reason to be grateful. Harper had already:

- Severed relations with, and cut tens of millions of dollars in aid to, the Palestinian Authority after Hamas, the more militant Palestinian faction, won a majority of seats in Palestinian legislative elections in 2006;[63]
- Condemned the abduction of Israeli soldiers by Hamas and Hezbollah in Southern Lebanon, supported Israel's right to defend itself, and characterized Israel's deadly response as "measured," later in the year;[64]
- Voted against a UN Human Rights Council motion condemning the Israeli offensive in the Gaza Strip

that killed 1,200 Gazans in response to Hamas rocket attacks in southern Israel in 2009.[65]

The same year, Harper marked Israel's sixtieth anniversary with a pledge of Canada's unshakable support, tying the two nations even closer together. "Our government believes that those who threaten Israel also threaten Canada," he told a crowd gathered to celebrate the birthday in the same auditorium Netanyahu would later visit. Harper drew a standing ovation as the audience cheered and whistled and waved Canadian and Israeli flags.[66] Six weeks later, Harper reiterated his government's staunch support for Israel. "Our support for her right to exist is unshakable," he said in a speech as he was awarded B'nai Brith International's highest honour, the presidential Gold Medallion for Humanitarianism. The media carried a photo of Harper lighting the last candle on the menorah.[67] The Harper–Netanyahu connection went well beyond the political. They spent time together on two occasions at Harrington Lake, the prime minister's official country residence. On the second visit, in March, 2012, wives Sara Netanyahu and Laureen Harper went snowshoeing together.[68]

So resolute has been Harper's support for Israel that critics parsed his every statement, seeking clues to his motivation. One explanation is that a focus on Israel would have the most obvious appeal to Canada's Jews. Harper's unwavering support for Israel's invasion of Lebanon won him enduring gratitude from the Jewish community, resulting in a steady migration of Jews from Liberal to Conservative ranks. This explanation, though, can account for only a small fraction of Harper's success. Jews make up just over 1 per cent of the Canadian population, about 380,000 in total. They comprise a significant segment of the electorate in only three federal ridings, Thornhill, north of Toronto, Mont-Royal on the Island of Montreal, and Winnipeg South Centre.

A second explanation for the Harper government's unrelenting commitment to Israel is that a much larger segment of the population is in play — evangelical Christians — partly because of its "strong traditional views of values and family," as Harper explained in his 2003 Civitas speech, but also because of its unyielding pro-Zionism (support for a Jewish state in Palestine). About four million Canadians — 12 per cent — are evangelical Christians[69] who believe in the need for personal salvation, the literal accuracy of the Bible, and the reality of the death and resurrection of the Son of God. Many believe Christ will return when the Jews have occupied the full extent of their Biblical homeland. Such an explanation is appealing because it correlates with the Straussian recipe for a strong state: religion and perpetual war. Unconditional support for Israel fits the bill on both counts: With an expansionist Israel as a close friend, there will always be Islamic enemies to face down. Former broadcaster Peter Kent, who would go on to become Harper's environment minister (see Chapter 5), won the Jewish-dominated Thornhill riding in 2008 and worked it well. As minister of state for foreign affairs, he told a Toronto Jewish magazine that "an attack on Israel would be considered an attack on Canada," inferring that, if Iran attacked Israel, Canada would go to war against Iran. Kent denied this is what he meant, but his statement remained in the realm of ambiguity and conjecture.[70]

***

In an editorial in the Thanksgiving 2012 edition of *The Weekly Standard,* William Kristol declared that "from Benghazi to Be'er Sheva, the West is under attack."[71] By the West he meant "those nations ... that carry the torch of liberal civilization." The United States "stands at the head" of this bunch. As for Israel, it is "the only country which as a country is an outpost of the West in the

East," he explained, quoting from a letter to the *National Review* written by Leo Strauss a half-century earlier (1956). Strauss spent a year teaching at the Hebrew University in Jerusalem and claimed that, even then, Israel needed American support, because it "is a country which is surrounded by mortal enemies of overwhelming numerical superiority."[72] Kristol was vague about the mortal enemies in his Thanksgiving piece, identifying "the terrorists of all stripes . . . who attack across the world and kill Jews, Christians, and Muslims alike." Their ultimate targets, though, are the United States and Israel, he reassured his readers. These countries "find themselves joined at the hip in a brotherhood that is more than a diplomatic or political or military alliance," and he warned that "should Israel perish, the holocaust will be upon us." He suggested that Thanksgiving shouldn't be about just thanking "the Almighty for our blessings here in America . . . We might also thank Him for restoring the homeland of the Jewish people."

In their concern for Israel's welfare, third-age neo-conservatives and evangelical Christians are also joined at the hip. For neo-conservatives, America's continued greatness depends on Israel's survival; for evangelical Zionists, the Second Coming depends on Israel's survival. For both, ridding Israel of its enemies is job one. Kristol makes no secret about Israel's current worst enemy — the state of Iran. In an earlier column he excoriated Iran for its "record of murder and mayhem"[73]— ignoring Israel's record of murder and mayhem — and its relentless pursuit of nuclear weapons — ignoring the fact that Israel already has nuclear weapons. Iran, meanwhile, was plotting to assassinate American diplomats in Azerbaijan, kill Israeli diplomats in the Republic of Georgia, Thailand, and India, and kill the Saudi ambassador (and American bystanders) at a Washington, D.C., restaurant, Kristol charged. The time for talk was long past. Kristol urged Obama "to ask Congress for an Authorization for Use of Military Force against Iran's nuclear program." And if Obama won't do it, Congress should act alone. It's that serious. The military option needs "to be front and centre and [we must ensure] it is seen as viable . . . The authorization would make it clear that the United States would come to Israel's aid in the event that it decides it needs to take action." There was an eerie similarity between what Kristol urged the Obama administration to do in Iran in 2012 and what he urged the Clinton and Bush administrations to do in Iraq more than a decade earlier: alleged nuclear weapons instead of alleged weapons of mass destruction was all that changed.

Harper didn't go as far as Kristol and call for war with Iran when he received the World Statesman Award from the Appeal of Conscience Foundation in New York in the fall of 2012. Officially the award was for his work as "a champion of democracy, freedom, and human rights." Unofficially, though, the award went to him largely because of his support for Israel and his criticism of Iran. It had to be for that reason, because many questioned Harper's record of defending democracy and human rights in his own country.[74] Iran received the brunt of his pointed remarks. He had already shuttered Canada's embassy in Tehran and expelled Iranian embassy staff in Ottawa. It wasn't just Iran's "appalling record of human rights abuse or its active assistance to the brutal regime in Syria or its undeniable support of terrorist entities or its determined pursuit of nuclear weapons," that made Iran "a clear and present danger," he insisted to the assembled dignitaries, which included a frail eighty-nine-year-old Henry Kissinger.[75] It was "the combination of all these things with a truly malevolent ideology," an ideology based on hatred of Israel. He gave the audience a lesson in history: "Those who single out the Jewish people as a target of racial and religious bigotry will inevitably be a threat to all of us."

In Harper's world, Canada is joined at the hip to both Israel and the United States. His affiliation to Israel, whether as third-age neo-con or evangelical Christian, is well-known. As for the U.S., it was "the best neighbour any nation could possibly have." That's because "our comparatively small country has . . . lived in secure peace and growing prosperity for almost two centuries . . . a testament to the enduring strength and essential benevolence of the U.S." Canada and Israel both benefit from American support; they might not exist without it. Iranian evil, American benevolence — a simple compass. The following day, Harper met with Netanyahu, in town to deliver a combative speech about Iran's nuclear ambitions to the United Nations General Assembly. Harper was "delighted" to see Netanyahu again, the *Canadian Jewish News* reported. Netanyahu replied, "Stephen, I think what you did, severing ties with Iran, was not only an act of statesmanship, but an act of moral clarity."[76]

Welding Israel's fate to that of Canada and the United States, neo-conservatives are working tirelessly to ensure that perpetual war continues and that Jews and evangelicals will be on board with the agenda. Stephen Harper's "moral clarity" is intended as a beacon to guide the avatars of Western civilization through the dangerous shoals of Islamic terror. Even the Obama administration, hardly a bastion of neo-conservatism, signed on to the perpetual-war frame to direct its international relations.[77] At a Senate Armed Services Committee hearing in May 2013, Michael Sheehan, the assistant secretary of defense for special operations and low-intensity conflict, admitted that the war on terror will last "at least 10 to 20 years." This was on top of the twelve years that had already passed since 9-11. It is as close as the administration has ever come to admitting it has adopted a doctrine of "endless war." As *Guardian* columnist Glenn Greenwald observes, "it is hard to resist the conclusion that this war has no purpose other than its own eternal perpetuation. This war is not a means to any end but rather is the end in itself." Leo Strauss would understand.

Harper, meanwhile, is making his own preparations for perpetual war. His government made public — on the day after Remembrance Day — its estimate that the full life-cycle cost of up to fifteen surface combat vessels will exceed $90 billion, plus another $8.6 billion for eight Arctic offshore patrol ships, and $7.1 billion for two ships to carry fuel, ammunition, vehicles, and cargo.[78] Then there will be $25 billion or more for F-35 Lightning jets or their replacements. *Discover Canada*, the Harper government's citizenship guide, has it right: war is the centrepiece of Canadian citizenship.

✳✳✳

Harper claims his mission is to make Canada into a more conservative and a more Conservative nation. And certainly, Harper government initiatives outlined in this chapter seem to promote a social-conservative agenda — war and patriotism, the Holy Land, and issues not discussed, such as appealing to traditional family values and attacking special interests that run counter to those traditional values. Undoubtedly these actions and policies appeal to a conservative temperament and a desire to return to older traditions.

Harper's neo-liberal program, on the other hand, cannot be considered conservative by any stretch of the imagination. His efforts to bring in free-market environmentalism and a new land-ownership regime for First Nations, are radical, not conservative. The agenda is to create and enforce markets, often where they didn't exist before. Such major transformations of Canadian society must be undertaken incrementally, so they don't look like revolution. Friedrich Hayek understood the nature of the project to impose what he called liberty on society. In a famous essay titled "Why I Am Not a Conservative," written as a postscript to his *Constitution of Liberty*, Hayek argues that conservatives want to keep things as they were, whereas he wants to change them dramatically. Conservatism is an "attitude of opposition to dramatic change,"[79] he writes, whereas neo-liberals see the urgent need for "a thorough sweeping away of the obstacles to free growth."[80] He had difficulty coming up with a label for his program, because the word radical usually applies to the left. And his party of liberty should be known as liberal, but that label has been appropriated by the American left.

Harper's social-conservative initiatives may not be so conservative either. He modelled much of his great-nation doctrine after third-age neo-conservatives in the United States. Their goal, as inspired by Leo Strauss, is to exploit conservative values to transform the United States into a more radical nation, one that is aggressive and hawkish in outlook and populated by compliant, patriotic citizens. Harper is doing the same in Canada, and in the process, is making the country unrecognizable.

CONCLUSION

Canada was a different place after Stephen Harper's first majority government than it had been in the 1980s when neo-liberalism first grabbed hold of federal government policy-making. The process accelerated under Harper and his unique brand of neo-liberalism — Harperism — would not be easily undone. For instance, by downgrading his government's capacity to undertake scientific research and minimizing the likelihood that scientific research might contradict his government's policy directions, Harper created an opening for new markets for "ecosystem services" to fill the void. A different prime minister could try to reverse the trend by hiring scientists and re-establishing government research stations. But where would the money come from? Harper's budget cuts meant that a new prime minister would have to raise taxes and there was little appetite among opposition leaders for that option. Besides, this would mean going back to what Canada had been before. Science was being irredeemably tarnished, so there could be no going back to an era in which the scientific enterprise had a stellar reputation. Meanwhile, the eco-system services market and free-market environmentalism were gaining a toehold.

The same problem would hinder a government that attempted to reverse Harper's efforts to bring private property ownership to First Nation reserves. Some First Nations would likely sign on to the First Nations Property Ownership Act, fracturing First Nations leadership and creating a new era in First Nation relation-ships in which government-to-government negotiations became a thing of the past. There was no going back here either.

Neo-liberals learned this lesson early. At their congregation in Mont Pelerin in 1947, they concluded that they couldn't go back to a nineteenth-century *laissez-faire* economy. Too much had happened between the nineteenth century and the end of the Second World War to consider a return to the good old days as a serious option. Government had dramatically increased its presence in the economy. Government interventions during the Great Depression, Franklin Delano Roosevelt's New Deal, crown corporations established by Liberal governments in Britain and Conservative governments in Canada, all presaged the centrality of government in the economy. The Mont Pelerin neo-liberals had to factor government into their emerging vision of a market state. It would, however, play a very different role, one focused more on serving the needs of the market and economy, and less on serving the needs of citizens. Instead of regulating markets — as socialism and social democracy saw the role of government — government would create and enforce markets and prop them up when they fail.

During the thirty years Keynesian demand management reigned supreme, the MPS worked quietly to refine its economic policies. Its time came in the 1970s, when Britain, the United States, Canada, and other developed nations experienced stagflation — high unemployment and high inflation combined with low or no growth. Political leaders cast around for alternative economic policies. The neo-liberals were ready. It was like the rewriting of French poet Victor's Hugo's famous observation that "nothing is more powerful than an idea whose time has come." In this case, though, the saying should be "when the time comes, make sure you have the ideas." Neo-liberals had the ideas and settled in for the next thirty years of ideological dominance.

But when neo-liberalism ran into its serious problems in 2007 and 2008 — skyrocketing unemployment, plummeting housing prices, millions of homeowners facing foreclosure, investment banks dropping by the wayside, too-big-to-fail banks on the verge of failing, and the economy on the precipice of a meltdown threatening to match the Great Depression, no coherent economic alternative presented itself. The time had come once again, but there were no new ideas. Governments turned back briefly to 1960s-style Keynesian stimulus spending but this couldn't be anything more than a temporary fix because the expectations about the appropriate roles of government and the private sector had changed since the sixties. Neo-liberalism quickly re-established itself. Stephen Harper gave the briefest of nods to stimulus before returning to his program.

If there's going to be a social and economic future besides neo-liberalism for Canada, a new role for government must be imagined, one that doesn't treat everything as an offshoot of the economy, but reincorporates social and political rights into its mandate, while addressing the dominance of the market in social and political life. It must then be developed into a serious policy contender. Such imaginings and discussions must take place on an international scale because of neo-liberal globalization. And they must be utopian in outlook — not typical political-party reactions to day-to-day policy issues — and take a long-term perspective, as the neo-liberals have done so well. The Institute of Economic Affairs, the first neo-liberal think tank, established the guiding principle for all its publications: make no concessions to existing political or economic realities, but stick to neo-liberal doctrine. Neo-liberalism's enemies must do the same if they ever hope to forge the ideas that will eventually replace neo-liberalism. Otherwise, Harperism will remain intact for years to come.

ACKNOWLEDGEMENTS

The genesis of this book was a request from Carleton University communications professor Kirsten Kozolanka to contribute a chapter to a book on the Canadian publicity state, which brings together current scholarship on the phenomenon of a federal government engaging non-stop in public relations, promotion, publicity, propaganda — call it what you will. This trend began well before Stephen Harper became prime minister. He has simply been better at it. That chapter, titled "From Hayek to Harper: The War on Ideas," appeared in *The Canadian Publicity State*, edited by Kirsten Kozolanka and published by University of Toronto Press in 2014. My thanks for permission to reprint material from that chapter.

I came across many of these ideas and the people who promoted them in the research for my earlier book *Not a Conspiracy Theory: How Corporate Propaganda Hijacks Democracy* (Toronto: Key Porter, 2009). I was concerned there about the success of corporate propaganda in persuading Canadians to believe ideas that went against their own interests. I rely on several texts in my efforts to unravel Harper's motivations. The first is Friedrich Hayek's wartime manifesto *The Road to Serfdom*, published three years before he founded the Mont Pelerin Society. Seventy years later it's still a bestseller. Hayek's important 1960 work *The Constitution of Liberty* had enormous impact on Margaret Thatcher. During a Conservative Party policy meeting in the late 1970s, Thatcher, the newly elected leader, interrupting a speaker, pulled Hayek's book out of her briefcase, held it up for all to see, slammed it on the table and exclaimed, "This is what we believe!" A third book that informs my understanding of Harperism is Milton Friedman's manifesto *Capitalism and Freedom*, also a perennial bestseller.

I want to acknowledge my partner, Mae Burrows, whose intellectual stimulation, organizational support, and loving encouragement made this book possible. And I want to thank publisher Jim Lorimer for believing in the book, and his competent staff, Kendra Martin and Morgan Tunzelmann, for bringing the manuscript to completion.

SELECT BIBLIOGRAPHY

Anderson, Terry and Donald Leal. *Free Market Environmentalism*. San Francisco: Pacific Research Institute for Public Policy, 1991.

Becker, Gary. "Crime and Punishment: An Economic Approach." *Journal of Political Economy*. Vol. 76, No. 2 (Mar.-Apr. 1968): 169–217.

Burgin, Angus. *The Great Persuasion*. Cambridge, MA: Harvard University Press, 2012.

Cockett, Richard. *Thinking the Unthinkable: Think Tanks and the Economic Counter-Revolution, 1931–1983*. London: HarperCollins, 1995.

de Soto, Hernando. *The Mystery of Capital: Why Capitalism Triumphs in the West and Fails Everywhere Else*. New York: Basic Books, 2000.

Flanagan, Tom. *First Nations? Second Thoughts*, 2nd ed. Montreal and Kingston: McGill–Queen's University Press, 2008.

Flanagan, Tom, Christopher Alcantara, and André Le Dressay. *Beyond the Indian Act: Restoring Aboriginal Property Rights*. Montreal and Kingston: McGill–Queen's University Press, 2010.

Friedman, Milton. *Capitalism and Freedom*, Fortieth Anniversary Edition. Chicago: University of Chicago Press, 2002.

Gutstein, Donald. "From Hayek to Harper: The War On Ideas." pp. 93–111 in Kirsten Kozolanka, ed. *Publicity and the Canadian State: Critical Communications Perspectives*. Toronto: University of Toronto Press, 2014.

Gutstein, Donald. *Not a Conspiracy Theory: How Corporate Propaganda Hijacks Democracy*. Toronto: Key Porter, 2009.

Gwartney, James, Robert Lawson, and Joshua Hall. *Economic Freedom of the World: 2012 Annual Report*. Fraser Institute, 2012. http://www.freetheworld.com/2012/EFW2012-complete.pdf.

Harper, Stephen. "Rediscovering the Right Agenda." *Citizens Centre Report*. Vol. 30, No. 10 (June 2003): 73–77.

Harper, Stephen and Tom Flanagan. "Our Benign Dictatorship." *Next City* (Winter 1996–1997): 34–40, 54–56.

Hayek, Friedrich. *The Road to Serfdom: Text and Documents*. Bruce Campbell, ed. Definitive Edition. Chicago: University of Chicago Press, 2007.

Hayek, Friedrich. *The Constitution of Liberty*. Chicago: University of Chicago Press, 1960.

Hayek, Friedrich. "Why I am Not a Conservative," pp. 397–411 in Friedrich Hayek, *The Constitution of Liberty*. Chicago: University of Chicago Press, 1960.

Hayek, Friedrich. "The Intellectuals and Socialism." *University of Chicago Law Review*. Vol. 16, No. 3 (Spring 1949): 417–433.

Hayek, Friedrich. "The Use of Knowledge in Society." *American Economic Review*. Vol. 35, No. 4 (Sept. 1945): 519–530.

Kenny, Alex, Stewart Elgie and Dave Sawyer. "Advancing the Economics of Ecosystems and Biodiversity in Canada." *Sustainable Prosperity.* June 2011. http://www.sustainableprosperity.ca/article1431.

Kristol, Irving. "The Neoconservative Persuasion." *The Weekly Standard.* Aug. 25, 2003. http://www.weeklystandard.com/Content/Public/Articles/000/000/003/000tzmlw.asp.

McDonald, Marci. "The Man Behind Stephen Harper." *The Walrus.* Oct. 2004. http://thewalrus.ca/the-man-behind-stephen-harper/.

Mirowski, Philip. *Never Let a Serious Crisis Go to Waste.* London: Verso, 2013.

Mirowski, Philip, and Dieter Plehwe, eds. *The Road from Mont Pèlerin: The Making of the Neoliberal Thought Collective.* Cambridge, MA: Harvard University Press, 2009.

Organisation for Economic Cooperation and Development, *Divided We Stand: Why Inequality Keeps Rising,* OECD Publishing, 2011. http://dx.doi.org/10.1787/9789264119536-en.

Peck, Jamie. *Construction of Neoliberal Reason.* New York: Oxford University Press, 2010.

Sustainable Prosperity. "Environmental Markets, 2012," Nov. 2012. http://www.sustainableprosperity.ca/article3228.

Stedman Jones, Daniel. *Masters of the Universe: Hayek, Friedman and the Birth of Neoliberal Politics.* Princeton: Princeton University Press, 2012.

Vaisse, Justin. *Neoconservatism: The Biography of a Movement.* Cambridge MA: Belknap Press of Cambridge University Press, 2010.

Wilkinson, Richard, and Kate Pickett. *The Spirit Level: Why Equality Is Better for Everyone.* Penguin Books, 2010.

ENDNOTES

INTRODUCTION

1   Paul Wells, *The Longer I'm Prime Minister* (Toronto: Random House Canada, 2013), 1.
2   Nigel Hannaford, "A Revolutionary in a Grey Suit Has Seen It All," *Calgary Herald*, Oct. 16, 2004, A23; Tom Olsen, "Take Up Health Battle, Harris Tells Klein," *Calgary Herald*, Oct. 14, 2004, A6.
3   Jamie Peck, *Construction of Neoliberal Reason* (New York: Oxford University Press, 2010); Philip Mirowski and Dieter Plehwe, eds., *The Road from Mont Pèlerin: The Making of the Neoliberal Thought Collective* (Cambridge MA: Harvard University Press, 2009); Angus Burgin, *The Great Persuasion* (Cambridge MA: Harvard University Press, 2012); Daniel Stedman Jones, *Masters of the Universe* (Princeton: Princeton University Press, 2012).
4   Richard Cockett, *Thinking the Unthinkable: Think Tanks and the Economic Counter-Revolution, 1931–1983* (London: HarperCollins, 1995), 173.
5   Molly Ball, "The Fall of the Heritage Foundation and the Death of Republican Ideas," *The Atlantic*, Sept. 25, 2013. http://www.theatlantic.com/politics/archive/2013/09/the-fall-of-the-heritage-foundation-and-the-death-of-republican-ideas/279955/.
6   Donald Gutstein, *Not a Conspiracy Theory* (Toronto: Key Porter, 2009), 186.
7   Brian Easton, "How Did the Health Reforms Blitzkrieg Fail?" *Political Science*, Vol. 42, No. 2 (Dec. 1994): 215. http://dx.doi.org/10.1177/003231879404600205.
8   Stephen Harper, "Rediscovering the Right Agenda," *Citizens Centre Report*, Vol. 30, No. 10 (June 2003): 78.
9   Ibid., 76.

CHAPTER 1

1   James Gwartney, Joshua Hall, and Robert Lawson, *Economic Freedom of the World: 2010 Annual Report*, Fraser Institute, 2010, 1. http://www.freetheworld.com/2010/reports/world/EFW2010_BOOK.pdf.
2   Fraser Institute, Economic Freedom: Spreading Prosperity and Growth, no date. http://www.fraserinstitute.org/programs-initiatives/economic-freedom.aspx.
3   James Gwartney and Robert Lawson, *Economic Freedom of the World: 1997 Annual Report*, Fraser Institute, 1997. http://oldfraser.lexi.net/publications/books/econ_free/countries/canada.html.
4   Government of Canada, "Address by Minister Van Loan to Fraser Institute," No. 2010/74, Ottawa, Sept. 23, 2010. http://www.international.gc.ca/media_commerce/comm/speeches-discours/2010/2010-74.
5   Miriam Henry, Bob Lingard, Fazal Rizvi, and Sandra Taylor, *The OECD, Globalisation, and Education Policy* (London: Pergamon, 2001), 59.
6   Friedrich Hayek, *The Road to Serfdom: Text and Documents*, Bruce Campbell, ed., Definitive Edition (Chicago: University of Chicago Press, 2007).
7   Milton Friedman, "Neo-liberalism and Its Prospects," *Farmand* (Feb. 17, 1951): 89–93.
8   Philip Mirowski, "Defining Neoliberalism," in Philip Mirowski and Dieter Plehwe, eds., *The Road from Mont Pèlerin: The Making of the Neoliberal Thought Collective* (Cambridge,

MA: Harvard University Press, 2009), 427.

9   David Harvey, *A Brief History of Neoliberalism* (New York: Oxford University Press, 2005), 2.

10   Timothy Mitchell, "How Neoliberalism Makes Its World," in Philip Mirowski and Dieter Plehwe, eds., *The Road from Mont Pèlerin: The Making of the Neoliberal Thought Collective* (Cambridge, MA: Harvard University Press, 2009), 386.

11   Friedrich Hayek, "The Intellectuals and Socialism," *University of Chicago Law Review*, Vol. 16, No. 3 (Spring 1949): 418.

12   Ibid., 419.

13   Mitchell, op. cit., 387.

14   Philip Mirowski and Dieter Plehwe, eds., *The Road from Mont Pèlerin: The Making of the Neoliberal Thought Collective* (Cambridge, MA: Harvard University Press, 2009).

15   Perry Anderson, "Renewals," *New Left Review*, 1 (2000): 13.

16   Marci McDonald, "The Man Behind Stephen Harper," *The Walrus*, Oct. 2004, 44; John Gray, "Will the Real Stephen Harper Please Stand Up?" *Canadian Business*, Mar. 2, 2009, 44–47; William Johnson, "The Outsider," *The Walrus*, Mar. 2009, 25.

17   Gerry Nicholls, "The Right Man for the Job," *National Post*, Mar. 5, 2009, A17.

18   Milton Friedman, *Capitalism and Freedom*, Fortieth Anniversary Edition (Chicago: University of Chicago Press, 2002), xv.

19   Ibid., 9.

20   Walter Block, ed., *Economic Freedom: Toward a Theory of Measurement.* (Vancouver, BC: Fraser Institute, 1991), xi.

21   Michael Walker, "Introduction: The Historical Development of the Economic Freedom Index," in James Gwartney, Robert Lawson, and Walter Block, *Economic Freedom of the World: 1975–1995*, Fraser Institute, 1996. http://oldfraser.lexi.net/publications/books/econ_free95/.

22   Michael Walker, "Setting the Scene," in Walter Block, ed., op. cit., 3.

23   Ibid.

24   Ibid., 4.

25   Richard Musick, ed., *The World Survey of Economic Freedom: 1995–1996.* (New Brunswick, NJ: Transaction Publishers, 1996), 7.

26   James Gwartney, Robert Lawson, and Joshua Hall, *Economic Freedom of the World: 2012 Annual Report*, Fraser Institute, 2012, 7. http://www.freetheworld.com/2012/EFW2012-complete.pdf.

27   Matt Naugle, "Profiles in Liberty: Dr. Robert Lawson of Southern Methodist University," *United Liberty*, Oct. 24, 2012. http://www.unitedliberty.org/articles/11667-profiles-in-liberty-robert-lawson-of-southern-methodist-university.

28   Dean Russell, "Who Is a Libertarian?" Foundation for Economic Education, *The Freeman*, Vol. 5, No. 5 (May 1955). www.fee.org/the_freeman/detail/who-is-a-libertarian.

29   Walter Block, ed., *I Chose Liberty: Autobiographies of Contemporary Libertarians.* (Auburn, AL: Ludwig von Mises Institute, 2010).

30   Brian Doherty, "Best of Both Worlds," *Reason*, June 1, 1995. http://reason.com/archives/1995/06/01/best-of-both-worlds.

31   Joshua Hall and Robert Lawson, "Economic Freedom of the World: An Accounting of the Literature," O'Neil Center for Global Markets and Freedom, Cox School of Business, Southern Methodist University, Working Paper, 2013–02, Mar. 2013. http://oneil.cox.smu.edu/detail/economic-freedom-of-the-world-an-accounting-of-the-literature.

32   Russell, op. cit.

33   Philip Mirowski, *Never Let a Serious Crisis Go to Waste* (London: Verso, 2013), 39.

34   Friedman, op. cit., 38.

35   Michael MacDonald and Darel Paul, "Killing the Goose that Lays the Golden Egg: The Politics of Milton Friedman's Economics," *Politics and Society*, Vol. 39, No. 4 (2011): 566.

36   Ibid., 567.

37   Ibid.

38   Ibid.

39   Ibid., 568.

40 Doherty, op. cit.
41 Walter Block, "Paul Craig Roberts on Empirical Measures of Economic Freedom: A Rejoinder," *International Journal of Social Economics*, Vol. 33, No. 7 (2006): 481.
42 Gwartney, Lawson, and Hall, op. cit., 8.
43 Timothy Mitchell, "How Neoliberalism Makes Its World: The Urban Property Rights Project in Peru," in Philip Mirowski and Dieter Plehwe, eds., The Road from Mont Pèlerin: The Making of the Neoliberal Thought Collective (Cambridge, MA: Harvard University Press, 2009), 386. Mitchell's important contribution is discussed in Chapter 4.
44 Greenpeace, "Charles G. Koch Foundation," 2013. http://www.greenpeace.org/usa/en/campaigns/global-warming-and-energy/polluterwatch/koch-industries/charles-g-koch-foundation/.
45 QMI Agency, "We're in the Top 5 for Global Economic Freedom," *Toronto Sun*, Sept. 18, 2012. http://www.torontosun.com/2012/09/18/were-in-the-top-5-for-global-economic-freedom.
46 Sarah Boesveld, "Canada Ranked in Top 5 for Economic Freedom," *National Post*, Sept. 18, 2012, A1.
47 Alvin Rabushka, "Philosophical Aspects of Economic Freedom," in Walter Block, ed., *Economic Freedom: Toward a Theory of Measurement* (Vancouver: Fraser Institute, 1988), 24.
48 Avilia Bueno, Nathan Ashby and Fred McMahon, "Selected Publications Using Ratings from Economic Freedom of North America," pp. 71-74 in *Economic Freedom of North America 2012*. http://freetheworld.com/efna.htm48   Paul Nyden, "Koch Brothers' Billions Reach West Virginia," *Charlestown Gazette*, Sept. 26, 2010. http://www.wvgazette.com/News/201009260391.
49 Paul Nyden, "Koch Brothers' Billions Reach West Virginia," *Charlestown Gazette*, Sept. 26, 2010. www.svgazette.com/News/202009260391.
50 Fred McMahon, "The History of Economic Freedom of the World," *Fraser Forum* (Nov. 2009): 14. http://www.fraserinstitute.org/research-news/research/display.aspx?id=13252.
51 Milton Friedman, "Preface: Economic Freedom Behind the Scenes," in James Gwartney and Robert Lawson, *Economic Freedom of the World: 2002 Annual Index*. Fraser Institute, 2002. http://www.freetheworld.com/release_2002.html.
51 Fred McMahon, ed., *Towards a Worldwide Index of Human Freedom*, Fraser Institute and Liberales Institut, 2012, v. http://www.freetheworld.com/2012/freedomIndex/Towards-Worldwide-Index.pdf.
53 Quoted in Michael Murray, "From Economic Freedom to Economic and Social Poverty," *Journal of Economic Issues*, Vol. 44, No. 2 (June 2010): 422.
54 Gary Mason, "Stephen Harper's Wildrose Soulmate," *Globe and Mail*, Apr. 5, 2012, A19.
55 Danielle Smith, "Danielle's Leadership Acceptance Speech," Oct. 17, 2009. http://www.wildrose.ca/speech/danielles-leadership-acceptance-speech/.
56 Jennifer Keene and Brooks DeCillia, "Vote Compass: Property Rights a Big Issue in Rural Alberta," *CBC News*, Apr. 18, 2012. http://www.cbc.ca/news/canada/albertavotes2012/story/2012/04/17/albertavotes2012-vote-compass-property-rights.html.
57 Armen Alchian, "Property Rights," in *The Concise Encyclopedia of Economics*, Library of Economics and Liberty, 2008. http://www.econlib.org/library/Enc/PropertyRights.html.
58 James Gwartney, Joshua Hall, and Robert Lawson, *Economic Freedom of the World: 2010 Annual Report*, Fraser Institute, 2010, 5.
59 Scott Reid and Randy Hillier, "Paths to Reform," Presentation to the Canadian Property Rights Conference 2012, Sept. 18, 2012. http://www.youtube.com/watch?v=P_fmOkAU0E0.
60 Robert Sibley, "Politicians to Call for Property Rights Protection in Charter," *Ottawa Citizen*, Feb. 24, 2011, A3; Scott Reid, Speech, Dec. 2, 2011.
61 Danielle Smith, "Day 1: Ottawa: Canadian Property Rights Conference 2012," Wildrose, Sept. 15, 2012. http://www.wildrose.ca/leader/day-1-ottawa-canadian-property-rights-conference-2012/.
62 Stuart Dryden, "Protect Property in Constitution, Says Conference," *Toronto Sun*, Sept. 15, 2012. http://www.torontosun.com/2012/09/15/protect-property-in-constitution-says-conference.
63 Scott Reid and Randy Hillier, op. cit.

64   "Harper Conservatives Use Majority to End Long-standing Wheat Board Monopoly," *Canadian Press*, Nov. 28, 2011.

65   Bruce Johnstone, "Rights Relative in Harper's World," *Regina Leader Post*, Aug. 4, 2012, B1.

66   Jennifer Graham, "Harper Pardons Convicted Farmers," *Globe and Mail*, Aug. 2, 2012, A5.

67   Robert Tamilia and Sylvain Charlebois, "The Importance of Marketing Boards in Canada: A Twenty-First Century Perspective," *British Food Journal*, Vol. 109, No. 2 (2007): 119–44.

68   Neil Reynolds, "The NDP Can Rest Content in Its Mission," *Globe and Mail*, Mar. 19, 2012, A11.

69   Neil Reynolds, "Kiwis Put Canada's Dairy Supply Management to Shame," *Globe and Mail*, Apr. 25, 2012, B2.

70   Martha Hall Findlay, "Supply Management: Problems, Politics — and Possibilities," *SPP Research Papers* Vol. 5, Iss. 19 (June 2012): 18–19.

71   Ibid., 18.

71   Kevin Cox, "Marketing Boards under Growing Fire," *Globe and Mail*, Nov. 30, 1981, P1.

73   Eric Beauchesne and Derek Abma, "Bad Policy Feeds Obesity Problem," *Ottawa Citizen*, Aug. 24, 2007, A5.

74   Brian Lee Crowley and Jason Clemens, "Impoverishing Canadians — As Consumers and Free-traders," *National Post*, June 22, 2012, A12.

75   Peter O'Neil, "Canada Walks Tightrope on Trade Fronts," *Vancouver Sun*, June 30, 2012, B1.

76   *Victoria Times Colonist*, *Vancouver Sun*, *Calgary Herald*, *Edmonton Journal*, *Leader Post*, *Star Phoenix*, *Winnipeg Free Press*, *Windsor Star*, *National Post*, *Ottawa Citizen*, *Montreal Gazette*.

77   Laura Rance, "Deregulation Looms as Possible Outcome of New Trade Talks," *Winnipeg Free Press*, July 14, 2012, B8.

78   Hall Findlay, op. cit., 1.

79   Jonathan Manthorpe, "Trans-Pacific Partnership Viewed with Skepticism," *Vancouver Sun*, June 25, 2012, C2.

80   O'Neil, op. cit.

81   Jim Stanford, "Trans-Pacific Partnership: A Few Questions," *The Progressive Economics Forum*, June 19, 2012. http://www.progressive-economics.ca/2012/06/19/trans-pacific-partnership-a-few-questions/.

82   Transport Canada, "Remarks by the Honourable Ed Fast, Minister of International Trade and Minister for the Asia–Pacific Gateway to the Canadian Manufacturers and Exporters Luncheon," Winnipeg, July 16, 2012. http://www.tc.gc.ca/eng/mediaroom/speeches-cme-6806.htm.

83   Lori Wallach, "Trans-Pacific Partnership: Under Cover of Darkness, a Corporate Coup Is Underway," *AlterNet*, June 29, 2012. http://www.alternet.org/story/156059/trans-pacific_partnership%3A_under_cover_of_darkness%2C_a_corporate_coup_is_underway/.

CHAPTER 2

1   James McGann, "2011 Global Go-to Think Tank Rankings," University of Pennsylvania, Jan. 18, 2012, 58. http://repository.upenn.edu/think_tanks/6.

2   Atlas Economic Research Foundation, "2012 Templeton Freedom Award Winners," Aug. 9, 2012. http://atlasnetwork.org/blog/2012/08/2012-tfa-winners/.

3   Macdonald–Laurier Institute, *Annual Report*, Dec. 31, 2010, 6.

4   Janet Ajzenstat, Brian Ferguson, Jack Granatstein, Patrick James, Rainer Knopff, Larry Martin, Chris Sands, William Watson.

5   Andrew Coyne, "Foreword," in Brian Lee Crowley, *Fearful Symmetry: The Fall and Rise of Canada's Founding Values* (Toronto: Key Porter, 2009), 11.

6   *The Next City* is out of print. Crowley republished the article on the Atlantic Institute for Market Studies website. See Brian Crowley, "The Man Who Changed Every-

one's Life," Atlantic Institute for Market Studies, no date. http://www.aims.ca/site/media/aims/Hayek.pdf. He also republished the article on the MLI site in 2012. See http://www.macdonaldlaurier.ca/commentary-celebrating-the-man-who-changed-everyone%E2%80%99s-life-f-a-hayek/.

7   Brian Lee Crowley, "We're All Hayekians Now," *National Post*, May 8, 2012, A15.

8   Quoted in Gerald Frost, *Antony Fisher: Champion of Liberty* (London: Profile Books, 2002), 40.

9   Frost, op. cit, 71.

10 Ibid., 77.

11 Ibid., 106.

12 Ibid., 103.

13 Brook Jeffrey, *Hard Right Turn* (Toronto: HarperCollins, 1999), 420.

14 Donald Gutstein, *Not a Conspiracy Theory* (Toronto: Key Porter, 2009), 122–23. See Fraser Institute, "Challenging Perceptions: Twenty-five Years of Influential Ideas," Vancouver, BC, 1999, 4–7.

15 See, for instance, how the Fraser Institute courted the British American Tobacco Co. for specific funding requests, Gutstein, op. cit., 165–67.

16 Atlas Economic Research Foundation, "How Did Atlas Start?" 2006. http://www.atlasusa.org/V2/main/page.php?page_id=319. No longer available.

17 Lawrence Soley, "Heritage Clones in the Heartland," *Extra*, Sept.–Oct. 1998. http://www.fair.org/index.php?page=1430.

18 Gillian Cosgrove, "Laurier Club Membership Has Its Privileges," *National Post*, Dec. 11, 1999, B11.

19 Atlas Economic Research Foundation, "Atlas Network 2013 Year in Review," Apr. 2014. http://atlasnetwork.org/wp-content/uploads/2014/04/Atlas_Network_Year_in_Review_2013_Final.pdf.

20 Atlantic Institute for Market Studies, "Annual Report 2006–07." http://www.aims.ca/site/media/aims/AR0607.pdf.

21 Atlantic Institute for Market Studies, "Charles Cirtwill," 2011. http://www.aims.ca/en/home/aboutus/authors/charlescirtwill.aspx.

22 Department of Finance Canada, "Clifford Clark Visiting Economist," Jan. 9, 2009. http://www.fin.gc.ca/comment/ve-ei-eng.asp.

23 Crowley, *Fearful Symmetry*, 20.

24 Industry Canada, "Federal Corporation Information – 4414993," Oct. 4, 2012. https://www.ic.gc.ca/app/scr/cc/CorporationsCanada/fdrlCrpDtls.html?corpId=4414993&V_TOKEN=1350 944505153&crpNm=macdonald%20laurier%20institute&crpNmbr=&bsNmbr=.

25 Patricia Best, "Flaherty a Big Fan of New Think Tank," *Globe and Mail*, June 18, 2009, B2.

26 Linda McQuaig, "Tories Keep the Faith, Such As It Is," *Toronto Star*, June 30, 2009, A19.

27 Jane Londerville, "Mortgage Insurance in Canada: Make It More Competitive," Macdonald–Laurier Institute, Nov. 18, 2010. http://www.macdonaldlaurier.ca/MortgageInsurance/; Jane Londerville, "Briefing on the Canadian Mortgage Finance System," MLI Policy Briefing, Macdonald Laurier Institute, Mar. 5, 2012. http://www.macdonaldlaurier.ca/new-paper-argues-first-time-homebuyers-may-be-subsidizing-ottawa%E2%80%99s-bottom-line/; Bill Curry and Sean Silicoff, "Feds Tighten Reins on CMHC," *Globe and Mail*, Apr. 27, 2012, A1; Tara Perkins, "Flaherty Eyes Privatization of CMHC," *Globe and Mail*, Oct. 22, 2012, A1; Stanley Hartt, "Why We Should Privatize CMHC," *National Post*, Dec. 17, 2013, FP11.

28 Because "civilization" suggests collective effort. See Brian Lee Crowley, "What's With Over-the-Top Reaction to Renaming of Museum of Civilization to the Canadian Museum of History?" *The Hill Times*, Oct. 22, 2012. http://www.hilltimes.com/true-north/2012/10/22/what%E2%80%99s-with-over-the-top-reaction-to-renaming-of-museum-of-civilization-to-the/32495.

29 John Ibbitson, "Think Tank Targets StatsCan's Falling Crime Rate Claim," *Globe and Mail*, Feb. 10, 2011, A4; Scott Newark, "Why Canadian Crime Statistics Don't Add Up," Macdonald–Laurier Institute, Feb. 9, 2011. http://www.macdonaldlaurier.ca/new-mli-

paper-canadian-crime-stats-don%E2%80%99t-add-up/; Scott Newark, "Police-Reported Crime Statistics in Canada: Still More Questions Than Answers," Macdonald-Laurier Institute, Feb. 2013. http://www.macdonaldlaurier.ca/is-crime-in-canada-really-declining-mli-study-questions-statscan%E2%80%99s-numbers/.

30   "Enhancing the Reporting of Crime Statistics in Canada," MLI Ottawa Scorecard, Macdonald–Laurier Institute, 2011. http://www.macdonaldlaurier.ca/mli-library/mlis-impact/.

31   "Ottawa Adopts MLI Migrant Smuggling Recommendations," Impact Report Card, Macdonald–Laurier Institute, 2012. http://www.macdonaldlaurier.ca/mli-library/mlis-impact/.

32   Brian Lee Crowley and Ken Coates, "The Way Out," Macdonald–Laurier Institute, May 2013. http://www.macdonaldlaurier.ca/rescuing-northern-gateway/.

33   Michael Watts, "Debunking the Myths: A Broader Perspective of the Canada Health Act," Macdonald–Laurier Institute, Sept. 20, 2013. http://www.macdonaldlaurier.ca/mli-report-debunking-the-myths-of-the-canada-health-act/.

34   In subsequent years, Donner's funding to MLI was: 2009 — $110,000; 2010 — $80,000; 2011 — $125,000; 2012 — $75,000.

35   Robert Remington, "Rice Stands by Bush Policies," Calgary Herald, May 14, 2009, A1.

36   Bloomberg Businessweek, "James Palmer: Executive Profile and Bibliography," Businessweek, no date. http://investing.businessweek.com/research/stocks/private/person.asp?personId=1200588.

37   See Marci McDonald, "The Man Behind Stephen Harper," The Walrus, Oct. 2004. http://thewalrus.ca/the-man-behind-stephen-harper/. See also Gutstein, op. cit., 150–59.

38   This may not be surprising, given that the SPP model is to utilize existing University of Calgary faculty, but the numbers are certainly skewed to the conservative side.

39   Stephen Joseph Harper, "The Political Business Cycle and Fiscal Policy in Canada," Thesis submitted to the Faculty of Graduate Studies in partial fulfillment of the requirements for the degree of Master of Arts," Department of Economics, University of Calgary, Sept. 1991, v.

40   David Hackett, et al., "Pacific Basin Heavy Oil Refining Capacity," School of Public Policy, SPP Research Papers, Vol. 6, Issue 8 (Feb. 2013). http://policyschool.ucalgary.ca/?q=content/pacific-basin-heavy-oil-refining-capacity; Bill Graveland, "Report Says Time Running Out for Canadian Oil Producers to Access Pacific Rim," Canadian Press, Feb. 6, 2013.

41   Jennifer Winter and Michal Moore, "The 'Green Jobs' Fantasy: Why the Economic and Environmental Reality Can Never Live Up to the Political Promise," School of Public Policy, SPP Research Papers, Vol. 6, Issue 31 (Oct. 2013). http://policyschool.ucalgary.ca/?q=content/green-jobs-fantasy-why-economic-and-environmental-reality-can-never-live-political-promise; Jennifer Winter, "The Myth of Green-Job Creation," Vancouver Sun, Oct. 28, 2013, A10.

42   Alan Gelb, "Should Canada Worry About a Resource Curse?" School of Public Policy, SPP Research Papers, Vol. 7, Issue 2 (Jan. 2014). http://www.policyschool.ucalgary.ca/?q=content/should-canada-worry-about-resource-curse.

43   Serge Coulombe, "The Canadian Dollar and the Dutch and Canadian Diseases," School of Public Policy, SPP Research Papers, Vol. 6, Issue 30 (Oct. 2013). http://www.policyschool.ucalgary.ca/?q=content/canadian-dollar-and-dutch-and-canadian-diseases.

44   Trevor Tombe, "The Taming of the Skew: Facts on Canada's Energy Trade," School of Public Policy, SPP Research Papers, Vol. 7, Issue 9 (Mar. 2013). http://policyschool.ucalgary.ca/?q=content/taming-skew-facts-canadas-energy-trade.

45   Sean Gordon, "Separatism Is Dead," Montreal Gazette, Sept. 10, 2003, A12.

46   Tom Olsen, "Take Up Health Battle, Harris Tells Klein," Calgary Herald, Oct. 14, 2004, A6.

47   Frontier Centre for Public Policy, 2009 Annual Report, 2010, 2. http://www.fcpp.org/annual-reports.

48   Krishna Rau, "A Million for Your Thoughts," Canadian Forum, July/Aug. 1996, 11–17.

49   Gutstein, op. cit., 161–62.

50   Stephen Harper and Tom Flanagan, "Our Benign Dictatorship," Next City (Winter 1996): 37.

51   Canada Revenue Agency, "Charities Listings," 2014. http://www.cra-arc.gc.ca/chrts-gvng/

lstngs/menu-eng.html.

52 Milton Friedman, "Public Schools: Make Them Private," *Washington Post*, Feb. 19, 1995, C07.

53 Children First, "Helping Families Afford the School of Their Choice," 2012. http://www. childrenfirstgrants.ca/.

54 Fraser Institute, "Fraser Institute and the W. Garfield Weston Foundation launch New Centre for Improvement in Education," June 28, 2012. http://www.fraserinstitute.org/ research-news/news/display.aspx?id=18504.

55 Munk Debates, "I Would Rather Get Sick in the United States than Canada," Nov. 26, 2009. http://munkdebates.com/debates/Healthcare: "Climate Change Is Mankind's Defining Crisis and Demands a Commensurate Response," Dec. 1, 2009. http://munkdebates. com/The-Debates/Climate-Change; "Foreign Aid Does More Harm than Good," June 1, 2010. http://munkdebates.com/The-Debates/Foreign-Aid.

56 Canada Revenue Agency, "Charities Listings," 2011. http://www.cra-arc.gc.ca/chrts-gvng/ lstngs/menu-eng.html.

57 Fraser Institute, "Fraser Institute Founder's Award Gala Dinner," June 3, 2010. http:// www.gifttool.com/registrar/ShowEventDetails?ID=180&EID=6152. No longer avilable online.

58 Gutstein, op. cit., 163–67.

59 Fraser Institute, *Annual Report 2012*. http://www.fraserinstitute.org/uploadedFiles/fraser-ca/Content/About_Us/Who_We_Are/fraser-institute-2012-annual-report.pdf.

60 Michael Walker, "Letter from Michael Walker to Adrian Payne regarding centre for studies in risk and regulation," Legacy Tobacco Documents Library, June 19, 2000. http:// legacy.library.ucsf.edu/tid/mbc53a99.

61 Fraser Institute, *Annual Report 2007*, 38. http://www.fraserinstitute.org/uploadedFiles/ fraser-ca/Content/About_Us/Who_We_Are/2007_Annual_Report.pdf.

62 Fraser Institute, *Annual Report 2002*, 25. http://www.fraserinstitute.org/uploadedFiles/ fraser-ca/Content/About_Us/Who_We_Are/2002-annual-report.pdf.

63 Gutstein, op. cit., 211–13.

64 Charlie Smith, "Fraser Institute Retains Photograph of Black," *Georgia Straight Online*, Dec. 13, 2003. http://www.straight.com/news/fraser-institute-retains-photograph-black.

65 Canada Revenue Agency, op. cit.

66 Krishna Rau, op. cit., 11; Miro Cernetig, "Neocons: Young Bucks of the New Right," *Globe and Mail*, Feb. 5, 1994, D1.

67 Manning Centre, "Council of Advisors," May 30, 2007. http://www.manningcentre.ca/en/ council. No longer available online.

68 Jeff Gray, "Ruling Upholds Limits on Free Speech," *Globe and Mail*, Feb. 28, 2013, A5.

69 Andrew Coyne, "Loose Talk on Free Speech: Top Court Ruling in Whatcott Case Beyond Belief," *National Post*, Feb. 28, 2013, A1.

70 Andrew Coyne, "In Limiting Free Speech, State Must Prove Its Case," *Montreal Gazette*, Mar. 2, 2013, B5.

71 Kevin Grandia, "Andrew Coyne's Connections to Free Market Think Tanks: Disclosure Lacking," DeSmogBlog, Oct. 2, 2012. http://www.desmogblog.com/2012/09/24/andrew-coyne-s-connections-free-market-think tanks.

72 Andrew Coyne, "Carbon Tax, Road Tolls, Electoral Reform? They Could All Be Possible," *Vancouver Sun*, June 4, 2013, B3.

73 Alejandro Chafuen, "We See Thee Rise: Canada's Emerging Role in Policy Leadership," *Forbes*, Aug. 6, 2013. http://www.forbes.com/sites/alejandrochafuen/2013/08/06/we-see-thee-rise-canadas-emerging-role-in-policy-leadership/.

74 Canadian Association of University Teachers, *Open for Business on What Terms?* (Ottawa: CAUT, Nov. 2013).

75 2013 mentions in the Canadian Newsstand Major Dailies database: Fraser Institute-820, Macdonald–Laurier Institute-311, University of Calgary School of Public Policy-274, Frontier Centre-131, AIMS-32, Montreal Economic Institute-30: total neo-liberal think tanks-1598. Canadian Centre for Policy Alternatives-316, Parkland Institute-55, Broadbent Institute-36: total progressive think tanks-407. Canadian Taxpayers Federation-782, C.D.

Howe Institute-382, Manning Centre-160, National Citizens Coalition-73: total neo-liberal allies-1337. Note: Some Calgary SPP mentions are not neo-liberal.

76 Dietmar Waber, "Examining the Examiners: Reflections on Non-Partisanship, the Fraser Institute and the Report Card on Schools," *Education Canada*, Vol. 46, Issue 3 (Summer 2006): 7.

77 Donald Gutstein, "Reframing Public Education," BC Teachers Federation, July 31, 2010. http://www.bctf.ca/uploadedFiles/Public/Issues/FSA/Gutstein-ReframingPublicEducation.pdf.

78 Eugene Lang, "Harper's Historic Tax-Cutting Legacy," *Toronto Star*, Dec. 27, 2013, A23.

79 Bill Curry, "By 2015, Harper Will Have Shrunk Government to Smallest Size in 50 Years," TheGlobeandMail.com, Nov. 19, 2013. http://spon.ca/by-2015-harper-will-have-shrunk-government-to-smallest-size-in-50-years/2013/11/19/.

80 Aaron Wherry, "Thomas Mulcair Versus Taxes," *Maclean's*, Aug. 8, 2013. http://www.macleans.ca/politics/ottawa/thomas-mulcair-versus-taxes/

81 Thomas Walkom, "Trudeau Clarifies Seven Policies for Prosperity," *Toronto Star*, Feb. 26, 2014, A12.

CHAPTER 3

1 Jefferson Cowie, "Out of Control: Reagan, Labor, and the Fate of the Nation," *Dissent*, Vol. 59, No. 1 (Winter 2012): 56.

2 Steven Greenhouse, "Share of the Work Force in a Union Falls to a 97-Year Low, 11.3%," *New York Times*, Jan. 24, 2013, B1; Barry Hirsch and David Macpherson, "Union Membership, Coverage, Density and Employment Among Private Sector Workers, 1973–2013," 2013. http://www.unionstats.com.

3 Emmanuel Saez, "Striking It Richer: The Evolution of Top Incomes in the United States (Updated with 2011 estimates)," Department of Economics, University of California, Jan. 23, 2013. http://elsa.berkeley.edu/~saez/saez-UStopincomes-2011.pdf.

4 Antonia Zerbisias, "Can Unions Save Middle Class" *Toronto Star*, Sept. 1, 2012, A1; Ross Eisenbrey and Colin Gordon, "As Unions Decline, Inequality Rises," Economic Policy Institute, June 6, 2012. http://www.epi.org/publication/unions-decline-inequality-rises/; David Madland, Karla Walter, and Nick Bunker, "Unions Make the Middle Class," Center for American Progress Action Fund, Apr. 2011. http://www.americanprogressaction.org/issues/labor/report/2011/04/04/9421/unions-make-the-middle-class/.

5 Rene Morissette, Grant Schellenberg, and Anick Johnson, "Diverging Trends in Unionization," *Perspectives*, Statistics Canada no. 75-001-XIE, Apr. 2005, 6; Sharanjit Uppal, "Unionization 2011," *Perspectives* on Labour and Income, Statistics Canada no. 75-001-X. http://www.statcan.gc.ca/pub/75-001-x/2011004/article/11579-eng.pdf.

6 Thomas Walkom, "Ottawa's Love Affair with Airline Abuses Law," *Toronto Star*, Mar. 10, 2012, A8.

7 Brent Jang and Kelly Grant, "Ottawa Readies Air Canada Back-to-Work Bill," *Globe and Mail*, Mar. 10, 2012, B9.

8 Vanessa Lu, "CP Rail Trains to Roll Again," *Toronto Star*, June 1, 2012, B2.

9 Bruce Campion-Smith, "Tories Talk Tough on Labour," *Toronto Star*, Oct. 13, 2011, A7.

10 Josh Rubin, "Labour Strife Set for 2012, Report Predicts," *Toronto Star*, Dec. 3, 2011, A16.

11 Tim Harper, "Public Service Muscles Up for 'Fight of Our Lives,'" *Toronto Star*, Nov. 7, 2011, A6.

12 Jane Taber, "Career Poised for Takeoff via Air Canada Dispute," *Globe and Mail*, Oct. 15, 2011, A6.

13 Brent Jang, "Ottawa Defends Air Canada Decision," *Globe and Mail*, Apr. 9, 2012, B3.

14 Campion-Smith, op. cit.

15 Randy Boswell, "A Change for Canada?" *Ottawa Citizen*, Oct. 29, 2011, A4.

16 Taber, op. cit.

17 Bradley Bouzane and Mark Kennedy, "Tories' Move to End Strikes a 'Sad Day,'" *Montreal Gazette*, June 16, 2011, B1.

18 Niels Veldhuis and Amela Karabegovic, "Reject Unions and Prosper," *National Post*, Sept. 10, 2010, FP11.
19 Friedrich Hayek, *The Road to Serfdom: Text and Documents* (The Definitive Edition), ed. Bruce Caldwell (Chicago: University of Chicago Press, 2007), 207.
20 Ibid., 208.
21 Yves Steiner, "The Neoliberals Confront the Trade Unions," in Philip Mirowski and Dieter Plehwe, eds., *The Road From Mont Pèlerin: The Making of the Neoliberal Thought Collective* (Cambridge, MA: Harvard University Press, 2009), 181.
22 Quoted in ibid., 182.
23 Ibid., 183.
24 Ibid., 188.
25 Alan Bullock and Stephen Trombley, eds., *The New Fontana Dictionary of Modern Thought*. 3rd ed. (London: HarperCollins Publishers, 2000), 630.
26 Steiner, op. cit., 183.
27 Ibid., 192.
28 Ibid., 195.
29 Milton Friedman, *Capitalism and Freedom*, Fortieth Anniversary Edition (Chicago: University of Chicago Press, 2002), 121.
30 Ibid., 122.
31 Milton Friedman and Rose Friedman, *Free to Choose: A Personal Statement* (New York: Avon Books, 1980), 9.
32 Ibid., 28.
33 Friedman, *Capitalism and Freedom*, 124.
34 Milton Friedman and Rose Friedman, *Free to Choose*, 236.
35 James Coates, "Will Coors Swallow the Union Label?" *Chicago Tribune*, Dec. 11, 1988. http://articles.chicagotribune.com/1988-12-11/business/8802230657_1_adolph-coors-william-coors-colorado-kool-aid.
36 "Joseph Coors," *Telegraph*, Mar. 19, 2003. http://www.telegraph.co.uk/news/obituaries/1424996/Joseph-Coors.html.
37 Daniel Stedman Jones, *Masters of the Universe: Hayek, Friedman and the Birth of Neoliberal Politics* (Princeton: Princeton University Press, 2012), 163.
38 Ibid., 162.
39 Thomas Edsall, *The New Politics of Inequality* (New York: Norton and Co., 1985), 217.
40 Ibid.
41 Charles L. Heatherly, ed., *Mandate for Leadership: Policy Management in a Conservative Administration* (Washington, DC: Heritage Foundation, 1981), 630.
42 Ibid., 631.
43 Jason Clemens, Amela Karabegovic, and Niels Veldhuis, *Measuring Labour Markets in Canada and the United States: 2003 Edition*, Fraser Institute, 2003, 3. http://www.fraserinstitute.org/research-news/display.aspx?id=13207. In the 2012 edition, the authors thanked the "supporters," rather than members who financed the project, but they, too, remained anonymous.
44 Amela Karabegovic, Nachum Gabler, and Niels Veldhuis, *Measuring Labour Markets in Canada and the United States: 2012 Edition*, Fraser Institute, 2012, 16. http://www.fraserinstitute.org/research-news/display.aspx?id=18788.
45 See Donald Gutstein, "Reframing Public Education: Countering School Rankings and Debunking the Neoliberal Agenda," paper prepared for the BC Teachers Federation, July 31, 2010. http://bctf.ca/uploadedFiles/Public/Issues/FSA/Gutstein-ReframingPublicEducation.pdf.
46 Roma Luciw and Terry Weber, "Alberta Labour Market Shows Strength," *Globe and Mail*, Aug. 29, 2003, B3.
47 Mark Mullins and Jason Clemens, "Labour's Real Need," *National Post*, Aug. 30, 2003, FP11.
48 Danielle Smith, "Right to Work: The Road to Prosperity," *Calgary Herald*, Aug. 31, 2003, A11.

49 See Luciw and Weber, op. cit.

50 Jesse Kline, "Labour Pains," *National Post*, Sept. 6, 2012, A19.

51 Amela Karabegovic, Nachum Gabler, and Niels Veldhuis, op cit., 41.

52 See Geoffrey York, "Union Wins Six-Year Battle on Spending Members' Dues," *Globe and Mail*, June 28, 1991, A5; Peter Edwards, "Unions Win Important Battle over Dues," *Toronto Star*, Feb. 1, 1989, A26; Rick Haliechuk, "Union Must Repay Dues of Dissenter Court Rules," *Toronto Star*, July 8, 1987, A1; Louise Brown, "Punching Out Unions' Political Clock?" *Toronto Star*, July 26, 1986, B6.

53 Marina Strauss, "Wal-Mart Says Union Means Retailer's 'Culture' Will Suffer," *Globe and Mail*, Feb. 13, 1997, B7.

54 Diane Francis, "Quebec Labour Laws Will Be Put to Test," *National Post*, Apr. 20, 1999, A4; R. *v.* Advance Cutting & Coring Ltd., [2001] 3 S.C.R. 209, 2001 SCC 70. http://scc. lexum.org/en/2001/2001scc70/2001scc70.html; Bill Stewart, "Hammering Away at Injustice," *Open Mind*, No. 10 (Spring 2002). http://www.meritalberta.com/dnn1/LinkClick. aspx?fileticket=IydqXRM-sQE%3D&tabid=109.

55 Richard Mackie, "School Tax-Credit Plan Hailed as a Money Saver," *Globe and Mail*, June 19, 2001, A5.

56 Raquel Exner and Bruce Cowan, "Klein Rejects Change to Labour Law," *Calgary Herald*, Nov. 10, 1999, B1.

57 Canada, Parliament, House of Commons, Bill C-377: *An Act to Amend the Income Tax Act (Requirements for Labour Organizations)*, First Reading, Dec. 5, 2011. http://www.parl. gc.ca/LegisInfo/BillDetails.aspx?Language=E&Mode=1&billId=5295287.

58 Canadian Bar Association, "Re: Bill C-377 — Income Tax Act amendments (requirements for labour organizations)," Letter to James Rajotte MP, Chair, Standing Committee on Finance, House of Commons, Ottawa, Sept. 17, 2012. http://www.cba.org/CBA/submissions/pdf/12-52-eng.pdf.

59 Louis Fortin, Youri Chassin, and Michel Kelly-Gagnon, "The Financing and Transparency of Unions," Montreal Economic Institute, Oct. 18, 2011. http://www.iedm.org/36452-the-financing-and-transparency-of-unions.

60 Kathryn May, "Unions Won't Have to Tell More About Finances," *Ottawa Citizen*, Nov. 5, 2011, A3.

61 Canada Revenue Agency, "Schedule 3: Compensation — The Fraser Institute," Jan. 30, 2013. http://www.cra-arc.gc.ca/chrts-gvng/lstngs/menu-eng.html. The U.S. Internal Revenue Service puts the Canada Revenue Agency to shame in this regard. In its filing requirements for non-profit organizations, names and dollar amounts must be provided for a variety of employees and directors. In 2012, the following Fraser Institute employees earned the following amounts: Michael Walker, senior fellow: $295,111; Niels Veldhuis, president: $275,935; Brett Skinner, former president: $260,376; Peter Cowley, VP – operations: $198,709; Fred McMahon, VP – international policy: $184, 552; Sherry Stein, VP – development: $167, 090. See Foundation Center, "The Fraser Institute," Return of Organization Exempt from Income Tax, Form 990, 2012. http://dynamodata.fdncenter. org/990_pdf_archive/980/980032427/980032427_201212_990.pdf.

62 Lori Theresa Waller, "Conservative Government Rams Through Anti-Union Bill C-377," rabble.ca, Dec. 13, 2012. http://rabble.ca/news/2012/12/conservative-government-ushers-anti-union-bill-c-377-through-house-commons.

63 Kelly McParland, "Senate Rebellion Against Union Bill Adds Insult to Expense Scandal Injuries," *National Post*, June 27, 2013. http://fullcomment.nationalpost.com/2013/06/27/kelly-mcparland-senate-rebellion-against-union-bill-adds-insult-to-expense-scandal-injuries/.

64 Bill Curry, "Tory Senators Balk at Union-Disclosure Bill," *Globe and Mail*, June 19, 2013. http://www.theglobeandmail.com/news/politics/tory-senators-balk-at-union-disclosure-bill/article12661697/.

65 Canada, Parliament, Senate, *Debates*, Feb. 14, 2013. http://www.parl.gc.ca/Content/Sen/Chamber/411/Debates/138db_2013-02-14-e.htm.

66 Charles McVety, "Karl Rove Keynote Speaker at G-20 Summit for Faith and Business

Leaders," Canada Free Press, June 18, 2010. http://canadafreepress.com/index.php/article/24428.

67 Jim Stanford, "Private Member Bill on Union Financial Disclosure," *The Progressive Economics Forum*, Oct. 4, 2011. http://www.progressive-economics.ca/2011/10/04/private-member-bill-on-union-financial-disclosure/.

68 "Conservative MP Russ Hiebert Introduces Anti-labour Bill," *Marketwire*, Feb. 17, 2012.

69 Elizabeth Williamson, "Labor Dept. Accused of Union Sabotage," *Washington Post*, Dec. 11, 2007, A19.

70 James Moore and Wayne Slater, *The Architect: Karl Rove and the Dream of Absolute Power* (New York: Three Rivers Press, 2007), 159–60.

71 Ibid., 161.

72 Bruce Cheadle, "Republican Operative Karl Rove to Join Circus Cast in Toronto During G20 Summit," *Canadian Press*, June 18, 2010.

73 John Geddes, "Union Made," *Maclean's*, May 23, 2011, 16.

74 Les Whittington, "NDP, Unions Blast Plan to Scrap Fair Wages Law," *Toronto Star*, June 1, 2012, A15.

75 Steven Chase, "Tories Defend Labour Provision in Budget," *Globe and Mail*, Oct. 23, 2013, A6.

76 "Stealth Blow to Workers," *Toronto Star*, Oct. 24, 2013, A26.

77 Milagros Palacios, Jason Clemens, Keith Godin and Niels Veldhuis, "Union Disclosure in Canada and the United States." Fraser Institute, *Studies in Labour Markets*, No. 3, Sept. 2006, 3. http://www.fraserinstitute.org/research-news/display.aspx?id=13564.

78 Ibid., 23.

79 Ibid., 5.

80 National Citizens Coalition, "NCC Update," no date. http://nationalcitizens.ca/doc_bin/bill_c377_letter.pdf. No longer available. Copy with author.

81 Brad Walchuk, "Labour Law in Harper's Canada: New Directions, New Challenges," *Canadian Dimension*, Oct. 26, 2011. http://canadiandimension.com/articles/4254.

82 Kathryn May, "Union Leaders Cry Foul Over MP's Plan," *Ottawa Citizen*, Sept. 6, 2012, A1.

83 "A Plan to Set Workers Free," *National Post*, Sept. 7, 2012, A16; John Ivison, "Expect a Lot of Noise About Union Dues Disclosure Bill," *National Post*, Sept. 12, 2012, A4.

84 Sunny Freeman, "Tories Right-to-Work Motion Marks 'Shift to the Far Right:' Critics," *Huffington Post Canada*, Nov. 5, 2013. http://www.huffingtonpost.ca/2013/11/05/tories-right-to-work-motion_n_4217842.html.

85 Benjamin Zycher, Jason Clemens and Niels Veldhuis, "The Implications of US Worker Choice Laws for British Columbia and Ontario," Fraser Institute, Sept. 2013. http://www.fraserinstitute.org/research-news/display.aspx?id=20.

86 Scott Taylor, "Kellogg's London Closure Adds Steam to Right-to-Work Debate," *MetroNews*, Dec. 10, 2013. http://metronews.ca/news/london/880630/kelloggs-london-closure-adds-steam-to-right-to-work-debate/.

87 Canadian Association of University Teachers, "Poll Results Show Majority of Canadians Hold Favourable Views of Unions," CAUT/ACPPU Bulletin Online, Vol. 60, No. 10 (Dec. 2013). https://www.cautbulletin.ca/en_article.asp?articleid=3754.

CHAPTER 4

1 Macdonald–Laurier Institute, "Tom Flanagan Discusses Beyond the Indian Act," Ottawa, Mar. 23, 2010. http://www.youtube.com/watch?v=sYOrEhFvISI.

2 Canada NewsWire, "'Who Should Own Reserve Lands?' Restoring First Nation Property Rights," Oct. 13, 2010; Macdonald–Laurier Institute, "Doing Property Properly and the Future of Canada's First Nations," Aug. 14, 2010. http://www.macdonaldlaurier.ca/doing-property-properly-and-the-future-of-canadas-first-nations/.

3 Tom Flanagan, Christopher Alcantara, and André Le Dressay, *Beyond the Indian Act: Restoring Aboriginal Property Rights* (Montreal and Kingston: McGill–Queen's University Press, 2010), 5.

4 Ibid., 6.
5 Macdonald–Laurier Institute, op cit.
6 Jonathan Montpetit, "Support Gathers for Proposed Law to Allow Private Property on Reserves," Canadian Press, June 9, 2010.
7 Keith Damsell, "$600M Project Set for Native Land," *Financial Post*, Jan. 30, 1996, 55.
8 Macdonald–Laurier Institute, "Manny Jules Discusses *Beyond the Indian Act*," Ottawa, Mar. 23, 2010. http://www.youtube.com/watch?v=uHrOi-woyBc.
9 Tom Flanagan and Christopher Alcantara, "Individual Property Rights on Canadian Indian Reserves," Fraser Institute, Public Policy Sources, No. 60 (July 2002): 16.
10 Ibid., 15.
11 Flanagan, Alcantara, and Le Dressay, op. cit., 7.
12 Macdonald–Laurier Institute, "Manny Jules."
13 Hernando de Soto, *The Mystery of Capital: Why Capitalism Triumphs in the West and Fails Everywhere Else* (New York: Basic Books, 2000), 5–6.
14 Ibid., 48.
15 Ibid., 6.
16 Alan Gilbert, "On the Mystery of Capital and the Myths of Hernando de Soto," *International Development Planning Review*, Vol. 24, No. 1 (2002): 3.
17 Christopher Woodruff, "Review of de Soto's *The Mystery of Capital*," *Journal of Economic Literature*, Vol. 39, Issue 4 (2001): 1222.
18 Timothy Mitchell, "How Neoliberalism Makes Its World," in Philip Mirowski and Dieter Plehwe, eds., *The Road from Mont Pèlerin* (Cambridge, MA: Harvard University Press, 2009), 390.
19 Ibid., 391.
20 Ibid., 392.
21 Ibid., 393.
22 Ibid., 402–06.
23 Brian Ballantyne, et al., "How Can Land Tenure and Cadastral Reform Succeed?" *Canadian Journal of Development Studies*, Vol. 21, No. 3 (2000): 693. Other critiques are cited in Jessica Dempsey, Kevin Gould, and Juanita Sundberg, "Changing Land Tenure, Defining Subjects," in Andrew Baldwin, Laura Cameron, and Audrey Kobayashi, eds., *Rethinking the Great White North* (Vancouver, BC: UBC Press, 2011), 233.
24 Mitchell, op. cit., 397.
25 Ibid., 396–99; States News Service, "Honoring Hernando de Soto and CIPE's Work on Promoting Private Enterprise," Oct. 26, 2009.
26 Owen Lippert, "Property & Poverty: An International Perspective on Canada's Aboriginal Title," *Fraser Forum*, Nov. 2000, 10. http://oldfraser.lexi.net/publications/forum/2000/11/section_04.html.
27 Hernando de Soto, "Explaining the Mystery of Capital," *Fraser Forum*, Sept. 2001, 24–25. http://oldfraser.lexi.net/publications/forum/2001/10/section_09.html.
28 Tom Flanagan, *First Nations? Second Thoughts*, 2nd ed. (Montreal and Kingston: McGill–Queen's University Press, 2008), 113.
29 Richard Pipes, *Property and Freedom* (New York: Alfred A. Knopf, 1999), 88.
30 Flanagan, op. cit., 113.
31 Terry Anderson, Bruce Benson, and Tom Flanagan, eds., *Self-Determination: The Other Path for Native Americans* (Stanford, CA: Stanford University Press, 2006).
32 Flanagan, op. cit., 114.
33 Ibid.
34 Ibid., 133.
35 Ibid., 196.
36 Ibid., 195.
37 Ibid., 198.
38 Tom Flanagan, "Property Rights on the Rez," *National Post*, Dec. 11, 2001, A18.
39 Tom Flanagan and Christopher Alcantara, op cit., 15.

40　See, for instance, Indian Taxation Advisory Board, "First Nation Property Taxation Review," 2000–2001 annual report. http://www.fntc.ca/index.php.

41　Indian Taxation Advisory Board, "Annual Report 2006–2007," 24. http://fntc.ca/index.php.

42　Ibid., 26.

43　Indian Taxation Advisory Board, "ITAB Annual Report 2008," 9. http://fntc.ca/index.php.

44　"Memorandum of Understanding Between the Tulo Centre of Indigenous Economics and the First Nations Tax Commission," Sept. 10, 2008. http://www.tulo.ca/docs/fntc-tulo mou signed.pdf.

45　First Nations Tax Commission, "Annual Report 2008–2009," 27. http://fntc.ca/index.php.

46　Ibid., 21.

47　Ibid., 20.

48　"Memorandum of Understanding: The First Nations Tax Commission and the Institute of Liberty and Democracy," July 19, 2009. http://fntc.ca/images/stories/mou/MOU FNTC - ILD Signed_2009 07 19.pdf.

49　Fraser Institute, "Media Advisory: Fraser Institute wraps up fall cocktail series with discussion on property rights and tax regimes on aboriginal lands," Calgary, Dec. 4, 2008. http://www.marketwire.com/press-release/Media-Advisory-Fraser-Institute-Wraps-Up-Fall-Cocktail-Series-With-Discussion-on-Property-926041.htm.

50　First Nations Tax Commission, "Annual Report 2009–2010," 2. http://fntc.ca/index.php.

51　Tom Flanagan, "Next Step: More Accountable and Transparent Native Governments," Globe and Mail, July 28, 2008, A13; Conservative Party of Canada, "Stand Up for Canada," Federal Election Platform 2006. http://www.cbc.ca/canadavotes2006/leadersparties/pdf/conservative_platform20060113.pdf..

52　Jason Warwick, "Ownership Remains the Issue for First Nations Housing," Leader Post, Sept. 26, 2006, A1.

53　Ibid.

54　Bill Curry, "Duncan's Reward," Globe and Mail, Aug. 7, 2010, A7.

55　Mia Rabson, "Top First Nations' Success to Be Studied," Winnipeg Free Press, Sept. 2, 2010, A6.

56　"Private Property for Natives," National Post, Sept. 3, 2010, A10.

57　Bill Curry, "Natives Fear Renewed Push for Privatized Land Ownership," Globe and Mail, Sept. 1, 2010, A1, A9.

58　"Private Property for Natives," op. cit., Sept. 3, 2010, A10.

59　This would not be the goal of many — but not all — academically-sponsored conferences where the objective is to bring forward various viewpoints and theories and thus move the discipline forward.

60　Meko Nicholas, "Deconstructing the First Nations Property Ownership Act — The Communications Strategy," First Nations in British Columbia, Jan. 4, 2011. http://fnbc.info/blogs/meko-nicholas/deconstructing-first-nations-property-ownership-act-communications-strategy.

61　First Nations Property Ownership Conference, "Featured Speakers," Oct. 20, 2010. http://www.fnpo.ca/newsletter.html. No longer available online.

62　Neskie Manuel and Emma Feltes, "World Bank Darling Promotes Privatization of Reserves," Vancouver Media Co-op, Oct. 28, 2010. http://vancouver.mediacoop.ca/story/world-bank-darling-promotes-privatization-reserves/4998.

63　Manny Jules, "Taking Ownership of Their Land," National Post, Nov. 1, 2010, A14.

64　First Nations Tax Commission, "Annual Report 2010–2011," 12. http://fntc.ca/index.php.

65　Canada, Parliament, House of Commons, Standing Committee on Finance, "Staying Focused on Canadian Jobs and Growth," Report, Dec. 2011, 41st Parl., 1st Sess. http://www.parl.gc.ca/HousePublications/Publication.aspx?DocId=5322386&Language=E&Mode=1&Parl=41&Ses=1.

66　Bill Curry, "Pros and Cons of Private Lands on Reserves Up for Debate," Globe and Mail, Dec. 16, 2011, A6.

67　Canada, "Budget Plan Chapter 3.4: Supporting Families and Communities," Budget 2012, March 2012. http://www.budget.gc.ca/2012/plan/chap3-4-eng.html.

68 John Ibbitson, "Tories Prepare New Native Land Plan," *Globe and Mail*, Aug. 6, 2012, A1.
69 Josh Wingrove, "First Nations and Land Ownership," *Globe and Mail*, Aug. 7, 2012, A4.
70 John Ibbitson, "Do Opponents of Native Property Rights Think Things Are Okay Now?" *Globe and Mail*, Aug. 8, 2012. http://www.theglobeandmail.com/news/politics/do-opponents-of-native-property-rights-think-things-are-okay-now/article4468909/.
71 First Nations Tax Commission, "Annual Report 2011–2012, 31. http://fntc.ca/index.php.
72 "Option to Own," *Globe and Mail*, Aug. 8, 2012, A14.
73 Brigitte Pellerin, "Feds to Introduce Law Allowing Property Rights on Reserves," *cnews*, Aug. 6, 2012. http://cnews.canoe.ca/CNEWS/Politics/2012/08/06/20072211.html.
74 "Reserve Property Ownership Long Overdue: Ex-Chief," *CTV News*, Aug. 7, 2012. http://www.ctvnews.ca/politics/reserve-property-ownership-long-overdue-ex-chief-1.906181.
75 Alexandra Paul, "First Nations Skeptical of Ottawa's Plan," *Winnipeg Free Press*, Aug. 11, 2012, A11.
76 Jason Fekete, "This Is a Big Oil and Mineral Land Grab," *Ottawa Citizen*, Aug. 17, 2012, A4.
77 Wab Kinew, "From a Grassroots Hashtag to a Real Opportunity for Change," *Winnipeg Free Press*, Dec. 6, 2012, C3; Doug Cuthand, "Next Year Critical to Native–Ottawa Relations," *Star Phoenix*, Dec. 7, 2012, A13.
78 John Ibbitson, "Protests Knock Harper Agenda Off Stride," *Globe and Mail*, Jan. 7, 2013, A4.
79 Richard Foot, "Bands Bank on Their Reserves," *Ottawa Citizen*, Aug. 15, 2010, A1.
80 Ibid.
81 Assembly of First Nations, "First Nations' Rejection of a 'Property Ownership Act,'" Resolution 44/2010, Annual General Assembly, Winnipeg, July 20–22, 2010. http://www.afn.ca/uploads/files/2010-res.pdf.
82 Bill Curry, op. cit.
83 Canada, Parliament, House of Commons, Debates, *40th Parl., 3rd Sess., Oct. 1, 2010*. http://www.parl.gc.ca/HousePublications/Publication.aspx?DocId=4669689&Language=E&Mode=1.
84 Canada, Parliament, House of Commons, Standing Committee on Aboriginal Affairs and Northern Development, Evidence, 40th Parl., 3rd Sess., Mar 8, 2011. http://www.parl.gc.ca/HousePublications/Publication.aspx?DocId=5023417&Language=E&Mode=1&Parl=40&Ses=3.
85 Richard Foot, "At Least 30 Chiefs Earn More than $110,000," *Calgary Herald*, Oct. 19, 2010, B11.
86 Sean Myers and Richard Foot, "Eighty Native Leaders Earn More than PM," *Calgary Herald*, Nov. 23, 2010, B7.
87 Troy Lanigan, "Influence Driven from 'the Outside,'" Canadian Taxpayers Federation, Oct. 3, 2009. http://taxpayer.com/blog/03-10-2009/influence-driven-outside. See also *Hill Times* online. http://www.hilltimes.com/.
88 Laura Stone, "First Nations Leaders Agree to Disclose Salaries to Members," *Edmonton Journal*, Dec. 15, 2010, A5.
89 Michael Woods, "First Nations Transparency Bill Signed into Law," *Ottawa Citizen*, Mar. 28, 2013, A4.
90 Michael den Tandt, "Federal Budget Will Stay the Course," *National Post*, Feb. 1, 2013, A5.
91 Miro Cernetig, "5.1 Billion Geared to Reducing Native, Métis Poverty Gap," *Vancouver Sun*, Nov. 26, 2005, A1.
92 Les Leyne, "Ottawa Agrees to a Tough New Deal," *Times-Colonist*, Nov. 26, 2005, A14.
93 Ira Basin, "Why a University of Calgary Professor Has Some Native Leaders Worried about a Conservative Government," *CBC Canada Votes Reality Check*, Jan. 17, 2006. http://www.cbc.ca/canadavotes2006/realitycheck/aboriginal.html.
94 Tristin Hopper, "Home Sweet Home," *National Post*, Nov. 9, 2013, A4.
95 Fraser Institute, "Ravina Bains." https://www.fraserinstitute.org/author.aspx?id=20022&txID=4778.
96 Tom Flanagan and Katrine Beauregard, "The Wealth of First Nations: An Exploratory

Study," Fraser Institute, June 2013, 25. http://www.fraserinstitute.org/uploadedFiles/fraser-ca/Content/research-news/research/publications/wealth-of-first-nations.pdf.

97   "Transcript: Peter Mansbridge Talks with Stephen Harper," *CBC News*, Jan. 18, 2012. http://www.cbc.ca/news/politics/story/2012/01/17/pol-mansbridge-interview-harper-transcript.html.

CHAPTER 5

1   Vaclav Klaus, "Current Global Warming Alarmism and the Mont Pèlerin Society's Long-term Agenda," *Economic Affairs*, Vol. 29, Issue 1 (Mar. 1, 2009): 45.
2   Ibid., 46.
3   Friedrich Hayek, *The Road to Serfdom: Text and Documents* (The Definitive Edition), ed. Bruce Caldwell (Chicago: University of Chicago Press, 2007), 99.
4   Friedrich Hayek, *The Constitution of Liberty* (Chicago: University of Chicago Press, 1960), 372.
5   Allin Cottrell and Paul Cockshott, "Information and Economics: A Critique of Hayek," Oct. 1994. http://reality.gn.apc.org/econ/hayek.htm.
6   Claude Shannon, *The Mathematical Theory of Communication* (Urbana: University of Illinois Press, 1949).
7   Hayek, *Constitution of Liberty*, 372.
8   Ibid., 374.
9   Ibid., 375.
10 See Donald Gutstein, *Not a Conspiracy Theory* (Toronto: Key Porter, 2009), Chapter 7 and references.
11 "Global Warming Skepticism Higher in U.S. and Britain than Canada," Angus Reid Public Opinion, June 27, 2012. http://www.angus-reid.com/polls/45431/global-warming-skepticism-higher-in-u-s-and-britain-than-canada.
12 James Powell, "Why Climate Deniers Have No Scientific Credibility — in One Pie Chart," DeSmogBlog, Nov. 15, 2012. http://desmogblog.com/6662.
13 John Cook, et al., "Quantifying the Consensus on Anthropogenic Global Warming in the Scientific Literature," *Environmental Research Letters*, 8 (2013).
14 DeSmogBlog, "Cato Institute," no date. http://desmogblog.com/cato-institute; Brendan Demelle, "Heartland Denial-a-Palooza Sponsors Have Received $67 Million from ExxonMobil, Koch and Scaife Foundations," May 22, 2012. http://www.desmogblog.com/heartland-denial-palooza-sponsors-have-received-67-million-exxonmobil-koch-and-scaife-foundations; Cato Institute, "Czech President to Join Cato Institute," Feb. 28, 2013. http://www.cato.org/blog/czech-president-join-cato-institute.
15 Mike De Souza, "Harper's Anti-Kyoto Letter Fuels Liberal Counterattack," *Ottawa Citizen*, Jan. 31, 2007, A3.
16 Bitumen is a more neutral term than either tar sands (the term used by "radical environmentalists") or oil sands (the term used by "apologists" for Big Oil and the Alberta and Canadian governments).
17 Robyn Eckersley, "Free Market Environmentalism: Friend or Foe?" in Piers Stephens, John Barry, and Andrew Dobson, eds., *Contemporary Environmental Politics: From Margins to Mainstream* (London: Routledge, 2006), 151.
18 Ibid., 152.
19 Steven Chase, "Peter Kent's Plan to Clean Up the Oil Sands' Dirty Reputation," *Globe and Mail*, Jan, 7, 2011, A10.
20 David Brock, *The Republican Noise Machine: Right-Wing Media and How It Corrupts Democracy* (New York: Crown Publishers, 2004).
21 Allan Woods, "'Dirty Oil' Anger Shocked Tories," *Toronto Star*, Dec. 23, 2010, A26.
22 Steven Chase, "'Dirty'? 'Ethical'? The Oil-Sands Fight Renews," *Globe and Mail*, Jan. 8, 2011, A3.
23 Ezra Levant, "Greenpeace Not Slick: Oilsands Bashing Ignores Problems of Other Options for Oil," *Toronto Sun*, Sept. 21, 2010. http://www.torontosun.com/comment/columnists/2010/09/20/15416881.html.

24 Claudia Cattaneo, "Saudi Oil's Ethical Warfare," *National Post*, Sept. 21, 2011, A1.
25 "Ethical Oil and OPEC," *Petroleum Economist*, Sept. 30, 2010. http://www.petroleum-economist.com/Article/2730961/Ethical-oil-and-Opec.html.
26 Ibid.
27 Ezra Levant, "America Over a Barrel: As an Ethical Source of Oil Imports, Canada Stands Alone," *Toronto Sun*, Sept. 14, 2010. http://www.torontosun.com/news/world/2010/09/10/15311826.html.
28 Levant, "Greenpeace Not Slick."
29 Ezra Levant, "James Cameron Gassing Up for Change," *Toronto Sun*, Sept. 26, 2010. http://www.torontosun.com/comment/columnists/2010/09/24/15467741.html.
30 Peter Foster, "Ethical Oil," *National Post*, Sept. 22, 2010, FP15.
31 Adam McDowell, "Alberta Sands Praised as 'Ethical Oil,'" *National Post*, Sept. 22, 2010, A8.
32 "Defending the Oil Sands," *National Post*, Sept. 23, 2010, A14.
33 Canada, Parliament, Senate, "Debates," 3rd Session, 40th Parliament, Oct. 27, 2010. http://www.parl.gc.ca/Content/Sen/Chamber/403/Debates/060db_2010-10-27-e.htm.
34 Canada, Parliament, Senate, "Debates," 3rd Session, 40th Parliament, Nov. 3, 2010. http://www.parl.gc.ca/Content/Sen/Chamber/403/Debates/063db_2010-11-03-e.htm.
35 Canada, Parliament, House of Commons, Standing Committee on Natural Resources, "Evidence," 3rd Session, 40th Parliament, Dec. 7, 2010. http://www.parl.gc.ca/HousePublications/Publication.aspx?DocId=4861242&Language=E&Mode=1&Parl=40&Ses=3.
36 Joyce Nelson, "Enbridge PR — Hill & Knowlton and Peter Kent," *Watershed Sentinel*, Vol. 23, No. 2 (Mar.–Apr. 2013). http://www.watershedsentinel.ca/content/enbridges-pr-firm-hill-and-knowlton-minister-environment-connection.
37 Mark Kennedy, "Harper Defends Oil Sands as Ethical," *Calgary Herald*, Jan. 8, 2011, A4.
38 Jane Taber, "Meet the Prime Minister's Oil-Sands Muse," *Globe and Mail*, Jan. 15, 2011, A12.
39 Colin Freeze, "Ex-Tory Message Maven Stays Political," *Globe and Mail*, July 28, 2011, A3.
40 Licia Corbella, "Website's Ads Hammer Myths About Canada," *Calgary Herald*, July 29, 2011, A1.
41 Shawn McCarthy, "Ethical Oil Ad Sparks Furor," *Globe and Mail*, Sept. 21, 2011, A6.
42 Gordon Hoekstra, "Ethical Oil.org Slams Environmental Groups for Taking U.S. Money," *Vancouver Sun*, Jan. 4, 2012, A7.
43 John Bennett, "Astroturf 'Ethical Oil' Files CRA Complaint Against Sierra Club Canada Foundation," Dec. 17, 2012. http://www.sierraclub.ca/en/blog/john-bennett/astroturf-%E2%80%98ethical-oil%E2%80%99-files-cra-complaint-against-sierra-club-canada-foundation.
44 "Glenn Solomon, Q.C., Managing Partner," *JSS Barristers*, no date. http://www.jssbarristers.ca/pages/people/solomon-glenn.cfm.
45 For Gore's presentation see Ivan Semeniuk, "No Such Thing as Ethical Oil," *Globe and Mail*, May 8, 2013, A6. For the follow-up survey, see Ivan Semeniuk, "On Topic : Al Gore and the Ethical Oil Debate," *Globe and Mail*, May 11, 2013, F8.
46 Claudia Cattaneo, "Canada's Energy Pitchman," *National Post*, Apr. 20, 2013, FP5.
47 "An Open Letter from Minister Oliver on Our Energy Markets and the Regulatory Process," Natural Resources Canada, Jan. 9, 2012. http://www.nrcan.gc.ca/media-room/news-release/2012/1/3525.
48 Laura Payton, "Radicals Working Against Oilsands, Ottawa Says," *CBC News*, Jan. 9, 2012. http://www.cbc.ca/news/politics/story/2012/01/09/pol-joe-oliver-radical-groups.html.
49 Greenpeace International, *Annual Report 2012*, 37. http://www.greenpeace.org/international/Global/international/publications/greenpeace/2013/GPI-AnnualReport2012.pdf.
50 Environmental Life Force, "Interview with ELF founder John Hanna," *ELF* (the original), Sept. 5, 2001. http://www.originalelf.org. No longer available online.
51 The Persuaders, "Interview Frank Luntz," *Frontline*, Nov. 9, 2004. http://www.pbs.org/wgbh/pages/frontline/shows/persuaders/interviews/luntz.html.
52 Luntz Research, "The Environment: A Cleaner, Safer, Healthier America," 2002, 142. http://www.motherjones.com/files/LuntzResearch_environment.pdf.

53   Ibid., 137.
54   Ibid., 142.
55   William Walker, "First of Four Parts," *Toronto Star*, Apr. 13, 1992, A15.
56   Bill Berkowitz, "Spurned by Washington Republicans, Frank Luntz Turns to Canada," *Media Transparency*, May 27, 2006. http://www.heatisonline.org/contentserver/objecthandlers/index.cfm?ID=5953&Method=Full&PageCall=&Title=Luntz%20Spins%20His%20Way%20Into%20Canadian%20Politics&Cache=False.
57   Elizabeth Thompson, "U.S. Guru Tells Tories to Talk Hockey," *Edmonton Journal*, May 7, 2006, A6.
58   Dennis Bueckert, "Conservative Climate Strategy Said to Be Inspired by U.S. Communications Expert," *Canadian Press*, May 14, 2006.
59   Canada, Parliament, House of Commons, "Debates," May 11, 2006. http://www.parl.gc.ca/HousePublications/Publication.aspx?DocId=2199068&Language=E&Mode=1.
60   Ibid.
61   Canada, Parliament, House of Commons, "Debates," May 3, 2006. http://www.parl.gc.ca/HousePublications/Publication.aspx?Language=E&Mode=1&DocId=2174969&File=0.
62   Peter O'Neil, "Block Foreign Eco-funding: MP," *Calgary Herald*, Feb. 10, 2012, D5.
63   Josh Rogin, "Canada Frustrated by 'Radical Environmentalists' Control Over Washington," *The Cable*, Apr. 13, 2012. http://thecable.foreignpolicy.com/posts/2012/04/13/canada_frustrated_by_radical_environmentalists_control_over_washington.
64   Marco Navarro-Genie, "Canadian Energy Strategy Would Invite Meddling," *Calgary Herald*, Feb. 13, 2012, A9.
65   Donald Gutstein, "Stephen Harper Repeats U.S. Republican Lines on Energy," *Georgia Straight*, Apr. 18, 2012. http://www.straight.com/news/stephen-harper-repeats-us-republican-lines-energy.
66   Leger Marketing, "Study on Canadians' Perceptions of Hydrocarbon Energy," Montreal Economic Institute, Sept. 24, 2012, 27. http://www.iedm.org/41036-study-on-canadians-perceptions-of-hydrocarbon-energy.
67   Ibid., 5.
68   Preston Manning, "A Fresh Start for a Fresh Decade," *Globe and Mail*, Jan. 25, 2010, A13.
69   Gloria Galloway, "How the Conservatives Dodged the Climate Bullet," *Globe and Mail*, Mar. 20, 2010, F3.
70   Clive Mather, Nancy Olewiler, and Stewart Elgie, "B.C.'s Carbon Tax Shift Is Smart Public Policy," *Globe and Mail*, Nov. 29, 2007, A21.
71   Sustainable Prosperity, "What We Do: Introducing Sustainable Prosperity: A Think Tank. A Do Tank," 2013. http://www.sustainableprosperity.ca/What+We+Do+EN.
72   Alex Kenny, Stewart Elgie, and Dave Sawyer, "Advancing the Economics of Ecosystems and Biodiversity in Canada," Sustainable Prosperity, June 2011. http://www.sustainableprosperity.ca/article1431.
73   Ibid., iii.
74   Robyn Eckersley, op. cit., 156.
75   Sustainable Prosperity, "Environmental Markets, 2012," Nov. 2012. http://www.sustainableprosperity.ca/article3228.
76   Gloria Galloway, "Canada a Global 'Laggard' in 'Environmental Markets,'" *Globe and Mail*, Nov. 17, 2012, A7.
77   Eric Roston, "Dumb Question: Is Environmentalism Annoying?" *Bloomberg*, June 5, 2013. http://www.bloomberg.com/news/2013-06-05/dumb-question-is-environmentalism-annoying-.html.
78   Terry Anderson and Donald Leal, *Free Market Environmentalism* (San Francisco: Pacific Research Institute for Public Policy, 1991), 3.
79   For a comprehensive list see John Dupuis, "The Canadian War on Science: A Long, Unexaggerated, Devastating Chronological Indictment," *Science Blogs*, May 20, 2013. http://scienceblogs.com/confessions/2013/05/20/the-canadian-war-on-science-a-long-unexaggerated-devastating-chronological-indictment/.
80   Canada, Statistics Canada, "Human Activity and the Environment: Measuring Ecosystem

Goods and Services in Canada, 2013," Ottawa: Minster of Industry, Dec. 2013, 4, *Statistics Canada Catalogue* No. 16-201-X.

81   Sustainable Prosperity "National Environment-Economy Research Network Launched," July 4, 2012. http://www.sustainableprosperity.ca/article2880.

82   Mike De Souza, "Biodiversity Threats Hover over Canadian Economy," *Ottawa Citizen*, July 18, 2013, A6; Canada, Environment Canada, "Departmental Overview: DM's Transition Binder," July 2012, Document released under the *Access to Information Act*, Request A-2012-01456.

83   Canada, Environment Canada, "Bob Hamilton, Deputy Minister," Aug. 21, 2013. http://www.ec.gc.ca/default.asp?lang=En&n=BC5E38F9-1.

84   European Commission, "The EU Emissions Trading System (EU ETS)," Oct. 2013. http://ec.europa.eu/clima/publications/docs/factsheet_ets_en.pdf.

CHAPTER 6

1   Compare Government of Canada, *Canada Gazette, Part 1*, June 20, 2010, 1731, and Government of Canada, *Canada Gazette, Part 1*, Apr. 16, 2005, 1245.

2   Shannon Proudfoot, "Canadian Census Change Will Shut Out Genealogists," *Calgary Herald*, June 30, 2010, A4.

3   "StatsCan Head Quits Over Census Dispute," *CBC News*, July 21, 2010. http://www.cbc.ca/news/canada/story/2010/07/21/statistics-canada-quits.html.

4   Canadian Press, "A List of Groups Opposed to Scrapping of Long-form Census," July 20, 2010.

5   Haroon Siddiqui, "Gutting of Census Stirs Opposition to Harper," *Toronto Star*, July 11, 2010, A13.

6   "Numbers Racket," *Ottawa Citizen*, June 2, 2010, A12.

7   Jason Hewlett, "Census Changes Leave Towns in Dark," *Kamloops Daily News*, May 17, 2013, A1.

8   Mia Rabson, "Province's Top Statistician Prods Feds to Hold 2016 Census," *Winnipeg Free Press*, May 17, 2013, A4; Mia Rabson, "Census Replacement Costs More, Gets Less Info," *Winnipeg Free Press*, May 13, 2013, A4.

9   Paul Saurette, "When Smart Parties Make Stupid Decisions," *The Mark*, July 23, 2010. No longer available online.

10   Tavia Grant, "StatsCan Analyst Quits, Citing Stifled Debate Over Census," *Globe and Mail*, Feb. 2, 2012, A7.

11   Philip Cross, "The Census Is Passé," *National Post*, May 9, 2013, FP11.

12   Dana Flavelle, "Business Split on Death of Long Survey," *Toronto Star*, July 21, 2010, B1.

13   COMPAS Inc., "Business Panel on Census Long Form Controversy: Apparent Reversal of Opinion, Almost No Support for the Status Quo," BDO Dunwoody Weekly CEO/Business Leader Poll, Aug. 9 2010. http://www.compas.ca.

14   Charles Lammam and Niels Veldhuis, "Census Too Intrusive," *National Post*, July 17, 2010, FP 19. See also Shannon Proudfoot, "Surveys Way to Go: Think-Tank," *Regina Leader Post*, July 17, 2010, A9.

15   Canada, Treasury Board Secretariat, "Statistics Canada," 2010–11 Main Estimates, Mar. 29, 2010. http://www.tbs-sct.gc.ca/est-pre/20102011/me-bpd/IC-CI-eng.asp#bm11.

16   Louise Egan, "StatsCan, or StatsCan't?" *Ottawa Citizen*, May 3, 2012, B12.

17   Gloria Galloway, "Budget Cuts Another Victory in Tory War on Information: Opposition," *Globe and Mail*, Mar. 30, 2012. http://www.theglobeandmail.com/news/politics/ottawa-notebook/budget-cuts-another-victory-in-tory-war-on-information-opposition/article4097001/.

18   "Omnibus Bill Sidelines MPs," *Saskatoon Star Phoenix*, June 12, 2012, A8.

19   Margaret Munro, "Environment Canada 'Muzzles' Scientists' Dealings with Media," *Ottawa Citizen*, Feb. 1, 2008, A1.

20   Margaret Munro, "Small Ottawa Army Handles Media Requests," *Vancouver Sun*, Sept. 17, 2010, B2.

21   Pallab Ghosh, "Canadian Government is 'Muzzling its Scientists.'" *BBC News*, Feb. 17, 2012. http://www.bbc.co.uk/news/science-environment-16861468.
22   Douglas Quan, "PM Urged to Stop 'Muzzling' of Federal Scientists," *Calgary Herald*, Feb. 18, 2012, A10.
23   "Frozen Out," *Nature*, Vol. 483, No. 7387 (Mar. 1, 2012): 6.
24   John Geddes, "Cracking Eggheads," *Maclean's*, Aug. 16, 2010, 20.
25   Ibid.
26   Friedrich Hayek, *The Road to Serfdom: Text and Documents* (The Definitive Edition), ed. Bruce Caldwell (Chicago: University of Chicago Press, 2007), 70.
27   Ibid., 200.
28   Ibid., 202, fn. 35.
29   "Science and the National War Effort," *Nature*, Vol. 146, No. 3702 (Oct. 12, 1940): 470.
30   Philip Cross, "Muzzling Government Scientists?" *National Post*, June 14, 2013, FP11.
31   Jon Ferry, "The Carbon-Tax Love Affair Is a Hot-Air Illusion," *The Province*, July 29, 2013, A6.
32   Brian Laghi, "Harper Would Get Tough on Crime," *Globe and Mail*, June 2, 2004, A8.
33   John Ibbitson, "The Tories Find Their Wedge Issue," *Globe and Mail*, Jan. 6, 2006, A6.
34   Stephen Harper, "Idle Talk Won't Save Lives," *National Post*, Dec. 30, 2005, A18.
35   Janice Tibbetts, "Tory Plan to Jail More People Will Cost Billions," *Ottawa Citizen*, Feb. 18, 2006, A5.
36   John Geddes, "Are We Really Soft on Crime?" *Maclean's*, Nov. 16, 2009, 22.
37   Tobi Cohen "Harper Hits Trudeau on Terror," *Montreal Gazette*, Apr. 26, 2013, A10; Steven Chase, "PM Steps Up Attack on Trudeau Over 'Root Causes' of Terrorism," *Globe and Mail*, Apr. 26, 2013, A5.
38   John Conway, "Thou Shall Not Commit Sociology," *Monitor*, Canadian Centre for Policy Alternatives, June 2013, 38.
39   Wayne MacDonald, "Bullying Political Tactics," *Ottawa Citizen*, Apr. 27, 2013, B5.
40   Ralph Bigio, "Harper Rapped for 'Committing Ideology,'" *Vancouver Sun*, May 1, 2013, A6.
41   Gary Becker, "Crime and Punishment: An Economic Approach," *Journal of Political Economy*, Vol. 76, No. 2 (Mar.–Apr. 1968): 169–217.
42   John Donohue, "Economic Models of Crime and Punishment," *Social Research*, Vol. 74, No. 2 (Summer 2007): 381.
43   Ibid, 382.
44   Public Health Agency of Canada, "Fetal Alcohol Spectrum Disorder (FASD)," 2005. http://www.phac-aspc.gc.ca/hp-ps/dca-dea/prog-ini/fasd-etcaf/faq/.
45   Kim Pemberton, "Mysterious Clues Led to Diagnosis," *Vancouver Sun*, Dec. 4, 2010, A10.
46   Svetlana Popova et al., "Fetal Alcohol Spectrum Disorder Prevalence Estimates in Correctional Systems: A Systematic Literature Review," *Canadian Journal of Public Health*, Vol. 102, No. 5 (Sept./Oct. 2011): 339.
47   Donohue, op. cit., 380. Becker's "Crime and Punishment: An Economic Approach" has been cited in over 10,000 books and articles, according to Google Scholar.
48   Emma Bell, *Criminal Justice and Neoliberalism* (New York: Palgrave Macmillan, 2011), 2.
49   Donohue, op cit., 405.
50   Andrew Mayeda and Mike De Souza, "PM Offers Peek at Next Election," *National Post*, Feb. 7, 2007, A4.
51   Mitchell Anderson, "Harper's Green Mirage," *The Tyee*, Jan. 24, 2007. http://thetyee.ca/Views/2007/01/24/GreenMirage/.
52   Mayeda and De Souza, op. cit.
53   Rick Salutin, "Adaptation Equals Doing Nothing," *Globe and Mail*, Feb. 9, 2007, A17.
54   Luntz Research, "The Environment: A Cleaner, Safer, Healthier America," 2002, 143. http://www.motherjones.com/files/LuntzResearch_environment.pdf.
55   Chris Mooney, *The Republican War on Science* (New York: Basic Books, 2005), 75.
56   Barry Wilson, "Harper Says Majority Necessary to Kill Long-gun Registry," *Western Producer*, Apr. 4, 2011. http://www.producer.com/daily/harper-says-majority-necessary-to-kill-longgun-registry/.

57 "PM Delivers Remarks at the 2012 National Fish and Wildlife Conservation Congress," Prime Minister of Canada Stephen Harper, May 30, 2012. http://pm.gc.ca/ENG/MEDIA. ASP?id=4832.

58 Brian Riddell of the Pacific Salmon Foundation and a former Fisheries and Oceans scientist, for one. See Fisheries and Oceans Canada, "Hunting and Angling Advisory Panel Meeting — May 2, 2013," Photo Gallery 2012. http://www.dfo-mpo.gc.ca/media/gallery-galerie-eng.htm.

59 Friedrich Hayek, "The Use of Knowledge in Society," *American Economic Review*, Vol. 35, No. 4 (Sept. 1945): 521.

60 Total deaths due to cigarette smoking in the U.S. is estimated at 443,000. Centers for Disease Control and Prevention, "Smoking and Tobacco Use," Mar. 21, 2011. http://www.cdc.gov/tobacco/data_statistics/fact_sheets/health_effects/tobacco_related_mortality/.

61 Warren Leary, "U.S. Ties Secondhand Smoke to Cancer," *New York Times*, Jan. 8, 1993, A14.

62 See Sheldon Rampton and John Stauber, *Trust Us, We're Experts* (New York: Jeremy P. Tarcher/Putnam, 2001), 238–241.

63 Heather Dewar, "GOP Ready to Dilute Environmental Laws: New Buzzwords Target Property Rights," *Houston Chronicle*, Nov. 12, 1994. Cited in Mooney, op. cit., 69.

64 See Donald Gutstein, *Not a Conspiracy Theory*. (Toronto: Key Porter, 2009), 234–36.

65 Shawn McCarthy, "Energy Exports to Asia a Priority," *Globe and Mail*, Sept. 14, 2011, B11.

66 Canada, Natural Resources Canada, "Canada and the United Kingdom: Growing Our Responsible Energy Partnership," Remarks by the Honourable Joe Oliver, Minister of Natural Resources, May 9, 2013. http://www.nrcan.gc.ca/media-room/speeches/2013/7159.

67 Canada, Natural Resources Canada, "Minister Oliver Promotes Canadian Energy Interests in Kuwait," Mar. 13, 2012. http://www.nrcan.gc.ca/media-room/news-release/2012/29/6051.

68 Canada, Natural Resources Canada, "Safety First: Canada's Commitment to Responsible Resource Development," Notes for remarks by the Honourable Joe Oliver, P.C., M.P., Minister of Natural Resources, at the Port Metro Vancouver, Sept. 7, 2012. http://www.nrcan.gc.ca/media-room/speeches/2012/6491.

69 Ecojustice, "Backgrounder: What Is BPA?" no date. http://www.ecojustice.ca/media-centre/media-release-files/backgrounder-what-is-bisphenol-a-bpa.

70 Tom Spears, "When the Market Jumps First . . . the Leaders Are Sure to Follow," *Ottawa Citizen*, 26 Apr. 26, 2008, B1.

71 Bill Schiller, "China Defends Canadians' Quarantine," *Toronto Star*, May 6, 2009, A7.

72 Tara Brautigam, "East Coast Fishery Will Hinder Cod Stocks, Experts Say," *Globe and Mail*, June 10, 2006, A10.

73 Gloria Galloway, "Coastal Nations Urged to Preserve Arctic Waters," *Globe and Mail*, May 13, 2011, A4.

74 "Junk science," *Oxford Advanced Learner's Dictionary*, 2013. http://www.oxfordlearnersdictionaries.com/definition/english/junk-science.

75 Adrian Berry, "Chilling Report Warns of Ice Age," *Vancouver Sun*, Dec. 19, 1989, A1.

76 Terence Corcoran, "Junk Science Looms Over Great Lakes," *Globe and Mail*, Feb. 18, 1994, B2.

77 Top five media mentions of junk science in the Canadian Newsstand Major Dailies database (as of June 6, 2014): *National Post*: 537 (38.8%), *Calgary Herald*: 112 (8.1%), *Globe and Mail*: 95 (6.9%), *Toronto Star*: 95 (6.9%), *Edmonton Journal*: 80 (5.8%). Total is 1385.

78 Terence Corcoran, "Attack of the Tomato Killers," *National Post*, May 4, 199, C7, 1999.

79 Terence Corcoran, "Women on Boards," *National Post*, June 11, 2013, FP13.

80 Ibid.; Susan Crockford, "Now We Have Too Many Polar Bears?" June 12, FP11; Peter Foster, "The Keystone XL Beetle Boondoggle," June 12, FP11; Roy Spencer, "Epic Climate Model Failure," June 13, FP11; Jesse Kline, "Ehrlich Bombs Again," June 13, FP11; Philip Cross, "Muzzling Government Scientists?" June 14, FP11.

81 Prime Minister's Office, "Red Tape Reduction Commission," Jan. 13, 2011. http://www.pm.gc.ca/eng/media.asp?id=3884.

82   Sam Stein, "Frank Luntz Pens Memo to Kill Financial Regulatory Reform," *Huffington Post*, Apr. 3, 2010. http://www.huffingtonpost.com/2010/02/01/frank-luntz-pens-memo-to_n_444332.html.

83   Frank Luntz, "The Language of Financial Reform," *The Word Doctors*, Jan. 2010, 12. http://www.huffingtonpost.com/2010/02/01/frank-luntz-pens-memo-to_n_444332.html.

84   Diane Jermyn, "Lobbying Effort Aims to Cut Red Tape," *Globe and Mail*, Jan. 10, 2011. http://www.theglobeandmail.com/report-on-business/small-business/lobbying-effort-aims-to-cut-red-tape/article561102/.

85   Railroaded, "Cando Contracting Ltd. Not Truthful," Aug. 12, 2012. http://railroaded.word-press.com/2012/08/12/cando-contracting-ltd-not-truthful/. See also Hanneke Brooymans, "Neighbour Not Told About New CN Rail Yard," *Edmonton Journal*, July 5, 2010, A1.

86   Canada, "Cutting Red Tape . . . Freeing Business to Grow," Red Tape Reduction Commission, Archived content, Oct. 2, 2012. http://www.reduceredtape.gc.ca/index-eng.asp.

87   Red Tape Reduction Commission, "Recommendations Report — Cutting Red Tape . . . Freeing Business to Grow," Jan. 18, 2012. http://www.reduceredtape.gc.ca/heard-entendu/rr/rrtb-eng.asp.

88   Canada, Treasury Board of Canada Secretariat, "Red Tape Reduction Action Plan," Oct. 1, 2012. http://www.tbs-sct.gc.ca/rtrap-parfa/rtrapr-rparfa-eng.asp.

89   Canada, Treasury Board of Canada Secretariat, "Speaking Notes for the Honourable Tony Clement, President of the Treasury Board of Canada, on the Occasion of Red Tape Reductions Announcements in Toronto," Jan. 21, 2013. http://www.tbs-sct.gc.ca/media/ps-dp/2013/0121-eng.asp.

90   Today's Trucking, "Feds Improving on Red Tape Reduction, Says Business Lobby Group," Jan. 23, 2013. htp://www.todaystrucking.com/feds-improving-on-red-tape-reduction-says-business-lobby-group.

CHAPTER 7

1   Adrian Wan, "HK Still Freest Economy, but Ranking at Risk," *South China Morning Post*, Sept. 21, 2011, 2.

2   Te-Ping Chen, "Hong Kong's Wealth Gap Gets Larger," *Wall Street Journal*, China Real Time Report, June 19, 2012. http://blogs.wsj.com/chinarealtime/2012/06/19/hong-kongs-wealth-gap-gets-larger/; Gus Lubin, "This City Has by Far the Most Inequality in the Developed World," *Business Insider*, June 26, 2012. http://www.businessinsider.com/inequality-in-hong-kong-2012-6.

3   Li Xueying, "Minimum Wage Helps HK's Poorest Workers," *Straits Times*, Oct. 10, 2012.

4   Enid Tsui, "Hong Kong to Introduce Competition Law," *Financial Times* (Asia-Pacific), June 15, 2012. http://www.ft.com/cms/s/0/2de35c52-b692-11e1-a14a-00144feabdc0.html#axzz22nJYwNDI.

5   Wan, op. cit.

6   Heritage Foundation, "Hong Kong Remains World Leader in Economic Freedom, 2012 Index Shows," Jan. 12, 2012. http://www.heritage.org/research/reports/2012/01/hong-kong-remains-world-leader-in-economic-freedom-2012-index-shows.

7   "Free Economy Balancing Act," *South China Morning Post*, Jan. 19, 2013, 14.

8   Central Intelligence Agency, "Distribution of family income — the Gini Coefficient," *The World Factbook*, no date. https://www.cia.gov/library/publications/the-world-factbook/fields/2172.html.

9   OECD, *Divided We Stand: Why Inequality Keeps Rising*, OECD Publishing, 2011. http://dx.doi.org/10.1787/9789264119536-en.

10   OECD, "Divided We Stand: Why Inequality Keeps Rising" (speech), Paris, Dec. 5, 2011. http://www.oecd.org/social/dividedwestandwhyinequalitykeepsrisingspeech.htm.

11   By income the OECD means disposable income adjusted for household size. This definition is meant to take into account the growing number of single and single-parent households, as well as households in which more members are working than previously.

12   OECD, "An Overview of Growing Income Inequalities in OECD Countries: Main Find-

ings," OECD Publishing, 2011, 22. http://www.oecd.org/els/soc/49499779.pdf.

13   OECD, "Divided We Stand: Why Inequality Keeps Rising," four-pager, OECD Publishing, 2011, 1, Figure 1. http://www.oecd.org/els/soc/49170768.pdf.

14   Conference Board of Canada, "Income inequality," 2013. http://www.conferenceboard.ca/hcp/details/society/income-inequality.aspx.

15   OECD, *Divided We Stand*, 99–104.

16   Ibid., 122, Figure 2.3.

17   Nicole Fortin, et al., "Canadian Inequality: Recent Developments and Policy Options," *Canadian Public Policy*, Vol. 38 No. 2 (June 2012): 132.

18   David Card, Thomas Lemieux, and W. Craig Riddell, "Unions and Wage Inequality," *Journal of Labor Research*, Vol. 25, No. 4 (Fall 2004): 555. Unions do not reduce wage inequality among women, because 1) unionized women are more concentrated in the upper end of the wage distribution, and 2) the union wage gap is larger for women.

19   OECD, *Divided We Stand*, 94–98.

20   The other 23 per cent of increased II is a result of increased non-unionized female employment at lower wages, plus other factors.

21   Fortin, et al., 131.

22   Ibid.

23   OECD, "An Overview of Growing Income Inequalities in OECD Countries: Main Findings," 36.

24   Fortin, et al., 124.

25   Ibid., 122.

26   Ibid., 127.

27   "Income Inequality Spikes in Canada's Big Cities," Canadian Centre for Policy Alternatives, Jan. 28, 2013. http://www.policyalternatives.ca/newsroom/news-releases/income-inequality-spikes-canadas-big-cities; "Alberta Is Canada's Most Unequal Province and Calgary the Most Unequal City," Parkland Institute, Jan. 28, 2013. http://parklandinstitute.ca/media/comments/alberta_is_canadas_most_unequal_province/.

28   Armine Yalnizyan, "Trickle-Down Would Work If It Weren't for the Sponges at the Top," Behind the Numbers — A Blog from the CCPA, Sept. 19, 2013. http://behindthenumbers.ca/2013/09/19/trickle-down-would-work-if-it-werent-for-the-sponges-at-the-top/.

29   Sheila Pratt, "Think-Tank Says Alberta Has Room to Hike Taxes on Wealthy Residents," *Edmonton Journal*, Jan. 29, 2013, A4; Jason Van Rassel, "Calgary's Wealth Gap Most Unequal in the Country," *Calgary Herald*, Jan. 29, 2013, B1; "Finding Fairness," *Calgary Herald*, Jan. 30, 2013, A18.

30   "Hug the 1 Per Cent," *Globe and Mail*, Jan. 30, 2013, A12.

31   Marc Lee, "Eroding Tax Fairness," Canadian Centre for Policy Alternatives, Nov. 2007, 16–17.

32   Friedrich Hayek, *The Constitution of Liberty* (Chicago: University of Chicago Press, 1960), 42.

33   Ibid., 43–44.

34   Ibid., 44.

35   Ibid., 85.

36   Ibid., 48–49.

37   Ibid., 49.

38   Ibid., 93.

39   Richard Wilkinson and Kate Pickett, *The Spirit Level: Why Equality Is Better for Everyone* (Penguin Books, 2010), 20.

40   Christopher Snowdon, "Fact-Checking *The Spirit Level*," The Taxpayers' Alliance, July 16, 2010. http://www.taxpayersalliance.com/economics/2010/07/factchecking-the-spirit-level.html.

41   Robert Booth, "*The Spirit Level*: How 'Ideas Wreckers' Turned Book into Political Punchbag," *The Guardian*, Aug. 14, 2010. http://www.theguardian.com/books/2010/aug/14/the-spirit-level-equality-thinktanks.

42   Nima Sanandaji, Arvid Malm, and Tino Sanandaji, "The Spirit Illusion: A Critical Analysis

of How 'The Spirit Level' Compares Countries," The Taxpayers' Alliance, July 7, 2010, 6. http://www.taxpayersalliance.com/spiritillusion.pdf.

43 Peter Saunders, "Beware False Prophets: Equality, the Good Society, and *The Spirit Level*," 2010, 8. http://www.policyexchange.org.uk/images/publications/beware false prophets - jul 10.pdf.

44 Ibid., 6.

45 Nima Sanandaji, et al., "Un-level Ground," *Wall Street Journal Online*, July 9, 2010. http://online.wsj.com/article/SB127862421912914915.html.

46 Peter Saunders and Christopher Snowdon, "Response: We're Not Wreckers. We Just Think *The Spirit Level* Is Bad Social Science," *The Guardian*, Aug. 26, 2010, 33.

47 Wilkinson and Pickett, op. cit., 299.

48 Statistics Canada, "Low Income Cut-offs," Publ. 75F0002M, June 3, 2009. http://www.statcan.gc.ca/pub/75f0002m/2009002/s2-eng.htm.

49 Chris Sarlo, "Redefining Poverty," *Toronto Star*, Aug. 31, 1992, A15.

50 "No More Poor People," *Edmonton Journal*, July 18, 1992, A8.

51 Geoffrey York, "Defending the Definition of Poverty," *Globe and Mail*, July 16, 1992, A1; Michael Kane, "Professor Purports to Prove Poor People Aren't Poor after All," *Vancouver Sun*, July 15, 1992, A1.

52 York, op. cit.

53 Brian Lewis, "Poverty Measure Disputed," *The Province*, June 12, 1996, 33.

54 *Calgary Herald*, Dec. 14, 1996; *Toronto Star*, July 17, 1997; *Edmonton Journal*, Dec. 30 1997; *Ottawa Citizen*, May 15, 1999; *National Post*, July 27, 2001.

55 United States Census Bureau, "Table F-4. Gini Ratios for Families, by Race and Hispanic Origin of Householder, 1947 to 2012," *Historical Income Tables: Income Inequality*, updated 17 Sept. 17, 2013. http://www.census.gov/hhes/www/income/data/historical/inequality/. The Gini coefficient continued to rise during the presidencies of Bill Clinton, George W. Bush, and Barack Obama, reaching 0.451 in 2012.

56 U.S. Department of the Treasury, Office of Tax Analysis, "Household Income Mobility During the 1980s: A Statistical Assessment Based on Tax Return Data," *Tax Notes* (June 1, 1992).

57 Paul Krugman, "The Rich, the Right and the Facts," *The American Prospect*, Vol. 3, No. 11 (Sept. 1992). http://prospect.org/article/rich-right-and-facts-deconstructing-income-distribution-debate.

58 Steven Mufson, "Treasury's Look at Income Mobility," *Washington Post*, June 3, 1992, A17.

59 Herbert Grubel, "Poverty Activists Fail to Consider Income Mobility," *Montreal Gazette*, Sept. 19, 2007, A19.

60 Jeffrey Simpson, "Do We Care That Ours Is an Unequal Society?" *Globe and Mail*, July 20, 2011, A17.

61 Conference Board of Canada, "Hot Topic: Canada Inequality," July 2011. http://www.conferenceboard.ca/Files/hcp/pdfs/hot-topics/caninequality.pdf.

62 Amela Karabegovic and Charles Lammam, "You Won't Be Poor for Long," *National Post*, Sept. 26, 2011, A10.

63 Milton Friedman, *Capitalism and Freedom* (Fortieth Anniversary Edition) (Chicago: University of Chicago Press, 2002), 171.

64 The Fraser Institute study refers specifically to Friedman's work in its discussion of why income mobility is important. See Charles Lammam, Amela Karabegovic, and Niels Veldhuis, "Measuring Income Mobility in Canada," *Studies in Economic Prosperity*, Fraser Institute, Nov. 2012, 5. http://www.fraserinstitute.org/uploadedFiles/fraser-ca/Content/research-news/research/publications/measuring-income-mobility-in-canada.pdf.

65 Niels Veldhuis and Amela Karabegovic, "At Conference Board, Poverty Is Forever," *National Post*, Sept. 25, 2009, FP11.

66 Niels Veldhuis and Charles Lammam, "'Poor' Getting Richer," *National Post*, Nov. 21, 2012, FP11.

67 Kathryn Blaze Carlson, "Poor Today, Rich Tomorrow," *National Post*, Nov. 21, 2012, A1.

68   Lammam, Karabegovic, and Veldhuis, op. cit., 16. Compare Table 2 and Table 3.
69   Ibid., 4, 18.
70   Ibid., iii.
71   Ibid., v.
72   David Macdonald, "The Rich Stay Rich: Fraser Institute," *Behind the Numbers*, Canadian Centre for Policy Alternatives, Nov. 20, 2012. http://behindthenumbers.ca/2012/11/20/the-rich-stay-rich-fraser-institute/.
73   Lammam, Karabegovic, and Veldhuis, op. cit., 8.
74   Niels Veldhuis and Milagros Palacios, "The Underclass Myth," *National Post*, May 2, 2008, FP13.
75   Michelle Malkin, "The Generational Theft Act of 2009," Creator's Syndicate, Jan. 7, 2009. http://michellemalkin.com/2009/01/07/the-generational-theft-act-of-2009/.
76   Matt Corley, "GOP Leaders Taking Cues from Malkin on Stimulus, Call It Generational Theft," ThinkProgress, Feb. 9 2009. http://thinkprogress.org/politics/2009/02/09/35962/malkin-mccain-boehner/.
77   John Boehner, "'Stimulus' Should Unleash America's Potential — Not Government's Appetite for Pork," AmericaSpeakOn.org, Feb. 8, 2009. http://americaspeakon.blogspot.ca/2009/02/representative-boehner-featured-blogger.html.
78   Tom Coburn, MD, "Coburn Fights Generational Theft Act, AKA Senate Stimulus Bill," Right Now, Feb. 3, 2009. http://www.coburn.senate.gov/public/index.cfm/rightnow.
79   Todd Thurman, "Sen. John McCain Speaks at Heritage on Generational Theft," Heritage Foundation, Mar. 26, 2009. http://blog.heritage.org/2009/03/26/live-john-mccain-speaks-at-heritage-on-generational-theft/.
80   Dustin Siggins, "The Debt-paying Generation Has Arrived," The Lobbyist, July 13, 2010. http://thelobbyist.net/lobby/archives/3712.
81   Crusader Patriot Store. "Generational Theft!" 2013. http://www.cafepress.com/crusader-patriot/6509526.
82   "Sarah Palin Gives Speech to Packed Calgary Crowd," CTV News, Mar. 6, 2010. http://www.ctvnews.ca/sarah-palin-gives-speech-to-packed-calgary-crowd-1.489579; Amanda Achtman, "Worthwhile," *Calgary Herald*, Mar. 9, 2010, A9.
83   Paul Delean, "Boomers' Selfishness Leading to Bust," *Montreal Gazette*, Jan. 27, 2012, B2.
84   Fazil Mihlar, "Think Like a Beaver," *Vancouver Sun*, Sept. 19, 2011, A11.
85   For an analysis of *Vancouver Sun* coverage of Occupy Vancouver, see Donald Gutstein, "How Canada's Corporate Media Framed the Occupy Movement," *Vancouver Observer*, Dec. 1, 2011. http://www.vancouverobserver.com/politics/commentary/2011/12/01/how-canadas-corporate-media-framed-occupy-movement.
86   Robert Wright, "Generation Lie," *Ottawa Citizen*, Dec. 3, 2011, B1.
87   Don Cayo, "Transferring Wealth Is Better Than Just Losing It," *Vancouver Sun*, Sept. 19, 2013, D2.
88   Paul Kershaw, "Forget Occupy, the Real Divide is Generational, *Globe and Mail*, Sept. 21, 2012, A17.
89   Paul Kershaw, "Movement Should Change Focus," *Vancouver Sun*, Oct. 18, 2011, A11.
90   Alessandro Speciale and Andrew Frye, "The Pope on Capitalism," *Ottawa Citizen*, Nov. 27, 2013, D2; Nicole Winfield, "Pope Francis Calls for Church to Move Away from Doctrine, Help Those in Need," *Globe and Mail*, Nov. 27, 2013, A15.
91   White House, "Remarks by the President on Economic Mobility," *The Arc*, Washington, D.C., Dec. 4, 2013. http://www.whitehouse.gov/the-press-office/2013/12/04/remarks-president-economic-mobility.
92   Sara Norman, "Federal Minister Says Child Poverty Not Ottawa's Problem," *News 1130*, Dec. 15, 2013. http://www.news1130.com/2013/12/15/federal-minister-says-child-poverty-not-ottawas-problem/.
93   Eugene Lang, "Harper's Historic Tax-Cutting Legacy," *Toronto Star*, Dec. 27, 2013, A23. See also Les Whittington, "PM's Tax Cuts Bite into Ottawa's Clout," *Toronto Star*, Jan. 19, 2011, A6.
94   Canada, House of Commons, Standing Committee on Finance, "Income Inequality in

Canada: An Overview," Ottawa, Dec. 2013. http://www.parl.gc.ca/HousePublications/Pub-lication.aspx?DocId=6380060&Language=E&Mode=1&Parl=41&Ses=2.

CHAPTER 8

1   Canada, Citizenship and Immigration Canada, *Discover Canada: The Rights and Respon-sibilities of Citizenship*, Ottawa, 2012. http://www.cic.gc.ca/english/pdf/pub/discover.pdf.
2   Donald Gutstein, "New Citizenship Handbook Twists 'The Canadian Story,'" *The Tyee*, Mar. 3, 2010. http://thetyee.ca/Mediacheck/2010/03/03/DiscoverCanada/.
3   Donald Gutstein, "Harper–Bush Share Roots in Controversial Philosophy," *The Tyee*, Nov. 29, 2005. http://thetyee.ca/Mediacheck/2005/11/29/HarperBush/.
4   Canada, Citizenship and Immigration Canada, *A Look at Canada*, Ottawa, 2001. http://publications.gc.ca/collections/Collection/Ci51-61-2001E.pdf.
5   Ibid., 4.
6   Laura Stone, "Citizenship Guide to Include More History," *Ottawa Citizen*, Nov. 11, 2009, A4.
7   Canada, Citizenship and Immigration Canada, *A Look at Canada*, 4.
8   Ibid., 7.
9   John Ibbitson, "Ottawa's Latest Citizenship Guide Restores Reference to Same-Sex Rights," *Globe and Mail*, Sept. 10, 2012. http://www.theglobeandmail.com/news/politics/ottawa-notebook/ottawas-latest-citizenship-guide-restores-reference-to-same-sex-rights/article615619/.
10 "Being Canadian with Vitality," *Globe and Mail*, Nov. 12 2009, A18.
11 "The Death of History," *Globe and Mail*, Sept. 23, 2000, A16.
12 "What Canada Means," *Winnipeg Free Press*, Nov. 13, 2009, A14.
13 "Who We Are," *Ottawa Citizen*, Nov. 13, 2009, A8.
14 "Standing on Guard for Our Values," *Calgary Herald*, Nov. 13, 2009, A18.
15 During the 1990s, Donner was known as Canada's paymaster to the right, supporting a host of social-conservative and neo-liberal organizations and activities, as described in Chapter 2.
16 Dominion Institute, "About," modified June 29, 2007. http://www.dominion.ca/about.htm. No longer available online.
17 Christoph Conrad, "Social History," in *International Encyclopedia of the Social and Behav-ioral Sciences*, ed. Neil Smelser and Paul Baltes, Vol. 21 (Amsterdam: Elsevier, 2001), 14299.
18 John Fraser, "… and the Rest is History," *National Post*, June 6, 2001, B3.
19 A.B. McKillop, "Who Killed Canadian History? A View from the Trenches," *Canadian Historical Review*, Vol. 80, No. 2 (June 1999): 269–99.
20 Paul Webster, "Who Stole Canadian History?" *This Magazine*, Mar./Apr. 2000, 28–31.
21 Andrew Cohen, "What Is Expected in Canada," *Ottawa Citizen*, Nov. 17, 2009, A14.
22 Sean Gordon, "Tories Axe Unity Council Funding," *Toronto Star*, Mar. 18, 2006, A9.
23 Randy Boswell, "Student Exchange Program Back On," *Edmonton Journal*, Aug. 1, 2006, A6.
24 Randy Boswell, "Legion Slams Ottawa Over Program Award," *National Post*, Aug. 11, 2006, A7.
25 Historica–Dominion Institute, "The Historica Foundation of Canada Announces the Appointment of Ann Dadson as Interim President and CEO, as Current President Colin Robertson Returns to Federal Government," Press release, Oct. 30, 2007. No longer avail-able online.
26 Encounters with Canada, "Our Youth Program," no date. https://www.ewc-rdc.ca/en/our_youth_program/index.html.
27 Public Works and Government Services Canada, *Public Accounts of Canada, 2012*, Vol. III, Sect. 6 - Transfer Payments. http://www.tpsgc-pwgsc.gc.ca/recgen/cpc-pac/2013/vol3/ds6/index-eng.html#un_1813.
28 Susan Delacourt, "Civilization Ends and History Begins," *Toronto Star*, Oct. 17, 2012, A12.

29 Randy Boswell, "Vandals Mar Macdonald Bicentennial Ceremony," *Regina Leader Post*, Jan. 12, 2013, B6.

30 Encounters with Canada, "Harper Government Invests in Encounters with Canada," Apr. 2, 2012. https://www.ewc-rdc.ca/en/news/article.html?id=404827.

31 Historica–Dominion Institute, "The Historica–Dominion Institute Calls for National Day of Commemoration," Press release, Feb. 19, 2010. https://www.historica-dominion.ca/content/historica-dominion-institute-calls-national-day-commemoration.

32 Daniel Leblanc, "Honouring His Wishes, Veteran's Family Refuses State Funeral," *Globe and Mail*, Feb. 20, 2010, A4.

33 Mike Blanchfield, "Harper Refuses to 'Cut and Run,'" *Calgary Herald*, Mar. 8, 2006, A1.

34 Mike Blanchfield, "Casualties Won't Deter Us, PM Says," *Calgary Herald*, Mar. 14, 2006, A1.

35 Archie McLean, "Harper Salutes Army Graduates," *Ottawa Citizen*, Apr. 14, 2006, A8.

36 So were the *Charter of Rights and Freedoms*, bilingualism, the Canadian flag, and multiculturalism.

37 Jane Taber, "Harper Spins a New Brand of Patriotism," *Globe and Mail*, Aug. 20, 2011, A3.

38 Lee Berthiaume, "Military Aims for Small Hubs," *National Post*, July 20, 2012, A4.

39 Rick Salutin, "Stephen Harper: The last Straussian?" *Globe and Mail*, Sept. 17, 2010, A19. Some Salutin supporters believe he was fired because of this column and his last one on Toronto mayor Rob Ford. See: David Beers, "Rick Salutin's Last Words," *The Tyee*, Sept. 30, 2010. http://thetyee.ca/Opinion/2010/09/30/RickSalutinLastWords/. However, Salutin thinks the motivation was marketing, not suppression. See: Amira Elghawaby, "Rick Salutin: Is Dissent Alive and Well in Canada?" rabble.ca, May 10, 2012. http://rabble.ca/news/2012/05/rick-salutin-dissent-alive-and-well-canada.

40 Stuart Ewen, *PR! A Social History of Spin* (New York: Basic Books, 1996), 166.

41 Shadia Drury, *The Political Ideas of Leo Strauss*, Updated ed. (New York: Palgrave Macmillan, 2005), xiii.

42 Shadia Drury, *Leo Strauss and the American Right* (New York: St. Martin's Press, 1999), 12.

43 Anne Norton, *Leo Strauss and the Politics of American Empire* (New Haven: Yale University Press, 2004), 178.

44 Shadia Drury, quoted in Jim Lobe, "Strong Must Rule the Weak, Said Neo-cons' Muse," CommonDreams.org News Center, May 8, 2003. http://www.commondreams.org/headlines03/0508-02.htm.

45 Drury, *The Political Ideas of Leo Strauss*, xi.

46 Earl Shorris, "Ignoble Liars: Leo Strauss, George Bush, and the Philosophy of Mass Deception," *Harper's*, June 2004, 68.

47 Donald Gutstein, *Not a Conspiracy Theory* (Toronto: Key Porter, 2009), 144–46.

48 Irving Kristol, "The Neoconservative Persuasion," *The Weekly Standard*, Aug. 25, 2003. http://www.weeklystandard.com/Content/Public/Articles/000/000/003/000tzmlw.asp.

49 Shawn McCarthy, "Ottawa: PM Rejects War Without the UN," *Globe and Mail*, Mar. 18, 2003, A1.

50 Canada, Parliament, House of Commons, *Debates*, Mar. 20, 2003, 37th Parliament, 2nd Session. http://www.parl.gc.ca/HousePublications/Publication.aspx?pub=Hansard&doc=74&Language=E&Mode=1&Parl=37&Ses=2#T1130.

51 Tonda MacCharles, "Aide Quits as Copycat Uproar Stings PM," *Toronto Star*, Oct. 1, 2008, A1.

52 The first age occurred during the 1960s, Vaisse says, when conservative Democrats railed against what they saw as the liberal excesses of Lyndon Johnson's Great Society, with its failed social policies and moral chaos. During the second age, these Democrats and some Republicans demanded a more hawkish foreign policy to fight and win the Cold War.

53 Justin Vaisse, *Neoconservatism: The Biography of a Movement* (Cambridge, MA: Belknap Press of Cambridge University Press, 2010), 228.

54 Robert Kagan, "Mission Possible," *The Weekly Standard*, Sept. 18, 1995, 22. http://www.weeklystandard.com/Content/Protected/Articles/000/000/007/097eaudk.asp.

55 Vaisse, op. cit., 12.

56   Bruce Cheadle, "Tory Insiders and Behind-Scenes Lobbying Pave Path to New 'Fox North' Launch," *Canadian Press*, June 14, 2010.
57   Bruce Cheadle, "Documents Show PMO Hired Fleischer a Second time for U.S. Media Advice," *Canadian Press*, Jan. 6, 2010.
58   Fred Barnes, "Triumph of the Conservatives," *The Weekly Standard*, May 16, 2011. http://www.weeklystandard.com/articles/triumph-conservatives_559362.html.
59   William Kristol, "Harbingers of Success," *The Weekly Standard*, June 6, 2011. http://www.weeklystandard.com/articles/harbingers-success_571609.html.
60   David Brinn, "PM Gets Warm Welcome in Toronto," *Jerusalem Post*, May 31, 2010, 1.
61   Juliet O'Neill, "Israeli PM Tells Canada Troops Acted in Self-Defence," *Calgary Herald*, June 1, 2010, A1.
62   Campbell Clark, "Canada Calls for Investigation before Condemnation," *Globe and Mail*, June 1, 2010, A12.
63   Janice Tibbetts, "Canada First to Cut Off Palestinian Regime," *Calgary Herald*, Mar. 30, 2006, A7.
64   Jane Taber, "Harper Defends Israel's Right to 'Defend Itself,'" *Globe and Mail*, July 14, 2006, A12.
65   Campbell Clark, "Canada Votes Against Resolution," *Globe and Mail*, Jan. 13, 2009, A11.
66   Melissa Leong, "Canada Will Not Abandon Israel: PM," *National Post*, May 9, 2008, A1.
67   Andrew Mayeda, "Harper Denounces Zimbabwe Election," *Ottawa Citizen*, June 28, 2008, A4.
68   Kathryn Blaze Carlson, "No Greater Friend," *National Post*, Dec. 8, 2012, A12.
69   The Evangelical Fellowship of Canada, "Statistics on Christianity in Canada," 2014. http://www.evangelicalfellowship.ca/page.aspx?pid=776.
70   Steven Chase, "Attack on Israel Is an Attack on Canada, Kent Says," *Globe and Mail*, Feb. 17, 2010, A4. See the analysis by former Canadian diplomat Gar Pardy, "Peter Kent Goes to War," *Ottawa Citizen*, Feb. 23, 2010, A13.
71   William Kristol, "The West Fights Back," *The Weekly Standard*, Dec. 3, 2012. http://www.weeklystandard.com/blogs/west-fights-back_663845.html.
72   Leo Strauss, "Strauss's Letter to the Editors of the *National Review*," Jan. 5, 1956. Republished in "The Achievement of Leo Strauss," Colloquium, Henry Salvatori Center for the Study of Individual Freedom in the Modern World, Monograph New Series, No. 1 (Jan. 2000). http://www.claremontmckenna.edu/salvatori/publications/pdf/LeoStrauss.pdf
73   Jamie Fly and William Kristol, "No Iranian Nukes," *The Weekly Standard*, June 25, 2012. http://www.weeklystandard.com/articles/no-iranian-nukes_647326.html.
74   Tim Harper, "Can't Escape the Symbolism," *Toronto Star*, Sept. 28, 2012, A10.
75   Appeal of Conscience Foundation, "Canadian Prime Minster Stephen Harper Receives World Statesman Award at 2012 ACF Dinner," Sept. 27, 2012. http://www.appealofconscience.org/news/article.cfm?id=100271
76   Andy Levy-Ajzenkopf, "Netanyahu Heaps Praise on Canada," *Canadian Jewish News*, Oct. 4, 2012, 1.
77   Glenn Greenwald, "Washington Gets Explicit: Its 'War on Terror' is Permanent," *The Guardian*, May 17, 2013. http://www.theguardian.com/commentisfree/2013/may/17/endless-war-on-terror-obama.
78   Stephen Chase, "Ottawa Reveals Full Cost of Ships," *Globe and Mail*, Nov. 13, 2013, A6.
79   Friedrich Hayek, "Why I am Not a Conservative," pp. 397–411 in Friedrich Hayek, *The Constitution of Liberty* (Chicago: University of Chicago Press, 1960), 397.
80   Ibid., 399

INDEX